MARXISM & SMART LIFE

A CRITICAL ANALYSIS OF MARXISM & AN INQUIRY INTO HUMAN SOCIETY

NIMA MAZHARI

MONTREAL 2024

◆ FriesenPress

One Printers Way
Altona, MB R0G 0B0
Canada

www.friesenpress.com

ISBN
978-1-03-830059-1 (Hardcover)
978-1-03-830058-4 (Paperback)
978-1-03-830060-7 (eBook)

1. POLITICAL SCIENCE, POLITICAL IDEOLOGIES

Distributed to the trade by The Ingram Book Company

Is Karl Marx Right

CONTENTS

Part II: Modern Human Smart Life
An Inquiry Into Human Society

PREFACE

Forty-two years ago, while I was teaching Karl Marx's *Capital* in Tehran, Iran, a comrade asked me a question about the fetishism of commodity. It was not the first time that someone had asked me this question. However, after I answered the question, it was the first time that I started questioning myself and my understanding of the book *Capital*. I have been studying Karl Marx's *Capital* ever since. In fact, I have read it more than one hundred times in four languages—Persian, English, French and German—as Marx likes the Latin proverb: *Repetitio est mater studiorum (Repetition is the mother of study.)*[1]

Although it is widely accepted that Marx's *Capital* consists of three volumes (Volume I, 1867; Volume II, 1885; Volume III, 1894), Marx died on March 14, 1883. Thus, he only published one book called *Das Kapital* in his lifetime. With all due respect to Friedrich Engels, collector and curator of Volumes II and III, the other two books are nothing more than hearsay. Eventually I came to the conclusion that I should focus my attention specifically on two documents: *Capital*, Volume I, published in 1867, and *The Communist Manifesto*, published in 1848. These I have read over and over again, and in this book, I have tried

---

1 Karl Marx, *Value, Price, Profit*, 20.

very hard to focus all my attention on Marx's words. Because of this, I have avoided using references either supporting or refuting Marx. Therefore, the bibliography is very short.

Marx was born on May 5, 1818. When he was twenty-three years old, in April 1841, Marx earned his PhD for his thesis, which was a comparative study on the atomism of Democritus and Epicurus' ideas on contingency. Marx, in his thesis, claimed that theology must yield to the superior wisdom of philosophy. In 1848, when Marx was thirty years old, he and his friend Engels wrote *The Communist Manifesto*. In 1867, when he was forty-nine years old, Marx published *Das Kapital*, Volume I. We also know that Marx was a trained philosopher, a full-fledged, fiery political journalist, an economist, a historian, and a cultured person in several languages. Karl Marx was an encyclopedically knowledgeable thinker. But despite all these qualities, Marx was trapped in his genius, for he was inflamed by the political current of his time. As a young, thirty-year-old, flamboyant revolutionary, Marx wrote *The Communist Manifesto,* but it was forty-nine-year-old sage Marx, who wrote *Capital*. The logical sequence should have been the other way around. For the preface to the German edition in 1872, Marx confirms that the Communist League commissioned him and his friend Engels to write "a detailed theoretical and practical programme for the party." He added that: "The Manifesto has become a historical document which we have no longer any right to alter." But he admits that it "would, in many respects, be very differently worded today." If we represent pictorially that a young Marx wrote the *Manifesto* and old Marx wrote *Capital,* the ideology of Marxism would look like a cart pulling horses rather than horses pulling a cart.

While I was in love with Marx in my heart, Marxism was not convincing me in my head. The fire of this contradiction burned in me for many years until I discovered the malign tumour of imaginary exchange-value upon which Karl Marx denied the use-value of commodity. For me, my discovery of serious and harmful defects in Marxism as an ideology and a solution for emancipating humanity from misery was hard and bitter proof that I had lost a half century of my life in vain. Mistakenly and ignorantly, I had sacrificed everything that I had—which was a lot. For I had three industrial factories (part making and machine tool building) that were making millions and millions, and I was spending all my money in the Marxist-Leninist organization, of which I was a member, called RAH-E KARGAR (Worker's Way) and my political activities for what I believed was the common good. I had the noble idea to end or at least reduce the injustice and oppression of those who are the most miserable, vulnerable, defenceless, and fragile in society. Nevertheless, the joy and satisfaction of seeing light and stopping wrongdoing and ignorance is priceless and immeasurable.

I am also happy and proud of myself that, during all those years of direct struggle under the ruthless suppression of tyrannic regimes in Iran—before and after the 1979 revolution—I was not killed for Marxism and did not kill anybody for Marxism, even though I had been trapped in some misadventures. For instance, the Marxist-Leninist political organization of which I was a member once provided me with a hitman if I deemed it necessary to kill one of our comrades who wished to leave the organization. Fortunately, before committing such an atrocity, I successfully solved the problem for both the organization and that comrade through personal connections and money. I also had a few experiences of falling into ambushes that, by sheer luck, I escaped without being killed or killing anyone.

In fact, naturally and personally, I do not have any tendency to be socially violent. My interest in becoming a front-runner, full-fledged, fiery Marxist fighter was not my personal choice. Rather, it was chosen for me or imposed upon me by SAVAK (the Iranian secret police under the previous regime) when they arrested me. At the time, I was just sixteen years old, and my brother, who is ten years older than me, was arrested for a political reason in which I was not involved and knew nothing about. I had not been living with my brother at the same address; therefore, I had no direct knowledge about his daily life. Moreover, at that time, the only social and political knowledge I had was from reading two books: one was called *Investigations into the Educational Problems of Iran*, written by Samad Behrangi, and the second was *Hurricane Over Sugar* in Cuba, written by Jean-Paul Sartre.

As a sixteen-year-old child, I don't think I had understood even 30% of either book.

In fact, SAVAK didn't even care what I had read. When a detective came to interrogate me, his main question was quite peculiar. He asked me **why I was not playing with other kids my age in the neighbourhood**. When I answered him that I go to school and then to work, so it is dark and late when I go home, he took my answer as mocking him, and he beat me more. But the incident that turned my life upside down was something that happened before the interrogation.

It was a late winter day, and in the dark and cold, about 100 metres from our house, I was going home when three SAVAK agents put me in a car and brought me to Evin prison, which was back then on the outskirts of Tehran. Right inside the door, a very nicely dressed man slapped me on the face, and in a very hostile voice, he said, **"You sister fucker came?"** I felt the cold humidity of my saliva on my lips. I also felt a bizarre feeling in my shaking legs, like my pants suddenly got too tight and narrow. I didn't realize why until I received a few kicks and a smack on the head and heard another voice saying, **"Mother fucker coward, you pee in your pants! If you don't have the balls, why do you play hero?"** Then I understood why there was water in my shoes.

After that, they put me in an empty room with just a few chairs. But that welcoming ceremony, before putting me in that empty room, even though wasn't long, just maybe ten or fifteen minutes; nevertheless it drastically disturbed my life even until today. I never dared to tell anyone that I peed in my pants. I was ashamed. In fact, I was ashamed and scared of everything and everyone around me. All my life, I have had a perpetual feeling that I owe a debt to the whole world and to everybody. I was scared of walls, doors, and windows. At night, when the roads were quiet, on my way home, I would walk in the middle of the road to be far from walls, doors, and windows. Even though I am smart and creative, I was always too scared to talk or ask or answer any questions. Even at school, I was scared of answering exam questions. Unceasingly, I tried to hide myself in front of everybody's eyes because I felt they would know I had peed my pants, even though they were dry and I was not in Evin prison. Although medically I was not born as an autistic child, SAVAK made me an autistic person in a social sense, even to this day.

Despite being a very hard-working, friendly, and harmless kid who was always interested in positive and creative activities, I was targeted by SAVAK, even though they absolutely never had any concrete reason for considering me a troublemaker. Nevertheless, they chased me everywhere at school and at work. My parents were both 100% illiterate and very poor Azeri immigrants in Tehran. Except for a few broken words, they could not speak Persian and had very little connection to society and the authorities, so they weren't able to help me.

Back then, in Iran we did not have the Ministry of Sport. Instead, we had a sport organization (Sazeman Varzesh), which was in charge of handling all major sporting facilities in the country. Two years earlier, at the age of fourteen, I had become an employee of the sport organization and started working in a soccer stadium called Aryamehr Stadium. At that time, it was one of the biggest soccer stadiums in the world. SAVAK learned about my work in the sport organization and told me that it was illegal for a fourteen-year-old kid to be an employee of government. I didn't know that. I even didn't know if it was true or if they were using it against me because I was just a naïve and defenceless kid.

Then, when I was seventeen years old, I became an employee of the Iranian Public Railway, another government office, and another illegal job for someone so young. This situation became even more critical when I became one of the security officers in the safety room of the countrywide Railway Network Surveillance (Moraghebat Vigeh Khotut-e Sarasari). This was again an illegal job in a sensitive position for someone whose name was on SAVAK's bad list. Again, I was chased, questioned, and eventually lost my job. As Hegel says, "Reason guided by divine spirit makes history." In my case, the fact that SAVAK targeted me made me become a political activist. The more they bothered me, the more deeply I hated the Shah and his regime. And since I was naturally never interested in religion, I became attracted to the Marxist ideology. At the time, this was one of the two major ideologies (Marxism and Islam) dominating political activities fighting against the tyrannic regime of the Shah in Iran. Later, I became friends with the late Abdol Majid Majidi, Minister of Finance and Agriculture in the Shah's regime, when he was living in exile in Paris. Knowing my entrepreneurial background, he once said that if SAVAK had given me a couple of thousand dollars and left me alone to pursue my economic and industrial ambitions, instead chasing me and making me into a guerrilla fighter, my case would have been much less of a headache for them. Indeed, he was right.

Although intellectually I am writing against Marxism, in my heart I love Karl Marx. In 1835, when he was only seventeen years old school-boy, in "Reflection on a Young Man's Choice of a Profession," he wrote: "History calls those men the greatest who have ennobled themselves by working for the common good; experience acclaims as happiest the man who made the greatest number of people happy." He added, "If we have chosen the position in life in which we can most of all work for mankind, no burdens can bow us down, because they are sacrifices for the benefit of all; then we shall experience no petty, limited, selfish joy, but our happiness will belong to millions, our deeds will live on quietly but perpetually at work, and over our ashes will be shed the hot tears of noble people."

Karl Marx was a noble person. All his life, he remained loyal to his commitment to work for the common good. Nevertheless, the denial of use-value is a carcinogenic foolishness in Marxist ideology that makes it incompatible with human society. If it is tried in any human society, no matter what the level of industrial development is, it will cause a terminal cancer of tyranny and corruption in that society. History has already taught us that, and we don't want to lose the lesson.

We definitely cannot prescribe any lifestyle for people who will live one hundred years from now, but we certainly can say that for our time, human society needs capitalism and capitalism needs employees and consumers. Therefore, we must find civilized, sustainable solutions for the excruciating economic, social, and political problems that are causing poverty and injustice in today's human society. It is clear that any solutions to the problems of human society must be material, and according to available resources, the solutions must cause tangible and immediate improvements in modern human life. Modern humans should not waste time dreaming up solutions designed for some perfect life in a future that will never happen. In the second part of this book, based on the available social means and institutions, I have designed a social mechanism that can create significant improvements for the common good by providing a smart life for modern humans. I don't believe that Marxism is compatible with a smart life.

Montreal, 2024

PART I:

IS KARL MARX RIGHT?

A CRITICAL ANALYSIS OF MARXISM

IS KARL MARX RIGHT?

Not at all; he is definitely wrong, and here is why.

But before all, right here, it must be said that Karl Marx is one of the greatest thinkers that modern history has seen. Since the Renaissance, no one has ever surpassed the five peaks of modern civilization: Karl Marx, Leonardo da Vinci, Charles Darwin, Sigmund Freud, and Albert Einstein. Leonardo da Vinci (1452–1519) created masterpieces in painting, sculpting, geography, mechanics, anatomy, physics, architecture, and weaponry. He proved to humankind that creativity, ingenuity, and originality have no limits. Charles Darwin (1809–1882) helped define humankind by telling us who we are. Karl Marx (1818–1883) taught humans to change life, instead recounting life. Sigmund Freud (1856–1939) revealed the roots and reasons for our behaviours, and Albert Einstein (1879–1955) showed us our whereabouts in space.

The unique and unparalleled beauty, richness, and power that these giant thinkers have bestowed upon human civilization has changed forever—beyond all race, culture, and tradition—the horizon of human thought and comprehension. The grandness and excellency of their contribution to human thought is such that life before and after them is not the same.

Now, let us examine what Marx said. For Marx, capitalism is a mode of production. In his theory of capital, he explains the mechanism by which the capitalist system functions. Within the mechanism of capitalism, Marx highlights the class contradiction between those who possess the means of production (the capitalist class) and those who are paid to operate them (the working class). This class contradiction causes class struggle (class conflict). As part of this class struggle, Marx says that the administration of the capitalist society is controlled directly or indirectly by the owners of the means of production in order to establish a kind of social structure that will protect and promote their interests.

Marx also believed that there is an inherent, eternal, antagonist tension between the capitalist class (bourgeoisie) and the working class (proletariat). Intrinsically, the capitalist class perpetually robs the working class, and therefore, the working class must fight the capitalist class in order to protect itself against the capitalist class' robbery (class warfare). In Karl Marx's theory of capitalism, the injustice and robbery (surplus-value) of the capitalist mode of production are the elements that sustain the life of the capitalist system, and it will never end. Therefore, the ultimate emancipation for the proletariat, in Marx's view, is a revolution that will assure the possession of the means of production in the hands of a kind of state (communist) that will be governed and controlled by the representatives of the working class.

However, we are here to study what is wrong in Karl Marx's theory. All that Marx said is based on one thing: **commodity**. This is the starting point in Marx's theory of capital. If we remove the commodity from Marx's theory, all the essential elements that make his theory—such as means of production, mode of production, use-value, exchange-value, labour-power, surplus-value, social class, and class struggle—will fall apart and, consequently, his theory will collapse. As a result, we have to investigate in detail the concept of commodity and its role in human life and society.

Consider the following question to better understand commodity: Is it possible to remove the commodity from Marx's theory? The answer is no. Marx is quite right that the commodity is important.

We cannot, and we do not need to, remove the commodity from the theory of capital. However, since human life and society cannot exist without commodities, and in general, commodities in human life are as necessary as oxygen and water (in a sense, themselves are commodities), the function and impact of commodities in the theory of capital therefore must be thoroughly examined. In addition, we must find out what the characteristics of commodities are, according to Marx, and if these can legitimately explain the structure of capitalism and could it justify the class struggle under the leadership of the working class (proletariats) against the bourgeoisie?

WEALTH AND COMMODITY

Marx said, "The wealth of those societies in which the capitalist mode of production prevails presents itself as 'an immense accumulation of commodities', its unit being a single commodity. Our investigation must therefore begin with the analysis of a commodity."[2]

In a conversational context, this statement could be heard and then quickly ignored. Or, in a naïve observation, we can imagine that in the very first lines of his book *Capital*, Marx relates commodities to an idea about wealth in society in order to start his argument. But this statement, despite its simple appearance, goes deeper.

First, it is not true because saying "the capitalist mode of production prevails" is not a marriage certificate between wealth and commodity—although every commodity has use-value because it is a usable thing, and therefore, it is wealth. But all wealth is not commodity-based, even if it is beneficial and useful, because not every kind of wealth is a result of human fabrication. Later, we will analyze this aspect of wealth more in detail.

Second, it is not an authentic foundation for a philosophical and scientific investigation. It does not have any proof or warranty. This

---

2 Karl Marx, *Capital*, Vol. 1, 43.

statement is not an axiom, and it is not a self-proven postulate. It is just a statement.

Third, as a basic idea, it is prophetic, for its legitimacy is not inherent and self-sufficient. It acquires its legitimacy merely from the reputation of the speaker, in the same way that the laws of the prophets are accepted just because the prophets who proclaimed them were deemed to be speaking with authority.

Of the above three reasons, the third one is the most important. The prophetic quality of Marx's opening paragraph is an extremely significant issue that starts on the first page of Marx's book and never goes away. Later, I will analyze this more extensively.

Here, I will briefly examine Marx's statement with a few simple examples. It is also useful to say that when talking of wealth and commodity, the mode of production is not an important factor. We know that in Marxist literature: "For things to be commodities, they must meet three conditions: first, they must have value in use; second, they must possess value in exchange; and third, things must be exchanged."[3] Marx, when talking about primitive human society at the beginning of civilization, said:

> The social division of labour, which forms the foundation of all production of commodities . . . Within a family, and after further development within a tribe, there springs up naturally a division of labour, caused by differences of sex and age, a division that is consequently based on a purely physiological foundation, which division enlarges its materials by the expansion of the community, by the increase of population, and more especially, by the conflicts between different tribes, and the subjugation of one tribe by another...calls forth the consequent gradual conversion of those products into commodities . . . where the physiological division of labour is the starting-point . . . principally owing to the exchange of commodities with foreign communities.[4]

---

3 Peter C. Dooley, *The Labour Theory of Value,* 167.

4 Marx, *Capital,* Vol. 1, 331–3.

Therefore, a commodity is a commodity no matter who makes or uses it: a slave, a peasant, or a proletariat. Marx said that for a product to become a commodity, 'It must not be produced as the immediate means of subsistence of the producer himself.'[5] As we know, slaves produced goods and services for their masters, peasants produced for their lords, and workers produced for their capitalists. And wealth is wealth, regardless of the mode of production or historical epoch: slavery, feudalism, or capitalism. In modern times, regardless of how rich or poor a society is, the only existing production mode on Earth is the capitalist mode of production. However, for the sake of our investigation, we will ignore this point.

To study the relationship between wealth and commodity, we can examine the two countries of Afghanistan and Australia. First, we note that Afghanistan (652,880 km^2) is twelve times smaller than Australia (7,692,220 km^2). The question is: Should Australia's huge quantity of land be considered as wealth for that country? If so, could it also be considered as an immense accumulation of commodities? Second, Afghanistan is a landlocked country with no access to open waters, whereas Australia is the opposite: every millimetre of its border has access to ocean and seas. Should this advantage be considered wealth for Australia? And is it an immense accumulation of commodities?

There are many similar examples. For instance, the African country of Tanzania is fortunate to have the highest, free-standing single mountain in the world (Kilimanjaro), which brings the country innumerable advantages and income. Can we consider this geographical privilege in Tanzania as wealth? Can it be considered as an immense accumulation of commodities?

Now, let us examine the issue of wealth in societies from a different perspective. For example, South Africa has significant, rich natural resources of diamond, gold, iron, platinum, manganese, chromium, copper, uranium, silver, beryllium, and titanium. In addition to the gemstones that Afghanistan is known for—such as rubies, emeralds, tourmalines, and lapis lazuli—we know that country has rich natural

---

5 Marx, *Capital*, Vol. 1, 166.

resources of iron, copper, lithium, cobalt, bauxite, mercury, uranium, chromium, and rare earth elements. There are other countries like Iran, Venezuela, Kuwait, and Russia that have very rich oil and natural gas resources. Here, the same question can be asked: Can all these important natural minerals and resources be considered wealth and an immense accumulation of commodities?

The issue of wealth and commodity is quite a ticklish subject and can be examined from a number of angles. For example, according to 2013 statistics, we know that the numbers of physicians per capita (per 10,000 people) in the following countries are as follows: Tanzania—0.3; Spain—49.5; Afghanistan—2.7; Germany—38.9; Ghana—1; Sweden—39.3; and Mozambique—0.4. No one can deny that one of the most basic human needs is medical care, and the most important element of this is access to a medical doctor. So the question is: Can the number of physicians in medically rich societies be considered wealth and, therefore, an immense accumulation of commodities?

Questions regarding the issue of wealth and commodities in societies based on their geographical advantages, natural resources, professional expertise, and different factors could be asked endlessly. There are several definitions for national wealth; for instance, Thomas Piketty says, "I define 'national wealth' or 'national capital' as the total market value of everything owned by the residents and government of a given country at a given point in time, provided that it can be traded on some market. It consists of the sum total of nonfinancial assets (land, dwellings, commercial inventory, other buildings, machinery, infrastructure, patents, and other directly owned professional assets) and financial assets (bank accounts, mutual funds, bonds, stocks, financial investments of all kinds, insurance policies, pension funds, etc.) less the total amount of financial liabilities (debt)." And he summarizes by saying that: "National wealth = private wealth + public wealth."[6] But here, we will abandon the issue of national wealth and we will start examining commodity.

---

6 Thomas Piketty, *Capital in the Twenty-First Century*, 61.

COMMODITY AND USE-VALUE

The most important property of a commodity is its use-value. Simply put, it has value because we can use it, in one way or another, to fill our needs or wants. A commodity without use-value is nothing but a useless object that is worthless. Hence, to understand what a commodity is, it is crucial to understand the concept of use-value. Marx said, "A commodity is, in the first place, an object outside us, a thing that by its properties satisfies human wants of some sort or another. The nature of such wants, whether, for instance, they spring from the stomach or from fancy, makes no difference." He also said, "Neither are we here concerned to know how the object satisfies these wants, whether directly as means of subsistence, or indirectly as means of production."[7]

Further, Marx wrote: "The utility of a thing makes it a use-value," and also, "use-values become a reality only by use or consumption: they also constitute the substance of all wealth, whatever may be the social form of that wealth."[8] The conclusion that we can draw is that the use-value of a commodity is conditioned by fulfilling human needs and wants of any kind. In other words, a commodity has use-value because it can be used to satisfy human requirements. But considering the matter more closely will show us that Karl Marx views this differently.

We know Marx said, "As use-values, commodities are, above all, of different qualities, but as exchange-values they are merely different quantities, and consequently do not contain an atom of use-value." He continued, "If then we leave out of consideration the use-value of commodities, they have only one common property left, that of being products of labour."[9] He also said, "A use-value, or useful article, therefore, has value only because human labour in the abstract has been embodied or materialized in it."[10]

---

7 Marx, *Capital*, Vol. 1, 43.

8 Marx, *Capital*, Vol. 1, 44.

9 Marx, Capital, Vol. 1, 45.

10 Marx, *Capital*, Vol. 1, 46.

There is something confusing here, in what Marx says, and that raises a question: Why does use-value owe its existence only to human labour? Earlier we learned that use-value becomes reality only by use or consumption, which is very natural and logical. Then we hear that use-value has value only because human labour in the abstract has been materialized in it. This does not make sense, although Marx's idea is partially correct because human labour is one of the elements embodied in a commodity and, thus, in use-value.

Let us examine this through an example. If, while hiking, we find edible wild berries and enjoy their juicy, sweet taste, are we not using or consuming them? Would it be logical for us, as civilized, thinking people, to deny the use-value of what we had just eaten? Why should we care that in those tasty wild berries, human labour in the abstract has not been materialized? Why should we not accept the usefulness and use-value of wild berries that were produced by nature? We know Marx has no objection to recognizing the use-value of natural things. Marx even said, "A thing can be a use-value, without having value. This is the case whenever its utility to man is not due to labour. Such are air, virgin soil, natural meadows, etc."[11] But this question is not as simple as it appears, and we will study the details of this question more closely.

Talking about use-value, commodity, and exchange-value, Marx told us: "Our capitalist has two objects in view: in the first place he wants to produce a use-value that has a value in exchange, that is to say, an article destined to be sold, a commodity."[12] Then he added that: "His commodity possesses for himself no immediate use-value. Otherwise, he would not bring it to the market."[13] And he made it clear that: "All commodities are non-use-values for their owners."[14] In these words, Marx was telling us that a commodity does not have use-value for the capitalist, the owner, because the capitalist wants to sell the commodity.

---

11 Marx, *Capital*, Vol. 1, 48.

12 Marx, *Capital*, Vol. 1, 181.

13 Marx, *Capital*, Vol. 1, 89.

14 Marx, *Capital*, Vol. 1, 89.

Now, let us look at this matter from a different point of view. Let us imagine a capitalist who wants to do business by using money. Our capitalist will buy labour-power, raw material, and all necessary means of production to produce his commodities (let's say T-shirts) and sell them all.

For the sake of our investigation, we will ignore the matter of fairness about private profit and surplus-value. If we consider that our capitalist's reason (want) for doing business was to accumulate wealth, his commodities (the T-shirts) are satisfying his want to make money. Thus, would it be logical for us to deny the immediate use-value of the T-shirts for our capitalist, even though he is not wearing them? He is using and consuming them by selling (exchanging) them, as it was his intent (want) from the very beginning. Why should we deny the want of this capitalist and the satisfaction that he enjoys in doing his trade? While we remember that the legitimacy of human want, even as a fancy want, was approved earlier by Marx.

Another significant point is that Marx's method for denying use-value of a commodity will end up denying his own sacred human labour. As we remember, Marx said without the use-value, commodities are products of labour, and a useful article only has value because it was produced by human labour. If we reverse these sayings, they become: A use-value, or useful article, therefore, has value only because human labour in the abstract has been embodied or materialized in it. If then we leave out of consideration the use-value of commodities, they have only one common property left, that of being products of labour.

The first phrase tells us that the use-value of commodity exists or has value because of the human labour that produced it. Thus, if, as the second phrase stipulates, we leave out of consideration the use-value, automatically and inevitably, we remove consideration of the abstract human labour that is embodied in it. When a material container disappears, so does its abstract content. Therefore, in Marx's reasoning, nothing will be the product of nothing. If use-value disappears, the commodity and the abstract human labour in it will disappear. Thus, labour is not prior to value, and value is not prior to use-value, as Marx indicated. The sense of this equation is totally the other way around. In fact, use-value is prior to everything because use-value determines and proves the existence, the value, and the legitimacy of everything.

Hence, Marx was definitely wrong when he said, "As use-values commodities are, above all, of different qualities, but as exchange-values they are merely different quantities, and consequently do not contain an atom of use-value."[15] Since this saying of Marx's has a pivotal importance in our analysis and we will repeat it several times in different parts of our investigation; therefore, here, I will repeat this very particular saying in German, exactly as Marx personally wrote it in his mother tongue. "Als Gebrauchswerte sind die Waren vor allem verschiedner Qualität, als Tauschwerte können sie nur verschiedner Quantität sein, enthalten also kein Atom Gebrauchswerte."[16]

Thus, from the moment a commodity is produced, it has a use-value because its properties can satisfy human needs or wants, regardless of by whom, where, or how, it is produced or used. The use-value springs with a commodity, lives with a commodity, and dies with a commodity. A commodity without use-value does not exist—even at the moment of being exchanged between capitalists or between the capitalist and the final individual consumer. Hence, in any moment, the use-value of an existing commodity is not deniable even by virtue of its exchange-value. Consequently, we can define a commodity as follows: **A commodity is a useful, human-made object outside or inside us, or a useful human-acquired subject inside or outside us that—so far as it is consumed, applied, or communicated—can satisfy human need, desire, or want of any kind.**

REAL VALUE VS. ABSTRACT VALUE

In terms of value, commodity has a dual character. It can appear as a use-value or as an exchange-value. The use-value of a commodity is a concrete and rather complex phenomenon. It is an intrinsic value that is an independent and inherent property of a commodity, apart

---

15 Marx, *Capital*, Vol. 1, 45.

16 Karl Marx, *Das Kapital* (Ananconda): 51.

from its exchange-value, and by its nature, it is not conditioned by exchange-value at all. It is an autarkic quality that solely stands on itself because it has gone through a particular production process with specific modifications and alterations in order to become an article with a certain function, which is capable of serving a human need or want. Thus, when a person uses a commodity, the use-value of that commodity is carrying out the responsibility that was delegated to it during the production process. The person who is being served by the use-value is naturally the use-value-user, which determines the kind of use-value. In fact, the relation between use-value and use-value-user can be described as:

Use-Value / versus / Use-Value-User

In this formula, use-value is versus use-value user because:

1. Existing of one is inexisting of the other (i.e., if one is, the other is not). The existence of a use-value separated from the use-value-user is automatically confirmation of its independence up until the arrival of the use-value-user. For instance, the existence of a loaf of bread or a pair of shoes is independent and definitive as long as it is not possessed or consumed by a use-value-user. But the moment that a use-value is in use, its decomposition begins, and from there on, the use-value no longer has an independent and definitive existence. It must be considered as a disappearing phenomenon. From the other side, the arrival of the use-value-user is a definitive replacement of the use-value by the use-value-user because, from this moment on, the use-value becomes part and parcel of the use-value-user.

2. One explains the other. The relation between the use-value and the use-value-user is mutual. Use-value, by its nature, provides a service that has been created by a specific process. And from the other side, a use-value-user is a source requiring a service. The nature of the use-value-user's requirements—either objective or subjective, or either real or artificial—makes no difference.

3. One confirms the other. The mere existence of a use-value is a definite confirmation that one day there was, is, or will be a user. Thus, the use-value confirms or justifies—regardless of if it is right or wrong—the existence of the use-value-user.

It is not surprising that Marx noted the importance of the kind of use-value and who uses it. Here is how he writes it: 'Labour uses up its material factors, its subject and its instruments, consumes them, and is therefore a process of consumption. Such productive consumption is distinguished from individual consumption by this, that the latter uses up products, as means of subsistence for living individual; the former...labour consumes products in order to create products, or in other words, consumes one set of products by turning them into means of production for another set.'[17]

Contrary to use-value, the exchange-value of a commodity depends on, or is conditioned by, the use-value of that commodity because no one will exchange or take an article if it is not usable. Marx understood this very well and said, 'The articles exchanged do not acquire a value-form independent of their own use-value.'[18] The relationship between the use-value and the exchange-value of a commodity is a peculiar issue. Exchange-value is an instrumental value; viz., it does not have the capacity to immediately serve anybody. However, it can play a decisive role in helping or causing the use-value to go from one side of a transaction to the other and become available to serve the exchangers.

In fact, exchange-value is an abstract intellectual concept that cannot exist if it is not defined by a complete, exercisable, and desired use-value. In other words, it is merely an abstract value that will satisfy both sides of a transaction to exchange a commodity. This means that there is always a desired use-value, even if hidden, in any given exchange-value. An exchange-value is merely a symbolic and abstract reasoning; it does not serve any human needs or wants directly because it does not have any material form. The exchange-value is just an

---

17 Marx, *Capital*, Vol. 1, 179.
18 Marx, *Capital*, Vol. 1, 92.

idealistic and intellectual balance of quantitative value-relationship in an agreed comparison between interested use-values in two sides of a transaction, which they call an exchange. However, it is certainly true that through a transaction, an exchange of use-values allows certain human needs and wants to be served. The significant point here is that the human need for consumers and the want for capitalists on both sides of an exchange are use-values.

To understand how the use-value can remain hidden in the exchange-value, Marx has a brilliant method to explain the elementary expression of the value. We will first look at this, and then we will adapt his method in our investigation. Marx said, "In order to discover how the elementary expression of the value of a commodity lies hidden in the value-relation of two commodities, we must, in the first place, consider the latter entirely apart from its quantitative aspect."[19]

To illustrate this, he offered an example: "Whether 20 yards of linen = 1 coat or = 20 coats or = X—that is, whether a given quantity of linen is worth few or many coats, every such statement implies that the linen and coats, as magnitudes of value, are expressions of the same unit, things of the same kind. Linen = coat is the basis of the equation."[20]

Then, this is how he dissected the conundrum. He wrote:

> But the two commodities whose identity of quality is thus assumed, do not play the same part. It is only the value of the linen that is expressed. And how? By its reference to the coat as its equivalent, as something that can be exchanged for it. In this relation the coat is the mode of existence of value, is value embodied, for only as such is it the same as the linen. On the other hand, the linen's own value comes to the front, receives independent expression, for it is only as being value that it is comparable with the coat as a thing of equal value, or exchangeable with the coat.[21]

---

19 Marx, *Capital*, Vol. 1, 56.
20 Ibid.
21 Ibid.

He further explained what really is happening: "If we say that, as values, commodities are mere congelations of human labour, we reduce them by our analysis, it is true, to the abstraction, value; but we ascribe to this value no form apart from their bodily form. It is otherwise in the value-relation of one commodity to another. Here, the one stands forth in its character of value by reason of its relation to the other."[22]

And here is where he sheds light on a crucial point:

> By making the coat the equivalent of linen, we equate the labour embodied in the former to that in the latter. Now, it is true that the tailoring, which makes the coat, is concrete labour of a different sort from the weaving which makes the linen. But the act of equating it to the weaving reduces the tailoring to that which is really equal in the two kinds of labour, to their common character of human labour. In this roundabout way, then the fact is expressed, that weaving also, in so far as it weaves value, has nothing to distinguish it from tailoring, and, consequently, is abstract human labour. It is the expression of equivalence between different sorts of commodities that alone brings into relief the specific character of value-creating labour, and this it does by actually reducing the different varieties of labour embodied in the different kinds of commodities to their quality of human labour in the abstract.[23]

We know Marx is a clever person. He understands what he said above does not cover the point completely, for he knows that the question of the labour character is a complex matter. Here is how he imparted the complexity of this issue:

> There is, however, something else required beyond the expression of the specific character of the labour of which the value of the linen consists. Human labour power in motion,

---

22 Marx, *Capital*, Vol. 1, 57.
23 Ibid.

or human labour, creates value, but is not itself value. It becomes value only in its congealed state, when embodied in the form of some object. In order to express the value of the linen as a congelation of human labour, that value must be expressed as having objective existence, as being a something materially different from the linen itself, and yet a something common to the linen and all other commodities.[24]

And finally, Marx knew better than anyone else that, when concerning value and commodity, all roads will end up in use-value. Marx drew a very clear conclusion and showed us how the validity and legitimacy of everything related to the value and exchange of a commodity originates from the use-value:

Hence, in the value equation, in which the coat is the equivalent of the linen, the coat officiates as the form of value. The value of the commodity linen is expressed by the bodily form of the commodity coat, the value of one by the use-value of the other. As a use-value, the linen is something palpably different from the coat; as value, it is the same as the coat, and now has the appearance of a coat. Thus, the linen acquires a value-form different from its physical form. The fact that it is value is made manifest by its equality with the coat.[25]

Marx understood that use-value is a material issue that is in the bodily form of commodity, whereas exchange-value is an imaginary issue that receives its credit and justification from use-value. Nevertheless, he made a very grave mistake. Thus, below, we will examine the phraseology of Marx's denial of use-value in comparison with exchange-value.

As you will recall, Marx said, "As use-values, commodities are, above all, of different qualities, but as exchange values they are merely different quantities, and consequently do not contain an atom of use-value."[26]

---

24 Marx, *Capital*, Vol. 1, 57–8.

25 Marx, *Capital*, Vol. 1, 58.

26 Marx, *Capital*, Vol. 1, 45.

Here, Marx suggested that, in certain conditions, a commodity does not contain use-value. To better understand this, we must recognize that Marx's saying has three parts:

1. As use-values, commodities are qualities.
2. As exchange-values, they are merely different quantities.
3. Consequently, they do not contain an atom of use-value.

First, we will study part 2 in relation to part 3. This relationship tells us that exchange-values, which are quantities, do not contain an atom of use-value that is quality. In other words, quantity does not contain quality, and even more simply said, quantity is not quality. They do not replace each other, and they do not eliminate each other.

Second, we will study part 1 in relation to part 3. This relationship tells us that use-values, which are qualities, do not contain an atom of use-value, which itself is also a quality. In other words, quality does not contain quality, and even more simply said, quality is not quality. Therefore, the final form is that the commodity as a use-value and as quality, despite being a commodity, is not a commodity. Here, we face a very serious question: Is a commodity a commodity? Or is it not a commodity? If a commodity is not a commodity, and it does not contain use-value, so what phenomenon is a capitalist selling to a consumer? And if it is not a commodity with use-value, why would a consumer buy it? This reasoning, in one shot, is denying both the capitalist and consumer in the production and distribution process.

Let us see what we have if we recompose Marx's words. We will rewrite all of his twenty-six words but in a slightly different order: **As exchange-values, commodities are, above all, of different quantities, but as use-values, they are merely different qualities, and consequently do not contain an atom of use-value.** Thus, the three parts will become:

1. As exchange-values, commodities are quantities.
2. As use-values, they are merely different qualities.
3. Consequently, they do not contain an atom of use-value.

Although all twenty-six words are the same, but in a different arrangement, what they are saying seems irrelevant and nonsensical. To understand the point, let us ignore number 1. Then remains number 2 and 3, which, in relationship with each other, becomes:

Use-values do not contain an atom of use-value

It is ridiculous, isn't it?

Let us try another rearrangement by replacing the word "exchange-value" with "surplus-value."

This time, our recomposed form will be: **As use-values, commodities are, above all, of different qualities, but as surplus-values, they are merely different quantities, and consequently do not contain an atom of use-value.** Thus, the three parts become:

1. As use-values, commodities are qualities.
2. As surplus-values, they are merely different quantities.
3. Consequently, they do not contain an atom of use-value.

But Marx never said this, for he knew very well that by denying use-value in this formula, which means denying use-value compared with surplus-value, in fact, the capitalist would be omitted from the equation and, consequently, exonerated from the crime of robbing the working class. Whereas, in his original formula, by denying use-value compared with exchange-value, Marx very intelligently incriminates capitalists for exploitation and robbery because lack of use-value compared with exchange-value will result in illegitimacy of exchange at all. Here, our complicated issue is the legitimizing power of use-value, and later we will examine this issue extensively.

But this issue has another troubling aspect that we will look at it by writing two phrases of Marx's one after the other: "As use-values, commodities are, above all, of different qualities, but as exchange values they are merely different quantities, and consequently do not contain an atom of use-value." And, "A use-value, or useful article, therefore, has value only because human labour in the abstract has been embodied or materialized in it."[27]

Then, the three parts from above will change to four parts, such as

1. As use-value, commodities are qualities.
2. As exchange-values, they are merely different quantities.
3. Consequently, they do not contain an atom of use-value.
4. A use-value has value only because human labour in abstract is embodied in it.

Since we have already analyzed points 1, 2, and 3, here we will focus our analysis on the relationship between parts 3 and 4. Thus, if a commodity does not contain an atom of use-value, it will not have value, and consequently, human labour in abstract will not be embodied in it. Thus, in the absence of value and human labour, the labourer is denied in the production process.

What we see here is that Marx is denying Marxism, for the most important element in the Marxist economy is the commodity, which is the core of the capitalist mode of production. Commodities are the reason that the production process exists, and then the most important entities in the production process are the capitalist and labourer. Marx wanted to show the world that production relations in the capitalist society, which are a result of commodity relations, are inhuman and unjust. Therefore, a proletarian revolution is a legitimate solution for overthrowing the capitalist system. However, by Marx's reasoning, in denying the use-value of commodity, he has consequently denied the commodity, labourer, capitalist, and consumer, and therefore, he has collapsed the whole structure of his own theory.

Thus, philosophically, Marxism was a dead ideology from its birth. Furthermore, we can understand that, for whatever reason that happens, the denial of the use-value of commodities is gravely harmful to human society.

Above, we examined Marx's phraseology regarding use-value and exchange-value. Now, we will study Marx's wording regarding

---

27 Marx, *Capital*, Vol. 1, 45–6.

exchange-value. In his book *Capital*, Marx explained exchange-value as: "Hence exchange-value appears to be something accidental and purely relative, and consequently an intrinsic value, i.e., an exchange-value that is inseparably connected with, inherent in commodities, seems a contradiction in terms."[28] Here, Marx uses the term "intrinsic value" in a doubtful manner, but he does not say definitively that exchange-value is not an intrinsic value nor that exchange-value is only an instrumental value. We know that an intrinsic value has the capacity to serve or be used immediately, whereas an instrumental value does not have the capacity to be used immediately—but as an instrument, it can make usable things available. Therefore, exchange-value is an instrumental value.

Marx knew that exchange-value is not an intrinsic value. As a writer whose trademark is to repeat his points in many different fashions and who mentioned the words *intrinsic value* while talking about exchange-value in the above quote, he never directly and unequivocally said that exchange-value is not intrinsic value.

By employing the words **intrinsic value**, which he knows is irrelevant, and without ever using the relevant term of "instrumental value" when explaining the nature of exchange-value, Marx has contaminated the environment of the discussion. This continues for more than a page, with him finally saying, "*they* [referring to commodities] do not contain an atom of use-value," which is an absurd assertion. Some individuals have said that Marx in the above quote did not mean commodities, but rather that the exchange-values do not contain use-values. We will need to ask ourselves, does Marx, who was a brilliant, erudite philosopher writer, really need an attorney or priest to interpret his sayings? Why should we not judge Marx's words directly as he wrote them? Especially as the history of the past 175 years testifies that Marx's words had and are having a very serious and destructive effect on human life and civilization. Marxism is a religion, and Marx is a prophet, isn't he?

---

28 Marx, *Capital*, Vol. 1, 44.

THE PHENOMENOLOGY OF USE-VALUE AND EXCHANGE-VALUE

Let us have a closer look at the phenomenology of use-value and exchange-value.

First, we will examine use-value. But we must remember that use-value is not peculiar to capitalism or the capitalist mode of production. We see that Marx was aware of this when he said, "Anyhow, whether the coat be worn by the tailor or by his customer, in either case it operates as a use-value."[29] Now we will study use-value through an example. In a shoe store, in early December, before the holidays, a pair of shoes was priced at $100. The same pair of shoes, after the holidays, in early January, with a 35% discount, was priced at $65. Eventually, a witty customer, through a skillful negotiation, made a good bargain and bought that pair of shoes for $55. The shoe seller's cost for that same pair of shoes was $50.

We will examine this story from two different points of view: 1. the shoe buyer's, and 2. the shoe seller's.

1. **The shoe buyer (a consumer)** is buying a shoe (a commodity) to wear (a natural human need)—in other words, to use the use-value of the shoe. The use-value of the shoe (for which it was produced) is to serve by covering and protecting the human foot (the honourable human intention in production by labour). The shoe buyer has the sincere intention to consume a use-value (by wearing the shoe). No matter what the price (any of the three prices that might be paid), the shoe buyer will get only one pair of shoes. How high or low the price is will have absolutely no effect; it will never increase or decrease the use-value of the shoe for the buyer. The shoe has a definite use-value, regardless of its price. As soon as the buyer has the shoe in possession, the shoe (definite use-value) will serve (meeting its promise) the shoe buyer.

   Furthermore, even if our creative buyer decides to make a sculpture with this pair of shoes (a natural human want, my own experience in Montreal-Bordeaux prison) instead of wearing

---

29 Marx, *Capital*, Vol. 1, 50.

the shoes, there is still only one definite use-value of the shoe that will honestly and sincerely serve the shoe buyer. Thus, in use-value, there is a clear responsibility and duty that has been delegated to the shoe during the production process to serve a human need or want.

Let us try to look at other circumstances in which this pair of shoes might become a subject of consumption. Imagine that because of poverty, mental illness, or character disorder (a natural human defect), an individual steals this pair of shoes from the shoe seller instead of paying for them. From the moment that the individual is out of the shoe seller's sight, he can wear the shoe and the shoes' use-value will serve the person in a very normal manner.

2. **The shoe seller (a capitalist)** is selling the shoes (a commodity) to make money—a profit (a natural human intellectual want), which is using the use-value of the shoe. For money is wealth, and wealth is use-value. As Marx said, "Use-values become a reality only by use or consumption: they also constitute the substance of all wealth, whatever may be the social form of that wealth."[30] But, the use-value of the shoes for the buyer is not the same as the use-value for the seller. Here, we start seeing the complexity and perplexing nature of use-value. This side of use-value is not as obvious as the other side, which was serving the shoe buyer, although both are the intrinsic virtues of the commodity. In the case of the shoe buyer, the shoe is a definite object that has been produced for a specific, naturally existing form and size (the aim of the production), and the shoe buyer's feet are specific human body parts that also are of a certain natural function, form, and size (the cause of human need). Thus, what concerns the shoe buyer is paying the agreed price and from there on enjoying the use-value of the shoe, which originates from the shoes' raison d'être. The point here is that from the moment a use-value commodity is out of the production process, it possesses a

---

30 Marx, *Capital*, Vol. 1, 44.

self-manifested identity free from labour because labour finishes when the production process ends. This is similar to how a child, from the moment of birth, has a self-manifested identity free from its parents.

But for the shoe seller, the service of use-value is not achieved so naturally and easily as it is for the shoe buyer. The shoe's use-value as profit does not have a self-manifesting capacity because it is a want in the shoe seller's mind versus a human survival need. Even if the labourer who produced the shoe dies, the shoe will still have its use-value for the consumer. But if the shoe seller dies, so will the shoes' use-value as a profit. Even though the shoes are still wearable, the profit can disappear, because a charity organization can give the shoe to someone in need without any charge.

So, let us get closer to the core of this issue. We have considered that the shoe seller's cost for the shoe was $50. Now, we will look at the possible outcomes of the three prices for which the shoe seller may sell this pair of shoes:

1. If the shoe is sold at $55, the seller will make a $5 profit.
2. If the shoe is sold at $65, the seller will make a $15 profit.
3. If the shoe is sold at $100, the seller will make a $50 profit.

These three outcomes tell us that the use-value as a profit for the shoe seller is not a definite thing. Quite the opposite. The use-value of a commodity in the context of profit is a variable matter that can be affected by several things, such as the season, neighbourhood, or market. There are many factors that make it possible to sell identical articles for different prices and, therefore, to make different profits for the seller (capitalist). For now, we will not spend time on the elements that cause variability of profit. Those elements are all artificial and can be manipulated. We will analyze them closely later on. Here, the important point to understand is that the use-value as a profit for the capitalist is, by its nature, changeable and depends on the greediness or intelligence of the capitalist.

This is what can allow capitalist activity to either become corrupt (a negative human want) or become the motivation for commodity production and wealth accumulation (a positive human want). Thus, it is a dirty but effective energy for growing the economy and creating wealth. The thirst for profit and making money and wealth is not a human need necessary for survival; it is a fancy human want. In fact, it is the result of the evolution of the human brain and, thus, human intellectual development. Humans have developed the idea that making and accumulating wealth is important and attractive. Thus, as time and technology advance, the human thirst for wealth will increase. The human thirst for making money and accumulating wealth is similar to the thirst of plant roots searching for water and minerals. Roots will go anywhere and do anything to acquire what they need, as humans will do for money and wealth. Therefore, nothing can hinder them and, of course, nothing should prevent them.

There are two aspects of the variability of use-value in the form of profit that we must study. One aspect is abstract or intellectual, and the second aspect is concrete or financial.

The analysis of the **intellectual** aspect of the variability of use-value in the form of profit reveals that in a production process, to produce a commodity for selling, the capitalist is the subject of the verb. The capitalist will produce or buy, which means the capitalist is in a power position. But in the exchange process to sell a commodity, the consumer determines if the commodity will be bought and determines the success of the exchange process. Thus, the consumer (buyer) is the subject of the verb to buy, and the capitalist (seller) becomes the object, which is subordinate to the consumer's subjectivity. The capitalist must wait and watch until the consumer makes the final decision to complete the transaction. However, the whole game of seeking benefit (profit) for the capitalist starts here because the matter of price—the most crucial matter for a capitalist—is what will give birth to a profit from the exchange process, if it is finalized. At this stage, the capitalist will play an intellectual role, concentrating all his efforts to convince, entice, or even lure (a negative human want) the consumer to take the commodity and pay the price. In this phase, to succeed in collecting a profit, the intelligence, knowledge, and experience of the capitalist comes into play, and the capitalist may bypass laws, regulations, or moralities.

The analysis of the **financial** aspect of the variability of use-value in the form of profit reveals (as we saw above in the shoe story) that from the moment that the shoe seller has the shoes in hand, his only want is to sell them as quickly as possible (in a quantity of time) at the highest price (for a quantity of money). Here, the capitalist remains the subject of the verb because he has the final word on the price to sell the commodity for, and the consumer is subordinate to the capitalist's satisfaction. This subordinate position of the consumer in relation to the capitalist because of the price of the commodity is similar to the position of the employee, who is subordinate to the capitalist's satisfaction because of the salary. To reach his goal, the capitalist has to take into consideration all the elements that can affect his pricing. Because of the shoe seller's want, he will try all possible tricks to sell the pair of shoes for the highest price that he can.

We will look at some of the options that the capitalist may have in mind. The shoe seller could consider making 100% profit, which would mean doubling the cost price, if he thinks he could convince his customers to pay that price. The shoe seller could even raise the profit to 200% or 300%, if he believes that he could convince his customers to pay that price. This is why we often see the same articles with different prices. Recently, I wanted to buy a small hand-held vacuum cleaner. Within a ten-kilometre radius, in the same city, I found three different prices for the very same hand-held vacuum cleaner. The first price ($149.99) was 80% more expensive than the third price ($82.99). The second price was $99.99. Not surprisingly at all, the shop that was closest to me, and which had the most expensive price, agreed to adjust the price and sell me the hand-held vacuum cleaner for $82.99 so as to not lose me as a customer. However, we all know that even with the lowest price, the seller was still making a profit. The story is even more hilarious, if I tell you that, just a few weeks later, the same shop priced the same hand-held vacuum cleaner at $199.99, and by generously offering a 50% discount, was selling it for $99.99. As you remember, I had already bought the same item from the same shop for $17 cheaper.

Playing with prices and creating false impressions about the practicality and function of commodities in order to lure and encourage consumers to buy (consume) more and/or to consume certain brands is called marketing in capitalist literature. Later, we will study the market and marketing in the capitalist mode of production. Here, though, it will suffice to say that marketing in the capitalist philosophy means the art of endlessly convincing and encouraging people to buy more. For capitalism without consumers and consumption cannot exist, and for that matter, never existed. Next, we will study the network nature (social nature versus class nature) of the capitalist mode of production.

NETWORK NATURE OF CAPITALISM

Under capitalism, a commodity travels through the labyrinth of human society, starting with production and ending up in the hands of the consumer, who buys the commodity for personal (immediate) use. Therefore, we can conclude that today the capitalist mode of production, contrary to previous historic epochs, is not a binary system. It is a network system. The binary mode of production is a one-way trajectory production mechanism in which all the services and products go directly from maker to taker, without any other partner.

We will now examine the slavery mode of production. But first, it is useful to state that when talking about a mode of production, we must consider the means by which the land and all other raw materials are made available to the system. Therefore, studying a mode of production in any historical epoch must include examining the various roles of humans in the mechanism of production and the consumption of the commodity to determine who is the maker and who is the taker and how justice has been respected or neglected. Slavery was a social system in which masters (enslavers) owned slaves as private objects and property. Slaves were bound to their masters through accepted social and legal rules, which included social terror and violence practised and enforced by social institutions and the ruthless brutality of masters. In the slavery mode of production, since slaves (as biomechanical objects) belonged to enslavers, the slaves' use-value—their intellectual and physical capacity—were totally and unconditionally taken by enslavers (owners). Masters and their slaves were two poles of one circuit (maker and taker) and made a complete set with each other. They could live and survive together without requiring anybody else.

In a feudal mode of production, the mechanism has two principal elements: the lord (taker) and the peasants (makers). The feudal mode of production, with its two elements of a lord and peasants, is a complete autarkical system that can survive on its own. The lord and peasants need each other and nothing else. The absence of either of these two elements would definitively terminate the feudal mode of production.

The capitalist mode of production depends on three elements: the employee (the worker or maker), the employer (the capitalist or taker), and the consumer (the loser). The capitalist mode of production produces more commodities than the capitalists and workers could ever use on their own, so the role of the consumer is important. The capitalist mode of production could not exist without these three elements. Therefore, Karl Marx was wrong when he reduced the class struggle in the capitalist mode of production to only two elements: the capitalist and the labourer. In Marx's formula, the third element of the mode of production, the consumer (a huge majority of society), is absent.

The three titles—employee, capitalist, and consumer—are the socio-economic names for the natural persons in a society that determine the legal economic status of every individual in the commodity production relations. The only entity that connects these three elements (in either objective or abstract form) is the use-value of commodities. All three principle elements of the capitalist mode of production expect use-value from each other. This use-value, in one way or another, presents itself in the form of a commodity. Therefore, the commodity is an essential corporate entity of the capitalist mode of production. Therefore, it is important to understand how the commodity's use-value (the fourth element) travels back and forth between the three principal elements (the three natural persons). Commodity relations create a network between the three principal elements of the capitalist mode of production. Within this network, the exchange of the use-value in the form of a commodity—money—creates satisfaction for each element in the relationship and, therefore, ensures the continuation of the capitalist economy in society. This network could be called the vascular (circulation) system of the use-value, in which money plays a decisive role. Later on, we will study the social impact of money in the network of commodity relations.

Now, we will look at the characteristics of each of the principal elements within the network.

1. **The employee** is a natural person who 'brings his labour-power to market for sale as a commodity.'[31] All human values and power—physical or mental, action or knowledge—are usable-values. In whatever given circumstances or conditions, when a natural person offers a human usable-value that serves another human need or want, that value, in any material or abstract form, is a commodity. If that commodity is offered on the condition of being exchanged with compensation (salary, use-value), the person offering the service is an employee. In other words, an employee is an individual that sells his human use-values.

   Hired by a capitalist, in the capitalist mode of production, an employee uses his human usable-values (human power)—either in fabricating a useful object or in rendering a useful service—to give a use-value (a commodity) to the capitalist. John Stuart Mill, in his book *The Principles of Political Economy*, has written meticulously about the use-value resulting from labour, which he calls the use-value of things 'serviceable to human beings.'[32]

   The quality and the quantity of the use-value that an employee makes in the form of goods or services must satisfy the desire of the capitalist, who is the buyer. In the relationship between the capitalist and the employee, the capitalist calls the shots. He

---

31 Marx, *Capital*, Vol. 1, 174.
32 John Stuart Mill, *The Principles of Political Economy*, 24.

determines both the working conditions and the quantity of the use-value compensation (salary). Usually, a person becomes an employee in order to make a living (human need). In the capitalist mode of production, the employee is subordinate to the capitalist's demands. On an economic map, the relationship between the employee and the capitalist is a road in front of the employee that delivers the capitalist's insatiable orders and demand. In exchange for the service that is offered to the capitalist, the employee often receives very little compensation (wage) on which to live. Karl Marx has written extensively about low wages, so we will not get into the details of this here.

2. **A capitalist** is a natural person, even if he or she is hidden behind a corporation. The capitalist has money or wealth (use-value) and invests it in production or services or both in order to make a private profit (use-value for a human want). The capitalist also uses his money to pay a salary (use-value) to one or several employees to produce useful objects (use-value, commodity) or provide useful services (use-value, commodity) for the inhabitants (consumers) of society. On the economic map, the capitalist has two roads in front of him. One of the roads is connected to the employee, along which goods and services (use-value, commodities) produced by the employee come to the capitalist. The second road connects the capitalist to the consumer. Through the second road, the capitalist sells the goods and services (use-value, commodities) to the consumer and collects money (price, use-value).

The capitalist is superior to the consumer because he fixes the price of the commodity and the conditions of the transaction. According to the market, which is controlled by a capitalist economy, the capitalist sells his goods and services at the most expensive price possible. Consequently, for every use-value of goods and services offered by the capitalist, he collects proportionally a much higher use-value (price, money) from the consumer. Thus, from one side, the capitalist gives little to the employee, and he collects a lot more from him. And from the other side, the capitalist gives a little to the consumer, and he collects a lot more from him. This is how a capitalist becomes a multi-millionaire or billionaire, and richer and richer. He accumulates wealth that comes from the pockets of both the employees and consumers.

Here, I come to the point of saying that Karl Marx was wrong to encourage only the workers to resist capitalism for the injustices put upon them. He was also wrong to say that the communist party is a worker's party and only the workers or their representatives should take over and run society. Any social change for good that is based only on workers (proletariats) will never work because it is not based on the whole truth. The truth in Karl Marx's theory is partial and prejudicious; therefore, it is collapsible and corruptible, as history has shown us.

3. **A consumer** is a natural person who requires goods and services (use-value, commodity) to live (natural human needs and wants). Under the capitalist mode of production, the only way to acquire goods and services is to buy them in the market, and the market is made and controlled by capitalists. The entity that connects the consumer to the capitalist is the price (money, use-value). The consumer, subordinate to the capitalist, has to obey the capitalist and, therefore, pay the price set by the capitalist to obtain the goods and services necessary for living. On the economic map, the relationship between the consumer and capitalist is a road with a toll imposed on the consumer to receive goods and services.

Here, we will compare, in a linear schematic, the Marxist social structure of society with the network social structure that we have examined above. In Karl Marx's theory, the social structure of human society and its relation to use-value under the capitalist mode of production has two entities (capitalist and labourer) and can be shown as:

Use-value of a commodity	for a capitalist (human individual) is	not an atom of use-value
Use-value of a commodity	for a labourer (human individual) is	use-value

Whereas, based on our detailed scrutiny, we have learned that the social structure of human society under the capitalist mode of production is, indeed, a network structure, which consists of three social classes: the employee, capitalist, and consumer. In relation to use-value, this can be shown as:

Use-value of a commodity	for an employee (human individual) is	use-value
Use-value of a commodity	for a capitalist (human individual) is	use-value
Use-value of a commodity	for a consumer (human individual) is	use-value

As a result, the legitimizing power of use-value will legitimize the social function of every social class. Therefore, the question of superiority and inferiority among the social classes that establishes the social apartheid of capitalism in human society under the capitalist mode of production is a serious issue that we will examine more closely.

THE MECHANISM OF SUPERIORITY AND INFERIORITY

Above, we introduced the three principle elements of the capitalist mode of production. Each of these represents a group (class) of people in a capitalist society:

1. Employees   2. Capitalists   3. Consumers

These positions can overlap and may become mixed with each other: for instance, a consumer can also be an employee; a consumer can also be a capitalist; and a capitalist can also be an employee. However, this overlapping is not a major issue or a concern for our analysis. The most important questions for determining a person's social group (social class) in a capitalist society are; first: how dominantly is the person making money (i.e., by selling his labour-power or by buying somebody's labour-power)? Second: with respect to commodity relations, how is the person spending his money to buy goods and services for his needs and wants (i.e., merely by buying commodity or by buying and selling commodity)?

The answers to these two questions will reveal how the economic structure of a capitalist society imposes social discrimination upon its members. This capitalist social discrimination—a capitalist apartheid—is above and beyond all other hitherto known discriminations. It is absolutely indifferent to the social, political, ideological, racial, gender, and ethnic identities of the individuals in the society. The key factor is that every individual, as a human animal, is a source of profit, either as an employee or as a consumer. Therefore, in the frame of the social capitalist network, a capitalist is eager to use the market system to extract the maximum possible profit from every individual. This capitalist apartheid emerges from money. It is a result of the superiority and inferiority that has been created and established among individuals by the commodity relations in the social network system of the capitalist mode of production.

The employee (worker) in capitalist society is a natural biological machine and a seller of usable human forces (use-value)—physical, intellectual, or both—in exchange for a usable thing: money (use-value) to buy what is necessary for human needs and wants. In this position, an employee can be seen in two ways. From one side, the employee is a victim of the basic survival needs and wants that nature imposes on humans, such as the need for food, clothing, and shelter, either individually or for one's family. On the other side, the employee only has natural corporal capacities to offer in exchange for money (use-value), which he can use to buy the necessary substances to tame the basic fatal human needs. The human needs linked to survival are involuntary requirements of the body; if they are not furnished, the life and health of an individual will be threatened and eventually lead to death. There are two important points here: the involuntariness of the needs (which means they are not chosen by anybody) and the lethality of them (which, again, is not chosen by anybody). They are decided and imposed by nature upon humans. Humans have no choice but to provide themselves with adequate life-sustaining materials. This is the machinery that makes an employee subordinate to money and, therefore, to whomever possesses money that can be provided to them. In a capitalist society, the capitalist is both the source of money and the buyer of human corporal capacities (labour-power).

The concerning point here is that the nature of the entities' motivation in this equation is not the same. A capitalist's want to make money and accumulate wealth is not a phenomenon imposed by nature for survival. A capitalist makes a decision to become a capitalist based on his free will. And, of course, no one will die if one is not capitalist and does not accumulate money and wealth. However, the employee needs to work to make money to buy a means of subsistence, which is a phenomenon imposed by nature for survival. The nature of a survival need and a human want are not the same. The common element connecting the employee to the capitalist is money, and this plays a role in determining power. Hence, the luxury of having money makes the capitalist superior, and vitally needing money makes the employee inferior.

Now, let us examine the situation of the consumer in commodity relations and the relation between the consumer and the capitalist. Consumers buy all kinds of things, but in this inquiry, we are only concerned with purchases that provide the consumer with the means of subsistence or improvements to their health and quality of life. The consumer (buyer) in capitalist society wants to stay alive and, therefore, is constantly buying what is needed (use-value) for human subsistence (human survival needs). In a capitalist society, the only possible place to buy commodities of any kind is the market, which is controlled by capitalists. The common value for any transaction (buying and selling) is money; therefore, the consumer must pay money (use-value) directly or indirectly to the capitalist in order to obtain the commodities (use-value) for his vital needs and wants. The survival needs of consumers are the same as those of employees. These needs are made and imposed upon humans by nature. The commodities that the consumer buys are either for his needs, which will assure his survival, or for his wants, which will improve his living conditions. These needs and wants are a constant source of anxiety and stress for the consumer, which makes the consumer vulnerable and, therefore, inferior and subordinate to the capitalist. On the other side, the capitalist, as a provider of vital commodities and controller of the market, is in the determining power player position. As a result, the capitalist becomes protected and superior to the consumer.

So far, we have only studied the economic aspect of the social apartheid of capitalism, but the other side of this issue is the social aspect of it. Here, the situation is very similar to the slavery system, in which there was a general and socially accepted idea that some people were superior and others were inferior. It was also accepted that superior people (masters) could possess inferior people (slaves) as belongings and use them for whatever purpose they deemed suitable. In a slavery society, the social institutions, laws, and security and legal systems are made to facilitate and protect the practice of slavery. Under the practice of slavery, everything from the slave goes to the master. Thus, we must first bear in mind that, in a capitalist society, everything is conditioned by money, and money makes decisions for everything. Therefore, similar to the slavery system, in the capitalist society, the social machinery—consisting of social institutions, laws, and legal systems, security means and mechanisms and governing administration—are made to support that. From one side,. the capitalist does not pay enough money to employees, and from the other side the capitalist takes too much money from the consumer. As a result, monetary apartheid becomes the structure of the capitalist society. In the chapter Bird's-eye View, we will have a closer look at this issue.

The capitalist, who has money and wealth, also has a thirst (a human want) for making more money through their natural capacity for thought and action called ambition. To do so, the capitalist buys employees' labour to produce goods and services and then sells these to consumers. Capitalists are wealth makers, and it is true that they make all kinds of useful and important wealth in human society. Although human society has no right to deny the work and role of capitalists in flourishing human society, nevertheless, the monetary apartheid in human society is a serious social disease, which must be cured. Hence, we need to study more the role of use-value and exchange-value in the capitalist mode of production.

LIFE AND DEATH OF COMMODITY

As we have already seen, commodity means use-value; therefore, to study commodity, we must study use-value. The use-value of a commodity has multiple functions that below we will look at them carefully.

An employee, by selling the labour-power in the production process, produces a commodity, which has use-value to a capitalist, receiving wage in exchange. At this stage, the use-value of the commodity is the outward consumption of the commodity for the labourer to make money for the survival need. The commodity will not die at this stage. It will continue its travel life through the labyrinth of production relations while satisfying the survival need of the employee. It will merely be exchanged between employee and capitalist. Thus, we will call it **transit-use-value**.

For a capitalist who produces or buys a commodity to sell or exchange, the use-value of a commodity is the outward consumption of the commodity in commercial want. We will call this **transit-use-value.** At this stage, the commodity will not die. It will continue its travel life through the labyrinth of the fancy social life of a nonessential want.

The use-value of a commodity for a consumer, who buys it to satisfy a survival need, is the definite consumption of the commodity. At this stage, the travel life of a commodity ends, and it will start its decomposition. We will call this **terminal-use-value**. Between these three functions of use-value, the exchange-value in the form of wage and price is what transforms the use-value of an employee to use-value of a capitalist, and then to the use-value of a consumer.

The use-value of a commodity is a complex and delicate matter for defining a commodity and commodity relation. The commodity—regardless of by whom it has been made, from what it has been made, and where it has been made—has a vital social significance in human life. Thus, human life in any form is not imaginable without commodities. Hence, in order to have a fair and harmonious human society in which every inhabitant can enjoy a good quality of life and well-being, monetary, apartheid-free commodity relations must be established in society.

Use-value and exchange-value are the entities that determine the character of a commodity. As a use-value, a commodity has an innocent humanitarian character, but as an exchange-value, a commodity has a corrupt political character. The character of a commodity originates from two different human activities employed with commodities: the production process and the exchange process. We will study each step more closely.

The production process of a commodity is a complex series of human-involved activities for humanitarian reasons. As humans naturally need to consume commodities to live, producing commodities has a humanitarian aim. To produce a commodity, a human thinks of a suitable material (which comes directly or indirectly from nature), envisages a suitable form that will fill a human need, contemplates available tools and human skills, and then eventually fabricates it. Marx's explanation for human workmanship in producing a commodity is splendid; thus, we will repeat it here.

> A spider conducts operations that resemble those of weaver, and a bee puts to shame many an architect in the construction of her cells. But what distinguishes the worst architect from the best of bee is this, that the architect raises his structure in imagination before he erects it in reality. At the end

of every labour-process, we get a result that already existed in the imagination of the labourer at its commencement. He not only effects a change of form in the material on which he works, but he also realizes a purpose of his own that gives the law to his modus operandi, and to which he must subordinate his will. And this subordination is no mere momentary act. Besides the exertion of the bodily organs, the process demands that, during the whole operation, the workman's will be steadily in consonance with his purpose... The elementary factors of the labour-process are: 1. the personal activity of man..., 2. the subject of that work, and 3. its instruments."[33]

A commodity is something—visible or not visible, tangible or not tangible, foreign to the human body—that either relates a human with the material world or, as a means of subsistence, accommodates a human directly or indirectly to stay alive.

Human life has elements of animal-human and social-human, complex and stupendous, with myriad details that create limitless physical or mental needs and wants for surviving or improving living conditions that are all nature-imposed. This is captured in Marx's admirable observation:

coats and linen, like every other element of material wealth that is not the spontaneous produce of Nature, must invariably owe their existence to a special productive activity, exercised with a definite aim, an activity that appropriates particular nature-given materials to particular human wants. So far therefore as labour is a creator of use-value, is useful labour, it is a necessary condition, independent of all forms of society, for the existence of the human race; it is an eternal nature-imposed necessity, without which there can be no

---

33 Marx, *Capital,* Vol. 1, 174.

material exchanges between man and Nature, and therefore no life.[34]

There are two magical points in Marx's observation regarding the relation between commodity use-value and the existence of the human race: 1. material exchanges between humans and nature, and 2. nature-imposed necessity, without which there can be no life. We have to spend more time to explore these points further.

Nature has made humans with needs and wants, as humans are made of body and mind. Thus, humans eat food and think ideas. All human needs and wants (physical or mental; indispensable or extraneous; objective or abstract) are legitimate, nature-imposed necessities independent of all forms of society. These may be for accommodating and protecting life, improving living conditions or making life more luxurious and rich, increasing and developing human knowledge or expanding human scientific and cultural capacity, or advancing human strength and ability to use, confront, and protect nature. In this context, if a human wants to accumulate wealth and money because of some mental activity and inspired passion, such a want is as nature-imposed, legitimate, and moral as a human need for food and shelter. Aristotle, very clearly and wisely, said, "Men seek after a better notion of riches and of the art of getting wealth than the mere acquisition of coin, and they are right."[35] Here, we will face a good question: Why should the want to accumulate wealth and money be considered a nature-imposed necessity?

First, let us consider if a capitalist has a want for accumulating wealth and money and is responding to his want, enjoying his business, and accumulating wealth and money. In such circumstances, would denying our capitalist's want be smart? Would it be realistic? Would not it be in repugnance to human nature and wisdom?

Let us examine what Aristotle says concerning the human want to accumulate wealth and money. He said, "There is another variety of

---

34 Marx, *Capital*, Vol. 1, 50.

35 Aristotle *Politics*, book one, IX, 13.

the art of acquisition which is commonly and rightly called the art of making money, and has in fact suggested the notion that wealth and property have no limit."[36] And he continues:

> A kind of barter which is still practiced among barbarous nations who exchange with one another the necessaries of life and nothing more....This sort of barter is not part of the wealth-getting art and is not contrary to nature, but is needed for the satisfaction of men's natural wants. The other or more complex form of exchange grew out of the simpler. When the inhabitants of one country became more dependent on those of another, and they imported what they needed, and exported the surplus, money necessarily came into use. For the various necessaries of life are not easily carried about, and hence men agreed to employ in their dealings with each other sometime which was intrinsically useful and easily applicable to the purposes of life, for example, iron, silver, and the like. Of this the value was at first measured by size and weight, but in the process of time they put a stamp upon it, to save the trouble of weighing and to mark the value.
>
> When the use of a coin had once been discovered, out of the barter of necessary articles arose the other art of wealth-getting, namely, retail trade; which was at first probably a simple matter, but became more complicated as soon as men learned by experience whence and by what exchanges the greatest profit might be made. Originating in the use of coin, the art of getting wealth is generally thought to be chiefly concerned with it, and to be the art which produces riches and wealth, having to consider how they may be accumulated.[37]

One crucial point that we can learn from Aristotle is the idea of accumulating wealth and money is not peculiar to modern history

---

36 Aristotle *Politics*, book one, IX, 12.

37 Aristotle *Politics*, book one, IX, 12-13.

and capitalism. Ever since early classical antiquity and the discovery of money (coin), humans have learned not only the practicality of using money to exchange necessary articles, but also the advantage of hoarding it to use in a greater profit-making relations. As Aristotle wrote, "For all getters of wealth increase their hoard of coin without limit."[38]

The cruciality of Aristotle's point is to understand that the want of accumulating wealth and money is not just a simple matter of malicious desire, emanating from an isolated mean person's greediness. It is, indeed, the advent of retail trade that taught humans the usefulness and effectiveness of accumulating wealth and money in trade and production. In this regard, we can comprehend that the thought and act of accumulating wealth and money has resulted in the progress of human civilization independent of all forms of society. To this day, it continues to be useful and effective, even more than it was at any time in the past.

Let us get back to our main question: Why must the want to accumulate wealth and money be considered a nature-imposed necessity? As we know, breathing is not a function chosen or controlled by human wishes. A human breathes because nature has imposed it as a vital task for survival. We also know that eating, which is also a vital task, is another function imposed on humans by nature. And, by the same token, we understand that thinking, regardless of how dull or sophisticated it might be, is a human brain function imposed by nature. Nobody can decide to think or not to think. Thinking is indispensable. The human brain thinks as the human heart beats. We think about what to eat; how and when to wash our hands; how to make or wear our clothes; how to travel; how and what to talk about with our parents, children, and friends; where and for what reason to do our shopping, etc. Doubtlessly, we understand that more educated, more experienced, and more active people can have more complex thoughts compared to uneducated, ignorant, and naïve people. Nevertheless, thinking is a nature-imposed function of the human brain. As to know "what thought (cogitation) is," René Descartes tells us: "By the word

---

38 Aristotle *Politics*, book one, IX, 14.

thought, I understand all that which so takes place in us that we of ourselves are immediately conscious of it; and accordingly, not only to understand (intelligence, entendre), to will (velle), to imagine (imaginary), but even to perceive (sentire, sentir), are here the same as to think (cogitare, penser)."[39]

The departure point for capitalists is their want to accumulate wealth and money. We have to bear in mind that capitalists are not a kind of Isaac Asimov-invented creature sent to Earth from the end of the galaxy to save human civilization. Capitalists are nature-made and as human as anyone else, like teachers, bus drivers, workers, doctors, lawyers, etc. Some people, as long as they work, make their living, and support their families, are happy and satisfied, but not capitalists. We are not here to understand why capitalists want to accumulate wealth and money; however, we know that it is the result of a specific way of thinking in their brains. Neither are we here to naïvely think that capitalists are angels on Earth to provide humanity with evolution, progress, and civilization. Although sometimes, directly or indirectly, the activities of some capitalists have caused very significant and decisive developments and progress in history.

Moreover, we have learned from Albert Einstein that "The world we have created is a product of our thinking."[40] John Locke also said: "No man ever tries to do something except on the basis of some view or opinion that serves as his reason for what he does; and whatever faculties he employs, the understanding constantly leads, doing so with whatever light it has; and all his operative powers are directed by that light, whether it is true or false."[41] Robert Lawrence Kuhn says, "Nothing; not science, not theology, not politics, not love: Nothing means anything without our brains. Everything we know and do, all the sense of human thought, all the feelings of human emotion, all

---

39 Rene Descartes, *Principles of Philosophy*, Part 1, IX.

40 New York Times, May 25, 1946, p. 11

41 John Locke, *The Conduct of the Understanding*, 1.

the questions of human existence—all are the product of the brains in our heads."[42]

Let us take a closer look at some of the human characteristics of our capitalists. These so-called "invisible hands"[43] are that capitalists, regardless of how big or small they are in the market, are a kind of rapacious people who do not want to work for somebody; they do not like having a boss over their head, giving them orders and directions. Capitalists are thirsty to control, create, be in charge, take risks, make decisions, order like army generals, fool, lie, exaggerate, and manipulate others, and look enigmatic, powerful, and impressive, even if it is not true. Among them, those who are more naturally hard-working, rigorous, original, witty, assiduous, logical, realistic, sharp, and less emotional consequently become bigger and richer in the market.

Capitalists do not care about production, although the side effects of their activities are always good for production. As Adam Smith said, "Every individual is continually exerting himself to find out the most advantageous employment for whatever capital he can command. It is his own advantage, indeed, and not that of the society, which he has in view. But the study of his own advantage naturally, or rather necessarily, leads him to prefer that employment which is most advantageous to the society."[44]

Marx employed an entertaining way to explain the involvement of the capitalist in production when he mockingly said, "The product appropriated by the capitalist is a use-value, as yarn, for example, or boots. But, although boots are, in one sense, the basis of all social progress, and our capitalist is a decided 'progressist,' yet he does not manufacture boots for their own sake. . . . His aim is to produce not

---

42 Robert Lawrence Kuhn, "How Do Human Brains Think and Feel?" *Science and Religion Today*, May 6, 2010, https://web.archive.org/web/20151211042135/http://www.scienceandreligiontoday.com/2010/05/06/how-do-human-brains-think-and-feel/comment-page-1/.

43 Adam Smith, *The Wealth of Nations*, Book IV, Chapter ll, 572.

44 Smith, *Wealth of Nations*, Book IV, Chapter ll, 569–570.

only a use-value, but a commodity also; not only use-value, but value; not only value, but at the same time surplus-value."[45]

It is clear that capitalists want the accumulation of wealth and money, period. If capitalists could find an island where it snows silver in winter and grows gold in summer, all of them, at once, would move to that island. All year round, they would keep shovelling those precious use-values that constitute the substance of all wealth, and they would absolutely not give a damn if all remaining people on Earth died because they did not have commodities to eat. It is also clear that humans wanting to accumulate wealth and money is a nature-imposed human phenomenon, independent of all forms of society, which will never stop or disappear. As long as social humans exist, they will always strive to accumulate wealth and money. Any attempt to prevent humans from accumulating wealth and money would inevitably gravely damage the health of human society and end in corruption and tyranny.

Now, let us return to transit-use-value and terminal-use-value in three different aspects.

1. Let us consider a mother who buys a jar of baby food (a commodity) for her baby girl. From the moment that this mother has the baby food in her possession until the moment that she is spoon-feeding her baby, she is a holder of a use-value that she is not using (not eating). We know that she will never eat it, but by buying the baby food, this mother is responding to her need: her want to feed her baby. The indispensable want of a mother to feed her baby is a natural, legitimate, nature-imposed want, for which the mother is consuming the transit-use-value of the baby food from the moment of purchase until the moment that her baby eats the baby food. Thus, the baby is consuming the terminal-use-value of the baby food by eating it in response to her indispensable want for nutrition. Here, the mother and baby have exchanged the baby food (a commodity), and the

---

45 Marx, *Capital,* Vol. I, 207.

mother has been paid by the assurance of the health and growth of her baby.

2. Let us consider a person who buys a dog coat (a commodity) for her little dog. Indeed, the reason that this person is buying the dog coat is that she wishes (her fancy want) to provide (transit-use-value) her dog with comfort and protection against the cold weather. Therefore, her dog will (indispensable want) wear (terminal-use-value) the dog coat and not her. Hence, this person and her dog have exchanged the dog coat (a commodity), and in return, this person will be paid by the well-being of her dog.

3. Let us consider a mother who wants to indulge her young child (a fancy want) by buying a necklace (a commodity) for her daughter. In the first step, before giving the necklace to her daughter, the mother is the consumer of the transit-use-value of the necklace, responding to her fancy want. In the second step, when the daughter receives the necklace, she is the consumer of the terminal-use-value of the necklace in wearing it, which, in fact, is responding to her fancy want to adorn her look. Thus, the mother and daughter have exchanged the necklace (a commodity) and, in return, the mother has been paid by the pleasure of making her daughter feel precious and loved.

In the three examples above, we have examined the three different relations between the transit-use-value and the terminal-use-value as follows:

1.	Transit-use-value for indispensable want
	Terminal-use-value for indispensable want

2.	Transit-use-value for fancy want
	Terminal-use-value for indispensable want

| 3. | Transit-use-value for fancy want |
| | Terminal-use-value for fancy want |

The use-value is the basic essential entity that creates the identity and, hence, the nature of the commodity. It is the necessary element that justifies the existence, the raison d'être, of the commodity. The use-value is the soul of the commodity, like the soul of a human. Therefore, intrinsically, it is an invisible but real, effective, and functioning subject, contrary to the body of the commodity, which can be either abstract or concrete, and sometimes even both.

In our first example, when the baby eats the baby food (a commodity), she is not aware of consuming the use-value existing in the baby food. She is eating the baby food (consuming the terminal-use-value) because of the indispensable want that her nature, instinct, has given her. The baby is not aware, either, of the quality of what she is eating. Whatever esculent the mother puts in her baby's mouth, the baby will eat it.

The situation for the mother, though, is different. Although it is the mother's natural and instinctive duty that creates her indispensable want to feed her baby, she consciously and cognitively controls her action and behaviour to find the best possible baby food (use-value) for her baby. The mother is aware that she, herself, will not eat the baby food. Nevertheless, she knows that she is consuming the transit-use-value of the baby food in giving it to her baby. She also cares, contrary to the baby, about the quality of the use-value, which she is transferring to her baby, and will try her best to get the best quality she can according to her budget.

In our second example, the person who buys a coat (a commodity) for her dog is purely following a want created by her mind, as humans naturally are not made to live with dogs. But, through the brain (thought), humans have developed the idea of enjoying the company of animals, and domestic animals have become a fancy part of human life. Hence, the person knows that she will not wear the dog coat herself, and she is cognizant of her consumption of the transit-use-value of the dog coat that she is giving to her dog.

The situation for the dog, though, is different. If a dog, because of the fancy human want of his master, is exposed to the severe cold weather for which his body is not naturally protected, he will need (indispensable want) a cover to keep him warm. This dog will wear the dog coat (consumption of the terminal-use-value) that his master bought him. However, he is not aware of the use-value existing in his coat.

In our third example, the mother wants to indulge her young daughter. Although the attention and love of parents toward their children is a totally natural part of human life, the idea of buying a gift, regardless of who it is for, is a human brain-made, cognitively fabricated fancy want. Moreover, the mother is aware of the use-value embodied in the necklace. She also knows that she will not wear the necklace herself but rather is giving it (consuming the transit-use-value) to her daughter.

The situation for the daughter, apart from being the consumer of the terminal-use-value, is not very different. The daughter is aware of the use-value of her gift (the necklace), and she knows that she will wear it (consume the terminal-use-value). In addition, it is obvious that decoration is not an indispensable need for the human body. Therefore, the daughter understands that her mother's gift will satisfy her fancy want of adorning herself.

You might ask: Why is so much fuss necessary about human want and use-value? This is a legitimate question. We will start with human want. (As a matter of fact, calling it human want or human need makes no significant difference.) Human needs and wants are the roots and reasons for every good and bad thing that occurs in human life and society. Since the very beginning, humans have ceaselessly looked for answers to satisfy their myriad needs and wants. The reason for all human needs and wants that keep humans alive is use-value. Without needs, wants, and use-value, humans would disappear from the surface of the Earth. As Hannah Arendt brilliantly says, "The objectivity of the world—its object—or thing-character—and the human condition supplement each other; because human existence is conditioned existence, it would be impossible without things."[46]

Let us have a quick look at the combination of our planet and humans. According to the available knowledge of today about the universe, Earth is the third planet in our solar system, situated about 150,000,000 kilometres away from the sun. Our planet consists of three structures: mineral, vegetal, and animal. Non-stop movement is circulating between these three structures. Vegetal eats minerals; animal eats vegetal; and mineral swallows animal and vegetal. As we know, everything comes from Earth, and everything goes to Earth. Among the three structures, animals have the shortest, the most fragile, and the most complex lives, with mysterious, puzzling, thinking humans at the peak, for "we are specimens of the most highly developed species of organic life."[47]

Every human individual was born one day, somewhere on Earth, without ever being asked for consent to come into this earthly world, just because two persons answered their want to make love. As a result of making love (the bio-social labour of two persons), a human individual springs into the world. Hence, the birth of a human individual is a biomechanical function of human corporal capacity, and a human baby is a concrete bio-commodity in which human bio-social labour has been embodied. Therefore, the birth of a human individual is a bio-social-use-value that has been produced by human bio-social labour.

Every day, more than 350,000 human individuals (bio-social-use-value) are born in the world. This huge number of bio-commodities has been produced by the bio-social labour of about 700,000 persons, which constitutes the largest labour force in the world producing one sort of commodity.

Every newborn human individual is an innocent creature that will grow and become an adult member of society. The relationship between a human individual and society is a complex subject on which we will later spend enough time to investigate closely.

---

46 Hannah Arendt, *The Human Condition*, 9.

47 Arendt, *The Human Condition*, 11.

THE LABOUR THEORY OF VALUE

Let us now examine the Labour Theory of Value more closely with materials from Marx. Before discussing value in the context of political economy, we will first make some clarifications about value in a broad sense.

Generally speaking, value is the subject matter of moral, social, economic, political, aesthetic, religious, ethical, and some other philosophies. In fact, when talking of value, we tend to draw the attention of our listeners to determine if the value is positive or negative. In other words, our aim is to create a sense of magnitude and also clarify the sort of quality as good or bad, right or wrong, useful or harmful, or as an object, act, or situation. In this regard, axiologically, value can appear as two different qualities: intrinsic or instrumental. An **intrinsic** value is a benefit or an asset that springs directly from the intrinsic property of something, such as the nutritive value of a banana or a sandwich. An **instrumental** value is a potential or a capacity that exists in something, which if activated or circulated, can lead to value, either good or bad. For example, money does not have a nutritive value but, as an instrument, it can buy food to satiate hunger.

There is also another significant aspect regarding the reality of value. We know from physics and chemistry that there are two groups of substances: elements and compounds. Elements are substances that can not be broken down into simpler versions of themselves. Compounds are created when elements combine and create completely new substances with totally different properties that can be broken into simpler substances. Another point that we need to shed light on is the difference between a mixture and a compound. In the mixture, two or more things are put together to make a new thing, but each part still retains its properties. For example, a shoe is made of a mixture of leather, plastic, glue, thread, etc., but each item still has its own properties. Whereas, in a compound, two or more elements bond together to make a new substance, which has totally new and different properties. For example, water (H_2O) has properties that are different than its two basic elements of hydrogen and oxygen.

The state of value in both nature and human society is another important issue that must not be ignored. Although we can imagine that all elements in the periodic table are pure values, thanks to the genius of Russian chemist Dmitri Mendeleev (1834–1907), the truth is different in the real natural world. In reality, apart from a few very rare and exceptional cases when elements are in their pure state (like gold, platinum, copper, silver, diamond, and graphite), values in general and in human society are always in a compound or mixture state. Even sunlight as a physical value, which appears to our eyes as a bright, shining light in one colour, is, in reality, a mixture value of several colours.

In the framework of our investigation, we are interested in the application of value in political economy. Since we will examine surplus-value, human labour is a pivotal subject. In this regard, Marx said, "Human labour creates value, but is not itself value. It becomes value only in its congealed state, when embodied in the form of some object."[48] However, this saying of Marx about human labour is not accurate, and it fails to explain the value structure of human labour in a comprehensive manner.

---

48 Marx, *Capital,* Vol. 1, 57.

First, human labour does have a limited but effective intrinsic value by virtue of the impact of its direct function. For example, if someone scratches someone else's itchy skin, the result of this labour (scratching) is that the irritated skin will be soothed (use-value of the applied human labour). Likewise, when a human caresses another human to exchange affection and pleasure, this has an intrinsic value because the direct effect of this human labour's use-value is to establish physical and mental communication between the two individuals. The same can be said for human sexual labour, which has a genuine intrinsic value, regardless of if it is exercised for personal pleasure, as a professional service for making money, or as natural labour for the reproduction of the human race.

Second, as Marx noted, the instrumental value of human labour has the capacity to create value (become congealed) whenever a human individual applies labour to a form of production. For instance, human labour does not have intrinsic value as a shelter for humans (as a house would), but human labour, as an instrumental value, can build a house, which can shelter humans.

Besides that, human labour itself carries out both intrinsic and instrumental values, and furthermore, it can be both in a compound and mixture state simultaneously. In fact, the value structure of human labour at work has a mixture state as the functions of skin, muscle, bone, blood, etc., although working together (mixing) with means of production; after production ends, they still retain their own independent properties. Whereas, it also has a compound state as the functions of body temperature, humidity in breathing, mental and physical energy, calories, feelings, etc. "bind" to the product and disappear as a result. Thus, human labour definitely has its own complex value attached to it, regardless of the form and sort of its product.

Here, we need to find out what surplus-value is and what it has to do with the Labour Theory of Value. To start, this is how Marx talks about surplus-value:

> The capital C is made up of two components, one, the sum
> of money c laid out upon the means of production, and the
> other, the sum of money v expended upon the labour-power;

c represents the portion that has become constant capital, and v the portion that has become variable capital. At first then, C = c + v: for example, if £500 is the capital advanced, its components may be such that has the £500 = £410 const. + £90 var. When the process of production is finished, we get a commodity whose value = (c + v) + s, where s is the surplus-value; or taking our former figures, the value of this commodity may be (£410 const. + £90 var.) + £90 surpl. The original capital has now changed from C to C′, from £500 to £590. The difference is s or a surplus-value of £90.[49]

Then Marx explains in more detail the components of his presentation as such:

Now we have seen how that portion of the constant capital which consists of the instrument of labour, transfers to the production only a fraction of its value, while the remainder of that value continues to reside in those instruments. Since this remainder plays no part in the formation of value, we may at present leave it on one side. To introduce it into the calculation would make no difference. For instance, taking our former example, c = £410: suppose this sum to consist of £312 value of raw material, £44 value of auxiliary material, and £54 value of the machinery worn away in the process.[50]

Marx comes to his conclusion by telling us the importance and role of each entity within his formula:

Let us return to the formula C = c + v, which we saw was transformed into C′ = (c + v) + s, C becomes C′. We know that the value of the constant capital is transferred to, and merely re-appears in the product. The new value actually created in the process, the value produced, or value-product, is therefore not the same as the value of the product; it is not,

---

49 Marx, *Capital*, Vol. 1, 204.
50 Marx, *Capital*, Vol. 1, 204–5.

as it would at first sight appear (c + v) + s or £410 const. + £90 var. + £90 surpl.; but v + s or £90 var. + £90 surpl., not £590 but £180.[51]

Marx continues in several pages, repeating over and over these numbers and words, as we are familiar with his tautology. Nevertheless, the final word of Marx for his presentation is as follows: "We know that surplus-value is purely the result of variation in the value of v, of that portion of the capital which is transformed into labour-power."[52]

Although Marx wrote about and fought against capitalism all his life, but the capitalist as an individual—which for him was negative and unjust—is absent in his formulation of capital. Rather, Marx divides capital into two sections: **constant capital**, which is the materials and instruments of production, and **variable capital**, which is the wage that will represent and explain the role and place of the labourer in the production process. In Marx's formulation of capital, the only role he has for a capitalist in the capitalist mode of production is as an automatic money machine. The capitalist's only function is to give money (capital) and to take money (surplus-value) and nothing else. Otherwise, Marx's original formulation of C = c + v (in numbers, C = £410 + £90) should have included Capitalist Individual (CI) + Capital, therefore, CI + c + v, and CI + £410 + £90. This is again another way to see how Marx is denying the use-value of commodity for capitalists and the use-value of capitalists in the production process.

Now, we will investigate Marx's account above on surplus-value. As we have seen earlier, there are four general criteria for recognizing, judging, and evaluating every value. These are: 1. intrinsic value, 2. instrumental quality of value, 3. compound state of value, and 4. mixture state of value.

We will now further examine Marx's statement. As we remember, he said, , "We have seen how that portion of the constant capital which consist of the instrument of labour, transfers to the production only a

---

51 Marx, *Capital*, Vol. 1, 205.
52 Marx, *Capital*, Vol. 1, 206.

fraction of its value." In this statement, the important points are **the constant capital** and **only a fraction of its value**. Marx did not say these words accidentally or aimlessly; therefore, we must examine them very carefully. To do this, it will be quite useful if we briefly look at the historical background of the idea of dividing invested money into different parts, according to its different roles in the production process. Although the division of capital did not start with Adam Smith, we will start with Adam Smith, and then we will adjust ourselves with the time sequences.

The human desire to use and make profit from wealth and money is a natural function of human intellectual capacities. As Adam Smith pointed out, it is a human intellectual reaction to the presence of an assuring quantity of wealth in a human's possession that ignites the idea of dividing the available money into separate parts—some of it for immediate use and some for rather creating more wealth and revenue. To describe this point, Adam Smith had a quite clear and reasonable way of explaining this desire of a human individual:

> When the stock which a man possesses is no more than sufficient to maintain him for a few days or a few weeks, he seldom thinks of deriving any revenue from it. He consumes it as sparingly as he can, and endeavours by his labour to acquire something which may supply its place before it be consumed altogether. His revenue is, in this case, derived from his labour only. This is the state of the greater part of the labouring poor in all countries.
>
> But when he possesses stock sufficient to maintain him for months or years, he naturally endeavours to derive a revenue from the greater part of it; reserving only so much for his immediate consumption as may maintain him till this revenue begins to come in. His whole stock, therefore, is distinguished into two parts. That part which, he expects, is to afford him this revenue, is called his capital. The other is that which supplies his immediate consumption.[53]

---

53 Smith, *Wealth of Nations*, Book II, 373.

In fact, Adam Smith called this 'the division of stock.'. Generally speaking, this is the first step of dividing the money in use into different parts according to its function in the reproduction of service and revenue.

Marx, however, goes further back to the French economist Francois Quesnay (1694–1774). In 1759, Quesnay published his *Economic Table*, in which he explains two different functions of expenditures in production, which he calls productive expenditures and sterile expenditures. In fact, Quesnay was investigating cultivators' production in agriculture, and his goal was to explain how different kinds of expenses can affect the annual revenue of farmers. For Quesnay, productive capital is the capital that is spent in the immediate production process, and he divides it into two categories: avances primitives and avances annuelles. Marx believed that: "In Quesnay's work, the distinction between fixed and circulating capital appears as one between avances primitives and avances annuelles."[54]

We see that Adam Smith said something similar: 'That part of the capital of the farmer which is employed in the instruments of agriculture is a fixed, that which is employed in the wages and maintenance of his labouring servants, is a circulating capital.'[55] Marx's criticism of Adam Smith was that he generalized Quesnay's idea and related it beyond agricultural production. He said, 'The only step forward taken by Adam Smith was to generalize these categories. In his work, they no longer relate just to one special form of capital, farmer's capital, but to every form of productive capital. . . . In Smith, therefore, avances annuelles are transformed into circulating capital, avances primitives into fixed capital.'[56] Marx added that 'It is impossible for him (Smith) to understand the distinction between variable and constant capital, and thus the capitalist process in general.'[57] Marx also blamed the British political economist and Member of Parliament David Ricardo,

---

54 Marx, Capital, Vol. II, 268.

55 Smith, *Wealth of Nations*, Book II, chapter I, 355.

56 Marx, *Capital,* Vol. II, 269.

57 Marx, *Capital,* Vol. II, 291.

who he believed was blindly following Smith: 'Ricardo's uncritical reception of Smith's confusion is more surprising.'[58] In fact, Marx mocks Ricardo and says, 'Ricardo introduces the distinction between fixed and circulating capital only in order to present the exception to the law of value.'[59]

But in reality, Marx's problem with Smith goes far beyond the question of just generalizing the category of Quesnay's idea of dividing capital into separate parts in order to learn more precisely which part can bring more revenue for the farmer. Indeed, Quesnay's method of dividing the capital into separate parts, and for that matter, Smith's and Ricardo's method of doing the same thing but each in their own way, is basically intended to create an accounting mechanism to better control the management of a production institution and make it more profitable. Whereas Marx's aim in dividing the invested money in commodity production into two parts (constant and variable capital) is totally different than Quesnay's, Smith's, Ricardo's, and others'. Marx, indeed, is travelling on a completely different road, and therefore, he will never arrive at the same destination as bourgeois economists. For this reason, he disappointedly stated, 'We can thus understand why bourgeois political economy held instinctively to Adam Smith's confusion of the categories 'fixed and circulating capital' with the categories 'constant and variable capital' and uncritically echoed it from one generation down to the next for a whole century.'[60]

But here we must be aware of what Marx is looking to prove, is indeed the class struggle within the capitalist mode of production. In fact, the class struggle is the essence of the working class revolution, which was Marx's agenda. Thus, in dividing capital into two parts, Marx is not looking for a method to improve production management and increase the revenue of the capitalist. To the contrary, Marx is looking to prove that real value is produced by labour and not by capital, and capitalists are robbing the working class, and therefore, we

---

58 Marx, *Capital,* Vol. II, 297.

59 Marx, *Capital,* Vol. II, 293.

60 Marx, *Capital,* Vol. II, 297.

need a communist revolution to establish justice. This is Marx's foundation for making a religion in which specific human labour (industrial labour) becomes sacred. While it is true that all human labour, regardless of how it is applied, is a natural and biomechanical value-making mechanism, but Marx's goal in defining variable capital is to imbue in his believers that a divine quality makes industrial human labour a value worth worshipping. Indeed, quite amazingly, Marx did his job very well, both intelligently and philosophically.

As Marx explains, his constant capital is everything in capital but wage, and whatever a capitalist pays to workers in order to bring the labour-power into production is the variable capital. However, the crucial point in Marx's theory of surplus-value is that he wants to convince society that labour is the only element or source that makes value. Of course, Marx was not the first person to say or believe that labour is the source of value. Since Aristotle, countless philosophers and economists have said that human labour is a value-making entity.

Earlier, we explained how the value structure of human labour is a complex and complicated phenomenon. But here, our two main questions are: 1. What is the role of human labour in commodity production? 2. Should human labour be considered the only and sacred value-producing element in the capitalist mode of production?

The answer to the first question is that the human body is a biomechanical machine. Hence, the human body as a machine—either mechanically, intelligently, or both—in any kind of production is nothing but a mechanical tool.

And the answer to the second question is that the human body enters into the production process as a mechanical tool. Thus, although the human body plays a major and important role in the commodity production process, human labour-power is not, and never should be considered, as the sole or sacred value in transforming elements into products.

Let us now analyze the issue of value transferring in the commodity production process in Marx's theory of surplus-value. However, because of the intricacy of the issue, we will need to do a few back-and-forth trips inside the subject in order to comprehend the essence of the matter.

As we have seen above, Marx divides capital into two parts: constant capital and variable capital. For Marx, the constant capital consists of the raw materials, tools, machines, equipment, and auxiliary materials used in the process of commodity production. The reason that he is separating these two parts from each other is that he is focused on the commodity after it has been produced and is standing in front of us. There, Marx looks at the real and tangible commodity and sees that the final produced commodity carries **only a fraction of the value** from the different elements, which are part of the constant capital that itself (constant capital) is part of the advanced capital. This observation of Marx's is only partially correct.

Let us examine in detail Marx's observation in order to see up to which point it matches the material truth of the creation of a produced commodity. As an example, we will consider a coffee table that is made mostly of wood, but also out of materials such as screws, paint, glue, etc. In addition to these materials, some tools, such as an electric saw, pneumatic drill, hammer, screwdriver, etc. were used. We will accept that these materials and tools are enough for our analysis. We will now consider labour-power. A healthy skillful cabinet maker does the job: Some wood is cut to suitable measures and shapes, and then it is glued and screwed into the proper form. In the end, to protect the wood and for decoration, the table is airbrushed with paint to the desired colour.

Now let us back up to the beginning and separate the constant and variable parts of capital. The constant part of capital—the wood, glue, paint, screws, and auxiliary materials—were paid for and used in production, but most importantly, everything still materially exists, except that the old use-value has changed to a new use-value in the form of a coffee table. As Marx said, "We have seen that the means of production transfer value to the new product, so far only as during the labour process they lose value in the shape of their old use-value."[61] Or, in

---

61 Marx, *Capital,* Vol. I, 199.

other words: "Each use-value disappears, but only to re-appear under a new form in a new use-value."[62]

Still, in the same constant part of capital, the electric saw, drill, hammer, screwdriver, and airbrush sprayer were paid for and used. They finished the job, and they were only slightly worn down from the work. This means **only a fraction of the value** of these tools was used. Marx's example for this issue is interesting:

> Suppose a machine to be worth £1000, and to wear out in 1000 days. Then one thousandth part of the value of the machine is daily transferred to the day's product. At the same time, though with diminishing vitality, the machine as a whole continues to take part in the labour-process. Thus it appears, that one factor of the labour-process, a means of production, continually enters as a whole into that process, while it enters into the process of the formation of value by fractions only. The difference between the two processes is here reflected in their material factors, by the same instrument of production taking part as a whole in the labour-process, while at the same time as an element in the formation of value, it enters only by fraction.[63]

We will now examine the variable part of capital. In this part, a labourer is paid a wage (let us suppose a wage for one day) to come and make the table, and then he leaves. All that a labourer can offer is the entirety of a human mind and body through the labour-process, and this mind and body execute the production of the coffee table. Here Marx observes a very magical thing: "By the simple addition of a certain quantity of labour, new value is added, and by the quality of this added labour, the original values of the means of production are preserved in the product."[64] The magical effect of Marxian labour-power is a significant issue, which is a very particular matter that goes far

---

62 Marx, *Capital*, Vol. I, 194.

63 Marx, *Capital*, Vol. I, 197–8.

64 Marx, *Capital*, Vol. I, 195.

beyond any understandable phenomenon. To explain this point, Marx said, "In so far then as labour is such specific productive activity . . . by mere contact, the means of production from the dead, makes them living factors [erweckt.... von den Toten—raised from the dead] of the labour process, and combines with them to form the new products."[65] This is astounding. The effect of labour is capable of bringing things from the dead to living factors and, therefore, producing a new commodity. This saying of Marx is definitely very important; therefore I will repeat exactly as he wrote it in his mother tongue "erweckt die Arbeit durch ihren bloßen Kontakt die Produktionsmittel von den Toten, begeistet sie zu Faktoren des Arbeitsprozesses und verbindet sich mit ihnen zu produkten." (Das Kapital, 201.) Further, Marx said:

> While productive labour is changing the means of production into constituent elements of a new product, their value undergoes a metempsychosis. It deserts the consumed body, to occupy the newly created one. But this transmigration takes place, as it were, behind the back of the labourer. He is unable to add new labour, to create new value, without at the same time preserving old values, and this, because the labour he adds must be of a specific useful kind; and he cannot do work of a useful kind, without employing products as the means of production of a new product, and thereby transferring their value to the new product.[66]

As we look to draw a conclusion, a few little phrases from Marx will be of great assistance. Marx wrote, "The owner of labour-power is mortal."[67] And somewhere else, he wrote, "Every day brings a man 24 hours nearer to his grave."[68] Even more obviously, Marx talked about living labour: "The real material of the capital laid out on wages is labour itself, self-acting, value-creating labour-power, living labour,

---

65 Marx, *Capital,* Vol. I, 194.

66 Marx, *Capital,* Vol. I, 199–200.

67 Marx, *Capital,* Vol. I, 168.

68 Marx, *Capital,* Vol. I, 197.

which the capitalist has exchanged for dead, objective labour, and incorporated into his capital, this being the way that the value existing in his hands is first transformed into a self-valorizing value."[69] While remembering what Marx said above about metempsychosis, our task is to find out what we can learn from Marx's observation.

In the context of constant and variable capital, what Marx wants us to take away is that all the elements comprising constant capital are tangible material objects, which, by going through the production process, change their form from one shape to another and change from an old use-value to a new use-value. Nevertheless, all the elements of constant capital will continue to physically exist.

Regarding variable capital, Marx said, "Labour-power is the form under which variable capital exists during the process of production."[70] We understand that variable capital represents a labourer—a mortal human being going through the labour-process—who is transferring a certain quantity of irretrievable human life to the product that becomes value by virtue of bringing things from dead to living factors. As Marx said very clearly, "If we look at the means of production, in their relation to the creation of value, and to the variation in the quantity of value . . . in which labour-power, the value-creator, incorporates itself."[71] As a result, a labourer's human life disappears forever in the commodity through the production process by becoming congealed in the commodity. This is the secret to understanding how the effect of labour by mere contact is capable of bringing things from the dead to living factors. In fact, with this, Marx was preparing to draw the conclusion that surplus-value is merely the result of labour-power, and therefore, labourers, by paying with their life, are inhumanly exploited. Indeed, this is another occasion for incriminating capitalists.

As he said above, Marx's point was that from total capital (£410 const. + £90 var.), merely £90 variable creates the surplus-value of £90. And for the accumulation of the surplus-value regarding the

---

69 Marx, *Capital*, Vol. II, 299.

70 Marx, *Capital*, Vol. I, 553.

71 Marx, *Capital*, Vol. I, 199–207.

working-day, he said: "Suppose the working-day consists of 6 hours of necessary labour, and 6 hours of surplus-labour. Then the free labourer gives the capitalist every week 6 X 6 or 36 hours of surplus-labour. It is the same as if he worked 3 days in the week for himself, and 3 days in the week gratis for the capitalist . . . the labourer in every minute works 30 seconds for himself, and 30 for the capitalist."[72]

As we delve more deeply into the issue of surplus-value, it is interesting to know that Marx says that he was the first to introduce the terms constant and variable capital in political economy. In a footnote, Marx said, 'I must here remind the reader that the categories variable and constant capital were first used by me. Political Economy since the time of Adam Smith has confusedly mixed up the essential distinctions involved in these categories, with the mere formal differences, arising out of the process of circulation, of fixed and circulating capital.'[73] In criticizing Ricardo on the matter of fixed and circulating capital, Marx said "that labour-power constantly creates value and surplus-value as long as it continues to function."[74]

In terms of capital, labour, and production Marx made an important point that must be given heed: 'It is similarly ignored that the portion of value that the capital laid out on wages adds to the product is freshly produced (and thus actually reproduced), while the portion of value that the raw material adds to the product is not freshly produced, and not really reproduced.'[75] Despite the fact that erudite Marx was a well-educated philosopher, one wonders if he had ever heard the famous saying of pre-Socratic philosopher Heraclitus (544 BC): 'No man ever steps in the same river twice.' Thus, every created or modified value is a new value; therefore, to say it is not freshly produced is nonsense.

Let us now examine Marx's saying through an example. If we cut a few nicely shaped pieces of wood out of rough lumber to make a dining table, can we say that the newly cut pieces are not freshly produced?

---

72 Marx, *Capital*, Vol. I, 227.

73 Marx, *Capital*, Vol. I, 572.

74 Karl Marx, *Capital*, Vol. II, 299.

75 Marx, *Capital*, Vol. II, 296.

Can we deny that their new, smoothly sanded shapes add a different value that, all together with other values, causes the creation of the table (and without which the table could not become a table)? It is clear that Marx is saying that wood is always wood, before or after it is cut, and therefore, nothing is new or fresh. But who is Marx trying to convince? Just because rough lumber and freshly cut and sanded pieces of wood possess the same natural characteristics, is it reasonable or right to deny the new values that have been produced? This statement by Marx sounds more like a joke than a political economic statement. Or might it be better called the words of a prophet to his believers? To understand them, reason is not required. Believers will accept them as a fact.

Regarding the relation between constant and variable capital and the act of sale and surplus-value Marx was able to see a very important connection. But in his explanation of the function of his categories, constant and variable capital, and the act of creation of surplus-value through the mechanism of sale, there is a crucial point that Marx abandons without any clarification. Marx said:

> The characteristic feature of variable capital is that a definite, given (i.e., in this sense constant) part of capital, a given sum of value . . . is exchanged for a force that valorizes itself and creates value—labour-power, which not only reproduces the value paid to it by the capitalist, but also produces a surplus-value, a value that did not previously exist and is not bought for an equivalent. . . . What is involved in both cases is a transfer of given, previously advanced values to the product, and their replacement when the product is sold.[76]

Here Marx shows us the relation between the capitalist and the labourer in the production process, within which the capitalist pays wages to labourer, and labour-power creates value and surplus-value. Then he tells us that value transfer to "replacement," meaning surplus-value, happens only when the product is sold. Although he admits that

---

76 Marx, *Capital,* Vol. II, 295–6.

a product must be sold in order to have the surplus-value released, he does not say who sells to whom. In the first part above, he makes it very clear that the capitalist pays and the labourer creates. But in the second part, he only says "when the product is sold" without telling us who sells the product and who buys it. Therefore, the role of the buyer (consumer) of the product in the creation of surplus-value is unclear. Or we might think it is deliberately ignored.

"Sell" is a verb and an action. Thus, an act of selling can never happen without one or several buyers. The act of selling requires two or more natural or legal persons. Thus, surplus-value cannot be created if a product is not sold. Consequentially, the capitalist mode of production, which is a system of mass production of commodities, cannot exist or function without selling the commodities that it produces and definitely cannot exist without buyers (consumers). Hence, the structure of the capitalist mode of production is that, in the first part, production happens between a capitalist and a labourer in a production process that takes place in production facilities or workshops. This is where commodities are born; these are commodities that did not exist before, although they were potentially available to be realized within the raw materials. In the second part, selling occurs between a capitalist and a consumer in the market. This is the place where surplus-values are born; these values that did not exist before, although they potentially were available to be realized within the commodities.

Would it make any difference in the relation between capitalist and consumer if it were studied based on profit instead surplus-value? To answer this question, we need to know the difference between profit and surplus-value and what these terms represent. As mentioned earlier, surplus-value is a Marxian term for profit for which Marx has his own way of calculating. Thus, by learning how these two entities are calculated mathematically in commodity production and distribution, we will understand the commodity relation between the people involved in the network.

First, profit is equal to the sold price of a commodity minus the total capital advanced for its production (cost price). If this number is positive, it is called profit, and if it is negative, it is called loss. Let us illustrate this with real numbers. Suppose a dining table costs a capitalist $100 to produce, and it is then sold in the market for $120. Here, the cost price (CP) was $100, and the sold price (SP) was $120. Therefore, SP − CP = profit / loss. In real numbers, $120 − $100 = $20. Second, as Marx divides advance capital into constant capital and variable capital, in this case, the raw materials and means of production cost $80 (constant capital) and the labourer's wage was $20 (variable capital). According to Marx, "the surplus-value is determined first by its rate."[77] Thus, if we calculate the rate of gain by dividing the profit to variable capital $\frac{\text{profit}}{\text{variable capital}}$, which, in real numbers, is $20/20 = 1 \times 100 = 100\%$.

Here, in Marx's view, the variable capital has been expanded 100%. Therefore, it has created $20 new value that Marx calls surplus-value. As he said, "The total mass of profit is equal to the total mass of surplus-value."[78] The end of the matter is that profit and surplus-value are the same thing. At the time of the transaction in the market, the consumer pays the sold price. Economically speaking, this is the advanced capital and profit, or according to Marx, the constant capital, variable capital, and surplus-value are included. Hence, since profit and surplus-value are not two different things, in the analysis of the relation between capitalist and consumer, the usage of either title does not change anything in the network structure of a society in which the capitalist mode of production prevails.

Again, we have to return to the basics, but this time, our task is to tear down the fortress that Marx has created on top of his constant and variable capital. The first point is that **constant capital** consists of two parts:

1. The elements that go through the production process, such as tools (e.g., saw, drill, hammer) and raw materials (e.g., wood, screws, paint), retain their original properties. Physically, their existence will continue the same. Marx said that the means of

---

77 Marx, *Capital,* Vol. III, 247.
78 Ibid.

production transfers **only a fraction** of their **value**; he liked to say 'bit by bit.'. Thus, we will call this part of the constant capital that continues to exist and retain its properties the **REMAINING constant capital**.

2. The elements that go through the production process, such as the electricity consumed by a saw or the air consumed by an airbrush and pneumatic drill, disappear into the product so that nothing of them remains. Thus, we will call this part of the constant capital that finishes and disappears in the product the **DISAPPEARING constant capital**.

The second point is that **variable capital** also consists of two parts:

1. The parts of the labourer's body that go through the production process and continue to remain alive and healthy and retain their properties after the work is finished, such as hands, legs, skin, blood, etc. Marx said these transfer only a fraction of their value (bit by bit) to the product. Thus, we will call this part of the variable capital that continues to exist and retain its properties the **REMAINING variable capital**.

2. The elements of the labourer's body that the labourer starts with when they come to work (such as physical and mental energy, calories, etc.) but that are consumed and/or disappear into the product during the production process so that nothing remains of them. Thus, we will call this part of the variable capital that finishes and disappears in the product the **DISAPPEARING variable capital**.

Indeed, what the analysis above is telling us is that some part of constant capital is variable and some part of the variable capital is constant. Thus, they are mirror images of each other, and as a result, what Marx says about surplus-value is just a childish story. In fact, Marx, in his concept of surplus-value, is not writing as an economist. Marx's definition of surplus-value does not have any merit to political economy because economically, it is absolutely nonsense and useless. First of all, mathematically, it is relative and not definitive. Second, it is arbitrary and based on Marx's personal ideas of dividing capital into two parts (constant and variable) and stating that only the variable part is making surplus-value (profit). Most importantly, it is partial and discriminative, for he attributes it totally to the labourer, and he deprives the consumer of their own legitimate share.

Marx was a person obsessed with radical antagonism; all he cared about was class struggle and a proletariat revolution. Therefore, what Marx is doing with surplus-value, in reality, is a legal motion presented by a defence lawyer that carries only a part of the truth. It may be good for the working class, but it is misleading for human society and harmful for human civilization.

Let us examine the basic structure of surplus-value as value and as well its relation to the commodity production process within the framework of political economy. To start, we will use one of Marx's conclusions that we have already reviewed. First, we must make it clear that in the real world, no value can be pure and isolated—surplus-value included. Hence, all usable-values are compound or mixture phenomena, or both.

In the commodity production process, philosophically surplus-value has a complex status. On one side, surplus-value (profit) is a cause of production because a capitalist wishes to invest money in production to collect the surplus-value at the end. On the other side, surplus-value is an effect that springs from the commodity production process. This complex cause-and-effect structure of surplus-value is a result of a production and distribution process in which several elements, activities, and individuals come together in a very specific and harmonious arrangement. If any of the participant entities are missing, it can cause an interruption in or even a total disappearance of surplus-value. Regarding the basic structure of surplus-value, the analysis above tells us that surplus-value is an instrumental value because it can be collected as a profit or income that will provide its owner with comfort and services. In addition, as an intrinsic value in the form of capital, surplus-value can be reinvested and returned to the production process. Further, surplus-value can appear in both a compound and mixture state because the format of surplus-value is not necessarily limited to a monetary form. Thus, the return, accumulation, and distribution of surplus-value can vary according to the kind of production process, distribution method, and consumption status.

Let us now examine the relation between surplus-value and the commodity production process. As we remember, Marx said in an example that capital = (£410 + £90), which made a surplus-value of £90. This £90 surplus-value is only partially a result of capital + capitalist. In more detail, this means the sum total of £410 + £90 + capitalist, and in a more precise form, this becomes £410 + labourer + capitalist. However, there is still a missing part here. Because the product, the actual commodity, has not yet reached the market and been sold, the £90 surplus-value has not been created, even though it has potentially been made. The surplus-value will not fall from the sky and fill the pocket of the capitalist the moment that a product is produced. At this stage, a commodity is in its pregnant state, which is carrying a fetus called surplus-value. Surplus-value at this stage is nothing more than some abstract potential that will encourage its capitalist to bring it to market. Hence, the missing part is an element that belongs to the market. As in the production process, we had the capitalist, capital, and labourer, in the market, we have the capitalist, capital (commodities), and consumer. The linear schema of these relations in production and consumption is:

Capitalist   capital (production process)   Labourer

Capitalist   capital (market)   Consumer

Simplifying the equation will yield:

Labourer   Capitalist   Consumer

The conclusion, therefore, is:

Labourer + Capitalist + Consumer = Surplus-value

Although while analyzing and exposing the rights and wrongs in the Marxist economy we have used the term "surplus-value," we must be aware that Marxian surplus-value is a mere mathematical expression of the proportion between two numbers that have been arbitrarily and artificially chosen based on Marx's personal judgment. The equation of this calculation consists of two variable parameters: capital and profit. Since the variable capital does not represent the whole capital invested for the entire production, it is not a real and complete parameter for calculating the profit. This is because, if we invest only variable capital without constant capital in a production process, there will not be any commodity produced, and consequently, there will not be any profit (surplus-value) collected either. Thus, the only real profit or surplus-value in the commodity production is the difference between the total invested capital for a certain amount of production and the total amount of revenue collected for the same amount of production.

THE MAKE OF HUMAN LABOUR

Still the question of constant and variable capital has another significant aspect that must be investigated. In this study we will be delving more into the Marx's wordology in describing the matter. To start, we will repeat Marx's words when he said

> That part of capital then, which is represented by the means of production, by the raw material, auxiliary material and the instruments of labour, does not, in the process of production, undergo any quantitative alteration of value. I therefore call it the constant part of capital, or, more shortly, constant capital.
>
> On the other hand, that part of capital, represented by labour-power, does, in the process of production, undergo an alteration of value it both reproduces the equivalent of its own value, and also produces an excess, a surplus-value, which may itself vary, may be more or less according to circumstances. This part of capital is continually being transformed from a constant into variable magnitude. I therefore call it the variable part of capital, or, shortly, variable capital.[79]

---

79 Karl Marx, *Capital*, Vol. I, 202.

Above, in Marx's saying regarding constant and variable capital, each has three parts, as such:

A: 1 – Means of production + raw material + auxiliary material + instruments =

2 – Does not . . . undergo any quantitative alteration of value =

3 – Constant capital

B: 1 – Labour-power =

2 – Undergo an alteration of value =

3 – Variable capital

In each part, we ignore the number 1, and we do our analysis by studding number 2 and 3 as:

Does not...undergo any quantitative alteration of value = Constant capital

Undergo an alteration of value = Variable capital

We simplify the equations as:

Any quantitative alteration = Constant

An alteration = Variable

Marx has never, directly and specifically, explained what quantitative alteration and alteration are. Or why they are different. And how they become different; therefore, how they, eventually, become constant and variable. Even though he has not explained this explicitly, it is possible to find this out.

Let us first start with constant capital. In fact, Marx's logic is that, in a production process, a phenomenon can create value or add value to something else if only that phenomenon itself has value previously and independently from the production process. Thus, he said, "In the labour-process it (means of production) only serves as a mere use-value, a thing with useful properties, and could not, therefore, transfer any value to the product, unless it possessed such value previously."[80] Marx also makes it clear that even the quantity of the value, which a phenomenon can add to something else could not be more than the value that itself had it before the production process. Hence, he said, "Therefore, the means of production can never add more value to the product than they themselves possess independently of the process in which they assist."[81]

Regarding human labour, Marx said something important that must be studied carefully. He said, "human labour, creates value, but is not itself value. It becomes value only in its congealed state, when embodied in the form of some object."[82] We remember Marx told us earlier that a phenomenon cannot create value if itself does not have value independently and previously. But here, he says labour does not have value, but it creates value. We will leave this contradiction here and, in this regard, we will examine another of his sayings. As we can read, Marx said, "The value of labour-power resolves itself into the value of a definitive quantity of the means of subsistence."[83] Here Marx is telling us that labour-power has value, and it can even resolve that value into something else. Then Marx said, "Though a use-value, in the form of a product, issues from the labour process, yet other use-values, products of previous labour, enter into it as means of production. The same use-value is both the product of a previous process, and a means of production in a later process. Products are therefore not only results, but also essential conditions of labour."[84] Again, here Marx is telling us that use-value issued from labour is a result and also conditioned by products, and it enters into the production process as part of the means of production. But the pivotal point in Marx's thought for dividing capital into constant and variable lies here: "In the labour-process, therefore, man's activity, with the help of the instruments of labour,

---

80 Marx, *Capital*, Vol. I, 199.

81 Marx, *Capital*, Vol. I, 199.

82 Marx, *Capital*, Vol. I, 57.

83 Marx, *Capital*, Vol. I, 169.

84 Marx, *Capital*, Vol. I, 176–77.

effects an alteration, designed from the commencement, in the material worked upon. The process disappears in the product; the latter is a use-value, Nature's material adapted by a change of form to the wants of man. Labour has incorporated itself with its subject: the former is materialised, the latter transformed."[85]

First, we will dissect what Marx is saying and then analyze them. Here Marx is putting the production process as equal to the labour-process, and he says that this process has two parts; from one side, nature's materials will be transformed into certain objects (commodities) according to human needs, and from the other side, labour-power will be incorporated into those objects (commodities), while, in fact, labour has been materialized in the creation of those objects. The very determining entities in this statement are two words that Marx is employing; one is transformed for raw materials and means of production. And the second is materialized for labour-power.

The cruciality of this statement is that using two words means separating two things. In fact, Marx is telling us that two different things are happening here.

A: The transformed ingredients from an old form (old use-value) to a new form (new use-value) is merely a formal modification of one already (old) existing matter to a freshly (new) changed matter. As a result, in this stage, the nature of the act of production is seldom a conversion from old to new, viz., a palpable material thing is changing to another palpable material thing. Thus, he says there is quantitative alteration of value or constant capital. Regarding this issue, we can read Marx as saying, "The reason why means of production do not lose their value, at the same time that they lose their use-value, is this: they lose in the labour-process the original form of their use-value, only to assume in the product the form of a new use-value. . . . Raw material forms the substance of the product, but only after it has changed its form."[86]

---

85 Marx, *Capital*, Vol. I, 176.
86 Marx, *Capital*, Vol. I, 196.

B: Materialized labour, which is incorporated into the commodity. In fact, in this context, Marx is expecting us to understand that labour is not a material thing; rather, it is an abstract value-creating energy or phenomenon. Marxian labour is a human potential capacity. When it becomes activated (motion) in the labour-process through the instruments of production, abstract labour turns into a material entity; in other words, it becomes materialized. As he said, "Human labour-power in motion, or human labour, creates value but is not itself value. It becomes value only in its congealed state, when embodied in the form of some object."[87] Hence, the materialized labour is a value-creating phenomenon or energy that becomes incorporated into the produced commodity, consequently, turning things from dead to living elements. As Marx wrote, "In so far then as labour is such specific productive activity . . . it raises, by mere contact, the means of production from the dead, makes them living factors of the labour-process, and combines with them to form the new products."[88] As a result, in this stage, Marx is teaching us that the nature of the role of labour in production is a value-creating source. In short, in the labour-process, something from abstract (not existing) becomes material (existing) viz., a non-material thing becomes material thing, therefore, materialized. Thus, he calls it an alteration of value or variable capital. Marx also admits that this issue is too complicated for ordinary minds to understand, as he said, "That this same labour is, on the other hand, the universal value-creating element, and thus possesses a property by which it differs from all other commodities, is beyond the cognisance of the ordinary mind."[89]

Now, we start our analysis. The bottom line is that Marx wants us to believe that labour is a mysterious, value-creating energy, not material, not palpable, and not easily comprehendible for ordinary minds. Therefore, it is a kind of God-like phenomenon with mysteriously creating power versus ingredients and the means of production, which are

87 Marx, *Capital*, Vol. I, 57.

88 Marx, *Capital*, Vol. I, 194.

89 Marx, *Capital*, Vol. I, 506.

just palpable objects. For his claim, Marx has only one reason; labour is not material, and it is not value because it is not palpable. Labour has the capacity to become value and become incorporated into an object, therefore becoming a materialized, palpable thing.

Hence, our analysis must be focused to find out if labour is a material thing or not. The simple and general answer to this question is that only in religious beliefs do non-material things with magical creating power exist. For, in the real world, according to the sciences, everything in our planet Earth, our galaxy, and the whole universe is material, regardless of whether it is palpable or not. And human labour is not an exception to this rule. Human labour is nothing but human physical capacity that exists in human biological organs, such as muscles, bones, brain, etc. This transformation of human labour to commodity is totally similar to the transformation of electricity from the means of production to commodities. Human labour is not a palpable entity, and neither is electricity. Since electricity is not a palpable thing, Marx never said that electricity, by becoming incorporated into a commodity becomes materialized because Marx never saw electricity in his life. Thus, human labour is a material use-value capacity in the human body, which in the labour-process, a labourer, by transforming this use-value to a new use-value that is the subject of his labour, therefore fabricates a useful object for satisfying human need. And in human labour there is absolutely nothing mysterious or immaterial of any kind that has divine or celestial capacity for bringing things from dead to life. Contrary to what Marx told us above.

Very briefly, we will add here that humans do not have any materializing capacity. Only nature can materialize things. For instance, humans cannot materialize or make oxygen, potassium, or any substance, for that matter. All humans can do or are doing is merely transforming and mixing materials (substances provided by nature) from one state to another according to human needs and wants. Hence, Marx is wrong in telling us that human labour, as a value-creating power, materializes value. For human labour merely fabricates and does not materialize a useful object for human needs and wants by transforming itself from one previous form to a new form through the production process. Thus, Marx's variable capital is seldom a personal arbitrary fabrication for mystifying and divinizing a very specific kind of human being; that is, his proletariat.

THE NATURAL CHARACTER OF HUMAN LABOUR

In nature, labour is not peculiar to humans. All animals, plants, and minerals work in their own ways. Furthermore, labour is not peculiar to the planet Earth, either. The sun works 24/7 to produce light and energy. The planets work 24/7 by rotating around the sun. All galaxies and spatial objects work according to their needs and conditions. All forms of human labour—regardless of whether it is skilled, unskilled, amateur, or professional—are merely physical, mental, and social effort that humans exert because of naturally or socially imposed necessities and requirements. Human labour is a natural and biological phenomenon without any religious, divine, or sacred quality. Moreover, human labour, similar to all other varieties of labour in the universe, without absolutely no superiority and inferiority, appears and eventually disappears into nature. In addition, human labour should never be a matter of superiority or inferiority among humans because dignity and decent living conditions are a human right. As we have seen earlier, to justify the proletarian revolution as a mechanism for establishing justice and equality in human society, Marx, by introducing the idea of variable capital (human labour) as the superior source of producing value, has implicitly fabricated a sacred and superior quality (God-like image) for industrial labour that has resulted in a religious structure in Marxist ideology. It was and is a very grave harm remaining from Marxism.

While there are a lot of serious problems in human society, including political and economic ones, human history has shown us that religions are not a solution for the socio-economic or political problems in human society. As history can testify, religions have been the cause of problems rather than the solution. Religions create false, fabricated value systems and ideals that divide people into hostile groups and nurture animosity and wars. In human history and civilization, religions and ideologies have killed and caused more harm and destruction than any disease or natural disaster. Thus, any attempt to fabricate a sacred quality for human labour under any social title (social class), camouflaged in divinely transcended economic niceties in order to artificially demolish a historical epoch—even in search of redemption for humanity—is wrong, inhuman, and unscrupulous. Human beings should never fall into this trap. Although we must find earthly and sustainable solutions for the serious problems affecting society, but human civilization definitely does not need a new religion. Or for that matter any kind of idealistic or materialistic religion at all.

MARKET AND PROFIT (SURPLUS-VALUE)

Today, the capitalist economy is known as a free market economy. The crucial point is that the capitalist mode of production cannot exist without a market. However, by definition, a free market economy is an economic mechanism in human society, which is free from government control and intervention. Theoretically, a free market economy is not an economy that is programmed by the government but rather functions based on the requirements imposed upon it by the mechanism of supply and demand. In a real free market economy, there must be free circulation of labour and capital so that individuals can freely and fairly compete with each other, and the right of private property must be legally recognized and protected.

While some may argue that we are living in a free market economy that follows the principles of supply and demand, the cold, hard reality of a capitalist society is different. Actually, the term "free market economy" is a softened, popularized version of a free jungle economy. The mechanism of the free jungle economy is based on money. In the capitalist mode of production, a market is a kind of machinery that changes smaller money into bigger money. In order to understand the role of money in the market, we need to know that there are two major players in the market who come to the market with money: the capitalist and the consumer.

In the mechanism of a free market economy, money plays a major role in procreating profit (surplus-value). Marx explained this as follows:

> More money is withdrawn from circulation at the finish than was thrown into it at the start. The cotton that was bought for £100 is perhaps resold for £100 + £10 or £110. The exact form of this process is therefore $M - C - M'$, where $M' = M + \Delta M$ = the original sum advanced, plus an increment or excess over the original value I call "surplus-value." The value originally advanced, therefore, not only remains intact while in circulation, but adds to itself a surplus-value or expands itself. It is this movement that converts it into capital.[90]

This is interesting. The money with which capitalists come to market is always smaller than the money with which they leave the market. This is how going in and out of the market, for a capitalist, is nothing more than changing smaller money into bigger money. Marx also reveals that the capitalist side of the market is always the supply side of the market, as capitalists come to market with their commodities. Even when banks lend money to their customers as financing for a project or as a mortgage to home buyers, their money is the commodity that they are supplying. But this is not the end of it. Examining this in closer detail shows us a bitter irony. When a capitalist goes to the labour market to buy the required labour-power to run a production process, the capitalist is not the demander of the labour. Indeed, the role that a capitalist plays in the labour market is as the supplier of a job. The job is the commodity offered by the capitalist to fill the need of the labourer who comes to the labour market to buy the job. The labourer pays with labour-time—as we know time is money—in order to buy the offered job. Marx explained this matter when he wrote:

---

90 Marx, *Capital*, Vol. I, 149.

> Suppose the working-day consists of 6 hours of necessary labour, and 6 hours of surplus-labour. Then the free labourer gives the capitalist every week 6 X 6 or 36 hours of surplus-labour. It is the same as if he worked 3 days in the week for himself, and 3 days in the week gratis for the capitalist . . . the labourer in every minute works 30 seconds for himself, and 30 for the capitalist.[91]

The point is that in the capitalist mode of production, employees (through the mechanism of the production process) and consumers (through the mechanism of the market) are both profit (surplus-value) providers for capitalists.

Let us now examine the authenticity of the freeness in the free market economy. In the framework of the contemporary capitalist mode of production, we have two terms: monopoly and oligopoly. To examine these terms, we must first study the state of perfect and imperfect competition in the capitalist mode of production.

To study competition in economic activities among human individuals, we can go back several thousand years in time to the time of Plato and Aristotle or, closer to our time, in the fifteen, sixteen, and seventeen centuries, when economic competitions between commodity producers were much simpler and more honest and equitable. Even in the early years of capitalism, producers could bring their commodities to the market and sell them without control and restrictions. Therefore, competition among commodity suppliers was based on who had the better product and who was selling the product for a cheaper price. It was a real free market that functioned based on the conditions imposed by the supply and demand mechanism. This is called perfect competition, as producers were competing in a fair and uncontrolled environment, and the criteria for success was based on the good quality and good price of the products.

However, this period ended long ago. The perfect fairness and uncontrolled environment in economic competition does not exist

---

91 Karl Marx, *Capital,* Vol. I, 227.

anymore. Since the mid-nineteenth century, the economic market has been ruled by the political and monetary power of huge multi-million-dollar (nowadays multi-billion-dollar) institutions. These have the decision-making power to change the rules and conditions according to their own well-being and interest, even though it might cause harm to other smaller companies or consumers. Hence, despite the term "free market," the market today is based on imperfect competition. This means a free market economy that is controlled by monopolies and oligopolies. In effect, the market structure of the modern free market economy is based on monopolistically controlled competition.

Let us briefly explain these terms. In a monopoly, there is only one seller and a mass of buyers, such as some pharmaceutical companies for certain medications. In an oligopoly, there are only a few sellers and a mass of buyers, such as oil or cell phone companies. Under the monopolistic structure of a free market economy, neither employees nor consumers have any say in the price and conditions of the commodities offered in the market. The mechanism of a free market economy funnels the profit from the pockets of employees and consumers to the pockets of capitalists without leaving any room for real, free competition. Competition cannot be free if restrictions are imposed by the stronger entities against the weaker ones. The second major player in the market is the consumer. A market without consumers does not exist. Although consumers are the second major player in the market, the consumer is not the power player in the market. The consumer goes to market with money and leaves the market without money. One part of the consumer's money is commodity, and the second part of the consumer's money is profit (surplus-value), which goes to the pocket of the capitalist.

SOCIAL EFFECTS OF USE-VALUE
AND SURPLUS-VALUE

In order to investigate the social effects of use-value and surplus-value, it would be useful if we refresh our minds about what use-value and surplus-value are. As we have already studied use-value, we know that it is an entity that proves the existence of a commodity, since a commodity cannot exist without use-value. Surplus-value is the positive monetary difference between what a capitalist spends for producing a commodity and the price for which he sells that commodity. In economic and accounting literature, this is called profit. But in the context of the Labour Theory of Value, the word surplus-value is a Marxian term meaning gain, as we read in *Capital*, Volume III: "The total mass of profit is equal to the total mass of surplus-value."[92] Because of surplus-value, money becomes profit and capital. To explain surplus-value, Marx said, "The capitalist, formerly a buyer, now returns to market as a seller, of commodities. He sells his yarn at eighteen pence a pound, which is its exact value. Yet for all that he withdraws 3 shillings more

---

92 Marx, *Capital*, Vol. III, 247.

from circulation than he originally threw into it . . . the production of surplus-value."[93]

Let us now return to the important issue of use-value. We will start by comparing use-value with surplus-value and analyzing their functions regarding the three principle elements of the capitalist mode of production.

We will first look at the relation between use-value and 1. the consumer, 2. the capitalist, and 3. the employee:

1. The relation between the consumer and use-value of a commodity is direct and very active. This relation can be seen in two separate stages. The first step is the moment when a consumer buys a commodity. It is obvious that the only reason that a consumer buys a commodity is to use it because of either an involuntary need or because of a self-made want. Thus, the consumer is deeply concerned about the quality and exactitude of the usefulness of the use-value of the commodity that he buys. The second step is after that transaction is done for the time the commodity belongs to the consumer. At this stage, the consumer will try to consume the use-value of his commodity to the best and maximum advantage of it. In short, the use-value of a commodity is the consumer's primary concern.

2. The relation between the capitalist and use-value of a commodity is direct and very active. The capitalist knows that if the commodity that he is producing does not have use-value, nobody will buy it. Thus, every smart capitalist wants to make sure that the commodity that he offers to the market carries a definite and obvious use-value. A good use-value will assure successful sales and, consequently, a successful business. Having a successful business means having steady, permanent profit, which is the motivation for every capitalist. In short, the use-value of a commodity is the capitalist's primary concern.

---

93 Marx, *Capital,* Vol. I, 189.

3. The relation between the employee and use-value of a commodity is direct and very active. An employee is employed because of their ability to fabricate use-value. Thus, the employee must create use-value, and the use-value is an entity that confirms the identity of the employee. As Marx said, "Nothing can have value, without being an object of utility. If the thing is useless, so is the labour contained in it; the labour does not count as labour, and therefore creates no value."[94] Hence, the use-value is the employee's constant preoccupation, and with which his role in the production of goods and services can be justified. In short, the use-value of a commodity is the employee's primary concern.

So here, in the frame of commodity relations, we need to examine the relation between surplus-value and the three natural persons (three principle elements) in the capitalist mode of production. As previously mentioned, the surplus-value is the profit: the positive extra gain from selling a commodity compared to the expense of buying or producing the same commodity. This is how Marx explained surplus-value: 'Our capitalist has two object in view; in the first place, he wants to produce a use-value that has a value in exchange, that is to say, an article destined to be sold, a commodity; and second, he desires to produce a commodity whose value shall be greater than the sum of the value of the commodities used in its production.'[95] Now, we will examine this issue in the same order as we did for use-value:

1. The consumer: In the commodity market, every consumer is looking for a commodity—a use-value—for the least possible price. The price of a commodity is the total addition of the expense of the production plus the profit (surplus-value). The equation is as such: expense + profit = price. Hence, if we intend to translate this equation into value language, the outcome is as follows: the expense of the production of a commodity is equal to the sum of the use-value of that commodity, which is the original

---

94 Marx, *Capital,* Vol. I, 48.
95 Marx, *Capital,* Vol. I, 181.

and legitimate part of the price for that commodity. Whereas the profit of a commodity is equal to the sum of the surplus-value of that commodity, which is the artificial and custom part of the price of that commodity. Therefore, the surplus-value of a commodity is a political and economic burden of the prevailing capitalist system in a society. Thus, the capitalist pays only the expense to produce the commodity. But to buy a commodity, a consumer must pay the price, which is the combination of the expense and the surplus-value. Thus, we understand that when a consumer wishes to pay the lowest possible price, the only shrinkable part in the price is the surplus-value. In a normal situation, a person does not expect to buy a commodity without paying the expense (cost price), which in principle would mean buying a commodity for free. The surplus-value is an onus forcefully imposed upon the consumer. Therefore, if one day, for whatever reason, surplus-value dies, the consumer would be happier and richer.

2. The capitalist: In the commodity market, the only reason that a capitalist offers goods and services is to collect the surplus-value, and for as long as possible. Marx was a genius and had a sense of humour. He put this issue in a very clear and hilarious way: "Use-value is, by no means, the thing 'qu'on aime pour lui-même' in the production of commodities. Use-values are only produced by capitalist, because, and in so far as, they are the material substratum, the depositories of exchange-value. . . . His aim is to produce not only a use-value, but a commodity also; not only use-value, but value; not only value, but at the same time surplus-value."[96] It cannot be clearer than this. Both the capitalist mode of production and the capitalist are alive, so far as the surplus-value exists. They depend on each other as opposite sides of the same coin. If, one day, for whatever reason, surplus-value dies in the commodity market, so would the role of the capitalist and the capitalist mode of production. Marx said, 'The

96 Ibid.

production of surplus-value, or the extraction of surplus-value, is the specific end and aim, the sum and substance, of capitalist production.'[97]

3. The employee: In the commodity market, an employee is a seller of human power and is paid to sell his labour-power while working for the capitalist. He is expected to produce and render the use-value in the form of goods and services. As Marx said, "The capitalist buys labour-power in order to use it . . . by setting the seller of it to work. In order that his labour may re-appear in a commodity, he must, before all things, expend it on something useful, on something capable of satisfying a want of some sort."[98] In dissecting this matter, we will see that the employee is the decisive and living element in the use-value production, and therefore, the surplus-value that is potentially embodied within it. All that an employee earns is the salary that has been decided and determined by the capitalist at the time of hiring the employee. The surplus-value, as the profit part of the price, will be realized only after the commodity is sold. Therefore, the only one who is lawfully entitled to sell the commodity and collect the surplus-value is the capitalist. Thus, the surplus-value is a matter of concern for the capitalist and not for the employee.

The timing in the relationship between the employee's salary and the moment when the surplus-value is collected is also a crucial matter with regard to the functionality of the surplus-value. In the process of production, an employee is paid after finishing the work. Then, the produced commodity will be brought to the market and sold to the consumer. This is when the price of the commodity is collected, in which the surplus-value is included. In this schema, we will see that the time from when the salary is paid until the time when the surplus-value is collected can be considered as being in the past. And from the other side, the time from when the surplus-value is collected until

---

97 Marx, *Capital,* Vol. I, 281.

98 Marx, *Capital,* Vol. I, 173.

the time when the salary is paid can be considered as being in the future. These two periods of time do not meet. In the first period, the employee and capitalist are present. In the second period, the capitalist and consumer are present. This schema can be written as follows:

employee – capitalist / capitalist – consumer.

The outcome is that, indeed, the employee is deprived of the surplus-value. Therefore, in any imaginable circumstances, the surplus-value is not a matter of concern for the employee.

Let us now examine the use-value against the surplus-value of the commodity. We have confirmed the cruciality of use-value for all three natural persons in the capitalist mode of production. And from the other side, we have explored why surplus-value is a merely and vitally concerning matter for the capitalist, to the point that the existence of the capitalist depends on surplus-value. But the consumer and the employee have nothing to do with surplus-value. If it were to disappear, it would not do any harm to either of them and might even be beneficial for them.

Thus, we do not need to be concerned about the social effects of surplus-value. But, quite contrary to surplus-value, the social effect of the use-value is a very significant matter. Use-value has the capacity to determine the legitimacy of human wants and, therefore, their functionality and position in human society. At the beginning of our investigation, in order to study the commodity as a basic element in the structure of the capitalist mode of production, we justified the legitimacy of the role of the commodity in human society through the ability of use-value to satisfy human needs and wants. In order to show this analysis in a linear manner, we must start with human needs and wants. Then, the commodity has the capacity to respond to human needs and wants, and finally, the reason for the capacity of the commodity is its use-value. If we put this reasoning in a linear schematic presentation, we have:

Human wants ===➔ commodity ===➔ use-value.

Philosophically, the above is deducing from the human want to the use-value. It depicts the legitimizing capacity of human want for necessity of commodity; therefore, use-value. The point is that use-value also, on its own, has the same legitimizing capacity. Use-value can impose itself upon its user. Use-value can create its user. To depict this legitimizing capacity, we must reverse our analysis to inducing from use-value to human want, which can be shown as follows:

Use-value ===➔ commodity ===➔ human wants

To continue our investigation, we must have a comprehensive understanding of the meaning of use-value; generally, in nature and, specifically, in human life.

In the universe, everything hitherto known by humankind, in any and all forms, in any location far or near, is use-value. Thus, in short, so far as humans know, everything in the universe is use-value.

Humans have learned that ceaselessly in the universe, everything is expanding, changing, and moving, either from one place to another or distancing from each other and some approaching each other. Hence, everything is constantly affecting everything or affecting each other. Therefore, at any given moment, things are either using or being used by others. As a result, everything is constantly changing from old use-value to new use-value. Use-value is a nature-made, independent phenomenon in the universe, which, up to a certain degree, is accessible to humans. Humans in nature are free to consume the available use-values as they wish. Nevertheless, humans are a part of nature. Therefore, despite humankind's ability to modify nature up to a certain point to make better living conditions, nature ultimately makes the decisions and humans obey.

Here, we will look at a few examples that can shed further light on the universality of use-value. As it is clear, humans are not flying animals, but we have made the airplane so we can fly. Airplanes are human-made mechanical machines that are capable of using air to fly. Thus, the air has a use-value for flying among several other use-values. It is obvious that air is not a human-made substance. It is an invisible, gaseous (mainly oxygen and nitrogen), nature-made substance that surrounds the planet and which is retained by Earth's gravity. Humans also, by inhaling and exhaling air, consume the oxygen (use-value) that exists in it.

Let us look at another example to explore use-value. In Science Daily research news, 'Astrophysicist Dr. Natasha Hurley-Walker, from the Curtin University node of the International Centre for Radio Astronomy Research, led the team that made the [mysterious] discovery.' A summary of the discovery is as follows:

> A team mapping radio waves in the universe has discovered something unusual that releases a giant burst of energy three times an hour, and it's unlike anything astronomers have seen before. Spinning around in space, the strange object sends out a beam of radiation that crosses our line of sight, and for a minute in every twenty, is one of the brightest radio sources in the sky…This object was appearing and disappearing over a few hours during our observation, she said…. And it's really quite close to us—about 4,000 light-years. It's in our galactic backyard. The object was discovered by Curtin University Honours student Tyrone O'Doherty.[99]

It is amazing to see how a source that is 4,000 light-years away from us can send us a usable beam (use-value) that human scientists can consume, observe, and draw certain scientific conclusions from or possibly eventually use in one way or another. Humans definitely did not produce the use-value of this beam, although humans can use it. This beam was not produced to come and be observed on our planet Earth. In the meantime, we can imagine that this beam, from its source, could have also gone 4,000 light-years away in the opposite direction, which means, in total, 8,000 light-years from our planet Earth. This beam has a use-value that, therefore, could affect something or someone in that remote imaginable place. This example shows us that use-value is

99 International Centre for Radio Astronomy Research, "Mysterious Object Unlike Anything Astronomers Have Seen Before," *Science Daily*, January 27, 2022, https://www.sciencedaily.com/releases/2022/01/220126122424.htm.

an independent and significant matter, which is not only for human use. Thus, we must not underestimate, neglect, or misinterpret it.

Let us now look at another example. As we know, rocks are made by nature and the process for sedimentary rocks to form can take millions of years. As we read in the article "How are rocks made?": "When soil and surface materials erode over time, they leave layers of sediments. Over long periods of time, layer upon layer of sediments form, putting intense pressure on the oldest layers. Under great pressure and heat, lower layers of sediments eventually turn into rocks."[100] In the process above, the eroded materials are the use-values for creating the sedimentary layers. These layers are the use-values that accumulate on top of each other, and creating great pressure. In addition, the heat coming from the Earth becomes the use-value to cook the sedimentary layer into the rocks. The similarity of this process of forming rocks in nature to that which we can see in factories constructing bricks is amazing.

The Brick Industry Association in Reston, Virginia, USA, in December 2006, published a Technical Note on Brick Construction, in which was written:

> This Technical Note presents fundamental procedures for the manufacture of clay brick...Clay is one of the most abundant natural mineral materials on earth...Then the clay or shale mixtures are transported to plant storage areas...To break up large clay lumps and stones, the material is processed through size-reduction machines...The clay is extruded through a die to produce a column of clay...An automatic cutter then slices through the clay column to create the individual brick...Bricks are fired between 10 and 40 hours... from 1,600 F to 2,400 F (871 C to 1316 C).[101]

---

100 "How Are Rocks Made?" *Wonderopolis*, Wonder of the Day #1620, https://wonderopolis.org/wonder/How-Are-Rocks-Made.

101 Brick Industry Association, *Technical Note on Brick Construction*, TN9: Manufacturing of Brick, 703-620-0010. https://www.gobrick.com/media/file/9-manufacturing-of-brick.pdf.

Here, we see the clay, a use-value, is brought to the factory to make the clay column. Then, the clay column has a use-value for being cut to create the individual bricks. Furthermore, the use-value of fire eventually cooks and hardens the brick. This shows the intrinsic sequential capacity of use-value. A brick is a commodity—a use-value in the hands of a mason to make walls or a façade for buildings. But, above, we saw that several kinds of use-values, small and big, in different ways and different sequences, had to come together to end up with the emergence of a brick. Even in nature, and completely independent of humans, we saw the same process for the creation of rocks. But going back to the brick again, we see the brick, which is the final product for the brick factory, is itself still a small use-value compared to the wall or façade that will be made with the bricks. And even there, the wall or the façade is a use-value to separate something or cover a building, which itself will be a use-value for people who live or work there.

The chain of use-value looks like the chain of DNA for the whole universe, and therefore, humans and society are just a little part of it. The point for our analysis is that even in the chain of use-value—no matter how many times the use-value is transferred, transacted, exchanged, or consumed from one form or situation to another—use-value is use-value. Use-value does not vanish because of commuting from one circumstance to another. Here, I want to relate the matter of the chain of use-value to a statement by Marx: 'As use-value, commodities are, above all, of different qualities, but as exchange-value they are merely different quantities, and consequently do not contain an atom of use-value.'[102] Marx's saying does not fit in the chain of use-value. Denying the use-value will cut the chain of use-value, and cutting the chain of use-value is equal to denying the existence of the commodity. Further, denying the existence of the commodity means denying the whole production. Consequently, if the whole production is denied, thus will be denied society and life, then nothing will remain to talk about.

---

102 Marx, *Capital*, Vol. 1, 45.

USE-VALUE AND ITS CAPACITIES

THE POWER AND EFFECTIVENESS OF USE-VALUE

Any use-value in any given moment is nothing but a potential usable-value, regardless of its surrounding circumstances. We will consider a bottle of almond milk as an example. Imagine a consumer buys a bottle of almond milk to eat with cereal the next morning and leaves this bottle of milk in the fridge. If the consumer goes to the fridge five times, for whatever reason, he will see a potential usable-value in the bottle of almond milk. We could also imagine a pile of clay in front of us that has the potential to become bricks in a brick factory or vessels in a pottery workshop, or the millions of tons of grains in Ukraine today that could feed millions of hungry people in African countries if they were not stocked in silos because of a war and not going anywhere. Nevertheless, the almond milk, clay, and grain have use-value in their present time, which means a potential usable-value.

Use-value is a matter of either existing or becoming. Consequently, our duty is to analyze the essence of use-value in progress. But first, let us consider a use-value that has already been used (in the past). It becomes something or exists because it was used; hence, it turns into a power. Let us consider the almond milk that was drunk by a consumer. As it goes through his digestive system, the use-value of the almond milk will become digested and eventually turn into calories (or a force), and therefore, part of a healthy body for the consumer. We can also consider eroded surface materials that become sedimentary layers as they are used. The sedimentary layer has a potential for some kind of force, which can be called energy or a power. By the same token, use-value of commodity, through the production and circulation process, becomes profit or wealth, which is power for the capitalist.

Let us also consider a use-value that could be used in the future. In this state, a use-value has the potential of evolving or transcending from one thing to another, if indeed it is used, and to become a power. As a concrete example, we can imagine a clay column that has been prepared to be cut to create individual bricks. In this state, we are predicting the usage of use-value to become something else. This is an evolvement of use-value.

Our intention here in dissecting use-value in every detail of its phenomenality is to draw a very specific conclusion. The point is that the effectiveness of any value is the result of its use-value in progress. But progress is not one thing in a moment of time; rather, it is changing from one thing to another thing over time. To shed further light on the process of progress of use-value, we will look at the function of blood in the human body, as noted in an article published by the Institute for Quality and Efficiency in Health Care in Cologne, Germany, under the title of "What does blood do?"[103], which has been shortened for our purposes:

> Blood is a vitally important fluid for the body...The blood transports oxygen from the lungs to the cells of the body, where it is needed for metabolism...Blood also provides the cells with nutrients, transports hormones, and removes waste products, which organs such as the liver, the kidneys, or the intestine then get rid of.

---

103 Institute for Quality and Efficiency in Health Care," What Does Blood Do?" *InformedHealth.org*, 2006 [Updated 2019 Aug 29], https://www.ncbi.nlm.nih.gov/books/NBK279392/.

. . . All red blood cells contain a red pigment known as hemoglobin. Oxygen binds to hemoglobin, and is transported around the body in that way. In tiny blood vessels in the lung, the red blood cells pick up oxygen from inhaled (breathed in) air and carry it through the bloodstream to all parts of the body. When they reach their goal, they release it again. The cells need oxygen for metabolism...

Red blood cells live for about 120 days. When they're too old or damaged, they're broken down in the bone marrow, spleen, or liver.

In adults, blood cells are mainly produced in the bone marrow.

Now, we will start studying the use-value of the blood circulation system in a human body. As we learned above, the cells in a human body consume oxygen for metabolism. In the lungs, oxygen binds to the hemoglobin of red blood cells, and then the red blood cells carry (present time) the oxygen use-value to different tissues in the human body. Although the red blood cells are not themselves consuming the oxygen, the oxygen that is being carried to other tissues does not lose an atom of its use-value. It has the same potential usable-value oxygen while moving forward in the blood vessels toward different organs.

We also know that red blood cells are produced in the bone marrow. As Dr. Brian Koffman, a clinical professor at the Keck School of Medicine, USC, writes, "The bone marrow makes more than 220 billion new blood cells daily."[104] Bone marrow is a living tissue in a human organ with metabolism, and therefore, will (at a future time) consume oxygen to survive and function. Some oxygen will be used by the bone marrow to make red blood cells; thus, without oxygen, red blood cells cannot exist. The use-value of oxygen is used in the creation of red blood cells. The process that allows the usability of the use-value of oxygen to occur in the creation of red blood cells, even though they, themselves, are not using it, is a force that takes oxygen from the air

---

104 Brian Koffman, "What is Bone Marrow?" *CLL Society*, September 29, 2016, https://cllsociety.org/2016/09/what-is-bone-marrow/.

in the lungs and releases it in the tissues. Here, our conclusion is that use-value never loses its usability just because it is going from one place to another or from one owner to another. The variations of usability of use-value do not negate each other, as, for example, the use-value of oxygen for organs in the human body is different than the use-value of oxygen in mixing with hydrogen in water. By the same token, the effectiveness and usability of the use-value of a commodity are different for the employee, capitalist, and consumer in the capitalist mode of production.

LEGITIMIZING POWER OF USE-VALUE

In general, a use-value is an independent and natural thing that exists in the universe. For instance, sunlight has a very powerful use-value that is used inside and outside of all planets that are turning around the sun. On Earth, all minerals are affected by sunlight, and all plants and animals use the sunlight in myriad ways. Every day, we learn and discover new usable things available in nature. In the meantime, the use-value is a conflicting matter between nature and human value judgment. In nature, nothing is right or wrong; things exist because they exist, and things come and go and change from one thing to another. Value judgment is a human-made phenomenon because humans are thinking animals with a huge brain capacity. Humans can understand the good and bad of profit and loss. Humans can create imaginary things out of words, even if they are not true, and then believe in them and live with them as if they exist or are true.

We will look at a few examples. For instance, the coronavirus has a very effective use-value for causing severe infection in human lungs. The coronavirus has a functioning use-value that naturally is neither good nor bad. But the coronavirus, from a human perspective, is a horrible thing because it can kill humans. Here, human value judgment enters the equation to determine that the coronavirus is bad and must be controlled.

A volcano eruption is another example. A volcano erupts from the accumulation of too much pressure because of steam, ashes, magma, and heat in the Earth's crust. The use-value of a volcano is to release the pressure, but for nature, in general, a volcano is neither good nor bad. However, for humans who live close to a volcano, eruptions are hazardous and very harmful.

Now, let us look at some more human examples. Opium, for instance, is a highly addictive narcotic, which is made from the poppy plant and naturally contains morphine and codeine. Morphine and codeine from opium have medicinal uses. In hospitals, doctors sometimes prescribe morphine as a painkiller to relieve or moderate severe pain. The use-value of morphine for a patient who is suffering from a painful health condition is the mitigation of the pain. However, we also know that some individuals in human society consume opium for pleasure and recreational purposes. This is a very dangerous idea with complicated and devastating side effects. Every year, around the world, several thousands of individuals lose their lives because of overdoses or health problems caused by opium. The important point here is that both use-values of opium have the power to create their users, therefore legitimizing their existence.

Let us look at this issue from a different angle. One of the very strange use-values of water, which is practised almost all around the world, is when a coin is thrown into a basin or body of water. Many cultures believe that throwing a coin into water will provide some kind of protection or good fortune. This is a human-made idea, which some believe and others do not, but nevertheless, when the opportunity arises, many people will throw a coin into a fountain. We see here the power of the use-value of the available water that can create its users, therefore legitimizing their existence.

One thing that we must clarify when using the word "legitimize" is that it indicates a value judgment. The legitimizing power of use-value is not a moral issue and, therefore, does not carry any value-judgment implication. It merely means that a use-value has a real and independent capacity for naturally creating its user. Human need or want also creates a legitimate motivation for a human individual to search for a satisfying use-value. This is a situation that is similar to that of the alternating current (AC) in electricity, which periodically reverses direction. In the case of use-value and human need and want, the situation is a dual back and forth, a returning current of cause and effect. From one side, human need and want legitimizes the creation of the use-value, and from the other side, the use-value legitimizes the existence of users.

Now, we will return to Marx to examine human need and want and use-value through his words. Talking about the capitalist, Marx said, "His commodity possesses for him no immediate use-value. Otherwise, he would not bring it to the market. It has use-value for others; but for himself its only direct use-value is that of being a depository of exchange-value."[105] This is amazing. The words 'direct use-value . . . being depository of exchange-value' clearly show that Marx knew that use-value can appear in different contexts to satisfy different human needs or wants. He even brings Aristotle as his witness, and in the footnote in *Capital*, he writes from Aristotle:

> For two-fold is the use of every object... The one is peculiar to the object as such, the other is not, as a sandal which may be worn, and is also exchangeable. Both are uses of the sandal, for even he who exchanges the sandal for the money or food is in want of, makes use of the sandal as a sandal. But not in its natural way. For it has not been made for the sake of being exchanged.[106]

Indeed, we see clearly that both Marx and Aristotle understand the usability of use-value in different contexts. As we said in our shoe example, a pair of shoes can offer three different use-values, such as being worn or sold or a piece of sculpture, according to the need or want of every different individual. We see Aristotle says about the sandal, "For it has not been made for the sake of being exchanged."[107] Simply, we can ask, why not? Although it is easily conceivable that Aristotle didn't know capitalism and mass production and industrial development; therefore, advanced systems of trade and the complicated

---

105 Marx, *Capital*, Vol. I, 89.
106 Aristotle in Marx, *Capital*, Vol. I, 89.
107 Ibid.

mechanisms of money-making and wealth-accumulating were an unknown phenomenon, for Aristotle. In our time, we understand that making sandals or any commodity, for that matter, for the sake of exchange and money-making, is possible, is happening, is effective, and is super good for human society. Another important point is that when Aristotle said, "he who exchanges the sandal for the money or food is in want of"[108] approves the legitimacy of human want for using (use-value) sandal in an exchange for money, and indeed, for Aristotle, using sandal for money is as use as that of using sandal for wearing or for food. And I believe in Marx's genius, though it is not for nothing that he is putting Aristotle's approvals in his book, even if only as a footnote.

We will continue swimming in Marx's words. In talking about human need and want, Marx said, "The nature of such wants, whether, for instance, they spring from the stomach or from fancy, makes no difference."[109] Marx knew very well, and he was also confirming, that human wants are limitless and absolutely boundary-less. To emphasize, on this issue, as a witness, he writes in the footnote from Nicolas Barbon (1696), "Desire implies want; it is the appetite of mind, and as natural as hunger to the body. . . . The greatest number (of things) has their value from supplying the wants of the mind."[110] In talking about human satisfaction, which means the practical effect of consumed use-value on human need or want, again, Marx knew it very well, and he was also confirming it, that it is limitless and absolutely boundary-less, as he makes it clear that it is not even questionable. Like he says, "Neither are we here concerned to know how the object satisfies these wants, whether directly as means of subsistence, or indirectly as means of production."[111]

In Marx's wording above, we understand that the kinds of use-value can be myriad, as can the kinds of human need and want. Thus, in this

---

108 Ibid.

109 Marx, *Capital*, Vol. I, 43.

110 Ibid.

111 Ibid.

complex network of myriads, it does not make any sense when Marx said, "As use-value, commodities are, above all, of different quantities, but as exchange-value they are merely different quantities, and consequently do not contain an atom of use-value."[112] We know that at the time of exchange, somebody (a capitalist) can extract some sort of use-value from a commodity for producing a profit; nevertheless, it is still use-value in the consumption of the commodity that very naturally and legitimately is responding to a human want.

Above, we see Marx is denying the use-value of a commodity when it is exchanged. Marx knew what he was doing because he had an agenda in mind. By denying the use-value of a commodity for the capitalist at the time of exchange, in fact, Marx is denying the capitalist. There is no use-value, so there is no user, and therefore, by denying the capitalist, Marx is denying the capitalist mode of production. Although Marx's denial of use-value at the time of exchange is an artificial fabrication of an idealistic desire, however, through this denial, he allows himself to claim that the capitalist mode of production should be replaced by a working-class mode of production. But this will never happen because the use-value of a commodity is not deniable in any circumstance. Therefore, the root of Marx's idea is wrong, and his theory is not compatible with human society.

Let us refresh ourselves on this issue. If we take our pair of shoes, as we did earlier, a consumer can buy them to wear to protect his feet; a capitalist can buy them to sell and make a profit; and a sculptor can buy them to make a sculpture. The use-value of the pair of shoes is just as valid, whether it is protecting feet, making profit, or being used in a sculpture. With one object—the same commodity—we see three different, undeniable use-values for every user. In a peaceful, balanced, and just human society, none of these users will give up their intention to consume these rightfully available use-values. Definitely, it is human right for an individual to freely choose how and for what purpose to use the use-value of any commodity. Denial of use-value of commodities for citizens, based on any excuse, is certainly a violation

---

112 Marx, *Capital*, Vol. I, 45.

of human rights. Certain harmful commodities for the collective interest of society, of course, could be prohibited by law for all inhabitants and not just certain groups in society. Thus, any endeavour to prevent the users from consuming their legitimately desired use-value would destroy peace, balance, and justice and establish corruption and tyranny in human society, as history has repeatedly proven.

But Marx's denial of use-value is quite a complex issue. In the first step, because of exchange-value, Marx denies the use-value of commodity for the capitalist. Then, in the second step, Marx denies the use-value of commodity by attributing it only to labour, as he said, "A use-value, or useful article, therefore, has value only because human labour in the abstract has been embodied or materialized in it."[113] This is a very systematic method of denying use-value that requires acute scrutiny.

SYSTEMATIC DENIAL OF USE-VALUE

To study this issue, we will take our pair of shoes as an example. In general, through the creation or production process, commodities are made of a combination of use-values. In the case of the shoe, the raw materials—such as leather, thread, glue, rivets, and human labour—are all (in this case, five) use-values combined together to make the shoe. Practically speaking, it is definitely clear that a lack of any of these five use-values will end up in the shoe not being made. Consequently, in the shoeness of the shoe, all these five use-values are equally necessary for the existence of the shoe, and none of them is superior or inferior to the other, while none of them is sacred either.

Here, we will look at how Marx explains human labour. Marx wrote:

> We pre-suppose labour in a form that stamps it as exclusively human. A spider conducts operations that resemble those of a weaver, and a bee puts to shame many an architect in the construction of her cells. But what distinguishes the worst architect from the best of bees is this, that the architect raises

---

113 Marx, *Capital*, Vol. I, 46.

his structure in imagination before he erects it in reality. At the end of every labour-process, we get a result that already existed in the imagination of the labourer at its commencement. He not only effects a change of form in material on which he works, but he also realizes a purpose of his own that gives the law to his modus operandi, and to which he must subordinate his will. And this subordination is no mere momentary act. Besides the exertion of the bodily organs, the process demands that, during the whole operation, the workman's will be steadily in consonance with his purpose. This means close attention.[114]

Marx emphasizes the exclusivity of human labour. Then, he compares human labour with that of other animals. In this example, he mentions a spider and a bee and claims human imagination distinguishes human labour from animals' labour because a human gets a result that was imagined at the commencement of the work. If we take a bee, for instance, we will see that bees also always make the type of cells that they need. The obvious point is that animals have needs and wants as well. Their means of working and their brains' participation in mastering these efforts are not always 100% similar to humans, but animals—like humans—succeed in feeding themselves and their babies and meeting other needs according to their power and abilities. All animals, including humans, survive, grow, and progress, generation after generation, because of their labour and their actions and counteractions with their environment and nature. All animals, including humans, use their labour, up to the point possible, to modify nature according to their own needs and intelligence. Is there really any room to apply a value judgment on this issue? But one thing is definitely clear: human labour is not sacred, divine, or theological, nor for that matter is all other animals' labour. Labour-power is a natural, material, biological, physical human or animal bodily function. And human labour is just a use-value, far from any chant of lamentation or praying.

---

114 Marx, *Capital*, Vol. I, 174.

We cannot ignore or deny the brain power application of animals in their work just because it is not completely similar to humans'. Let us consider beavers. The engineering and mechanisms that beavers employ for building their dams are very complicated and effective. When beavers carve and cut wood pieces, branches, and trees, it is very similar to factory work. Beavers have a very sophisticated technique of mixing mud and branches to build walls in their dams. They also have an astonishing method of listening to the sounds of water to inspect and find holes in their dams, and an effective technical solution to fix the holes. At the end of their labour-process, beavers get the result for which they put themselves to work. And mesmerizingly they remain in consonance with the purpose of their dam building and lodge making up to the end of it.

We are still in the basket of use-value. In fact, we are curious to know where this systematic denial of use-value is going. But first, in order to clarify the situation, we need to do some technical homework.

In talking of an elementary or accidental form of value, Marx started with four lines:

x commodity A = y commodity B, or

x commodity A is worth y commodity B.

20 yards of linen = 1 coat, or

20 yards of linen are worth 1 coat[115]

Simplifying the first line will end up as A = B, which by itself does not mean anything. Marx knows this, so he helps the reader by saying in the second line that A is worth B. But, still, it does not mean anything except that someone accepts or believes that A is worth B. In the third line, Marx gives more detail as 20 yards of linen = 1 coat, and in the fourth line, Marx terminates the process by saying 20 yards of linen are worth 1 coat. Just in the frame of four lines, we can imagine that, between two sides of the equation, there is barter exchanging 20 yards of linen against 1 coat. This means that two people came to an

---

115 Marx, *Capital,* Vol. I, 55.

agreement for such an exchange. On another occasion, it is imaginable that two other people can agree to barter 25 or 15 yards of linen for 1 coat. This is an agreement that can happen between individuals, and it does not mean anything specific or important. It can also be considered as a market value or pricing value that 20 yards of linen is equal to 1 coat. Up to this point, the value in question is an equivalent value based on the agreement between the individuals or as a market value imposed by the market.

This is clear that the pricing value or equivalent value for trading commodities is a technical issue that is still being studied by economists every day. Even low-educated people in simple stores in remote villages deal with this issue daily. But the question of value for political economy is a different matter. For the value issue, Marx criticizes the bourgeois economists, talking of S. Bailey in a footnote in *Capital*,[116] saying that they exclusively give their attention to the quantitative aspect of the question. This shows that Marx clearly understood that in studying the value, it is important to distinguish the quality and quantity aspects of the value of a commodity. For Marx, the quality of value was important:

> The whole mystery of the form of value lies hidden in this elementary form…Here two different kinds of commodities (in our example the linen and coat), evidently play two different parts. The linen expresses its value in the coat; the coat serves as the material in which that value is expressed. The former plays an active, the latter a passive, part. The value of the linen is represented as relative value, or appears in relative form. . . . It is not possible to express the value of linen in linen . . . the use-value linen.[117]

Although I am very much concerned about the word **mystery** that Marx has used here, but for now we will leave it aside and take care of use-value. Marx used two commodities as an example, linen and

---

116 Marx, *Capital*, Vol. I, 56.

117 Marx, *Capital*, Vol. I, 55.

a coat, and he said that it is not possible to express the value of linen in linen. Therefore, the linen expresses its value in coat. But the question is: Why does one commodity need another commodity to express its value? Is it possible to say water expresses its value in ice, for it is not possible to express the value of water in water? Or to say water expresses its value in steam, for it is not possible to express the value of water in water? Or, if a person drinks water, can we say water expresses its value in the person, for it is not possible to express the value of water in water. But a person is not a commodity, so where does the value of water go? In this case, can we say water does not have value? Since water is a natural material, we will try this same method with another more obvious commodity.

Take mozzarella cheese, for instance. Is it possible to say mozzarella cheese expresses its value in pizza, for it is not possible to express the value of cheese in cheese? Or is it possible to say mozzarella cheese expresses its value in turkey sandwich, for it is not possible to express the value of cheese in cheese? Or, if a person eats mozzarella cheese, can we say mozzarella cheese expresses its value in the person, for it is not possible to express the value of cheese in cheese? But a person is not a commodity, so where does the value of cheese go? Can we say in this case that mozzarella cheese does not have value?

We will try to get closer to this issue, so we'll return to Marx's example. If linen expresses its value in coat, then where is the place for the coat to express its value? Would it be the person who will wear the coat? If coat could not find a place to express its value, can we then call the coat a valueless commodity?

Let us now look at the phenomenology of the value of the commodity. The value of a commodity springs from the "commodity-ness" of a thing. The commodity-ness of a thing is a quality that makes something useful, which can satisfy a human need or want; therefore, it is the identity and, thus, the value of commodity. If a commodity cannot express its identity in itself, it therefore expresses its identity in another commodity. This must mean that a commodity in itself is identity-less, and consequently, in the case of Marx's coat, if it is worn by a person, it will remain eternally identity-less and valueless, and therefore, it will never become a commodity. Is this really possible?

We'll continue our analysis in the conceptual framework, trying to understand the cognitive sense of this value denial and value fabrication. Although intelligently, Marx said that we cannot reverse this accidental placement, for commodities cannot simultaneously play the two active and passive roles in representing their value, still a question remains to be asked. Why does this accidental positioning only go in one direction? Therefore, is this really an accidental relationship, or is it an organized or maybe artificially made accidental relationship?

We'll examine the accidental relationship between commodities in Marx's example. Marx said the 20 yards of linen expresses its value in a coat. In the meantime, we cannot simultaneously say a coat expresses its value in 20 yards because, by accident, linen is first and the coat is second. If we translate this example in the cheese and pizza example, it will become that mozzarella cheese expresses its value in pizza, but pizza cannot express its value in cheese because cheese is first and pizza is second, and the relationship is not reversible. As good believers, if we say, *Ok, alles ist klar,* there is no reason to resist or contest this statement? Still if, we ask ourselves, what if we remove these two pages about "the two poles of the expression of value" from *Capital* ?[118] Would the removal of these two pages cause unforgivable damage to *Capital*? Even without these two pages, absolutely and definitely nothing would be missing from *Capital*. However, we can still wonder why Marx is talking about the poles of expression of value.

Here, we face the problem of the independency of use-value and value; therefore, we have a serious question. Why is it not possible to express the value of linen in linen? We see Marx wrote the use-value linen. So, if the value of linen is not represented by linen, why did Marx call it the use-value linen? And the question becomes more interesting when Marx denies the value in the form of calling it a mystery. What is the mystery of it? All evidence confirms that we need more digging into the grounds of denying use-value. We will again read what Marx said,

---

118 Marx, *Capital,* Vol. I, 55–56.

"If we say that, as value, commodities are mere congelations of human labour, we reduce them by our analysis . . . to the abstraction."[119] Then Marx said that "Human labour creates value, but is not itself value. It becomes value only in its congealed state, when embodied in the form of some object."[120]

Here then, very amazingly, Marx returned to the expression of value and said, "In order to express the value of the linen as a congelation of human labour, that value must be expressed as having objective existence, as being a something materially different from the linen itself."[121] In talking of value, Marx knows better than anyone that nothing and nobody in the universe can escape use-value. Therefore, he made a bridge: "The value of the commodity linen is expressed by the bodily form of the commodity coat, the value of one by the use-value of the other."[122] Next, Marx crossed over the bridge and said, ". . . is told us by linen itself, as soon as it comes into communication with another commodity, the coat. . . .In order to tell us that its own value is created by labour in its abstract character of human labour, it says that the coat, in so far as it is worth as much as the linen, and therefore is value, consists of the same labour as the linen.'[123]

All that we have seen above is nothing but a very well-prepared systematic denial of use-value which has been done purposely. First, I will go quickly through the steps of this denial system. As we have already seen, at the beginning, Marx starts with the commodity, and he tells us that a commodity is important because of its use-value that can serve human needs and wants. Then he denies the use-value of commodity for the capitalist because of exchange-value. Then it comes to the commodity itself, and Marx denies the value of the commodity by attributing it to the congelation of human labour. And finally, Marx says human labour creates value, but it is not value by itself. This is

---

119 Marx, *Capital*, Vol. I, 57.

120 Ibid.

121 Marx, *Capital*, Vol. I, 57–58.

122 Marx, *Capital*, Vol. I, 58.

123 Ibid.

how purposefully Marx directs us to a labyrinth from which the only way out is believing that human (proletariat) labour is, mysteriously (meaning sacredly), the source of all values in human life and society.

Marx knew that this would pave the road for his further intentions. Marx was well aware of two things: one was the legitimatizing power of use-value, and the second was his prophetical intention. Thus, by denying use-value, step by step (bit by bit), from the capitalist toward the labourer and concentrating it in the industrial working class, Marx has used the legitimatizing power of use-value to establish a theologizing mechanism to create a sacred impression for his proletariat and himself as the messenger of the Marxist ideology. As Marx was a trained philosopher, he well knew the theologizing mechanism that has its roots in the Abrahamic religions. In this mechanism, the founder of the cult fabricates a legitimized power centre with a holy character (in most religions, they call it God). Marx chose the working class as his holy character. Then, there is a book of instructions that lays out the legitimizing process. Marx was a genius; he knew very well why he was stripping the capitalist and commodity of use-value, and centralizing the power centre in the victimized working class. Bingo! Marx created the working class revolution as God created Adam and Eve. And indeed, Marx should be rightfully called Moses-Jesus-Muhammad al Marx.

In order to free ourselves from Marx's labyrinth regarding value, we need to set the record straight. Therefore, here is what value is: in the limit of the intellectual capacity of the human brain, in the universe that humans know today, all values are use-value in one way or another, for, the valuableness of value springs from its usefulness or usability. Hence, a value that is not use-value does not exist. This means a value cannot be called a value if it is not usable. All values are independent, and every value stands on itself. Human value judgment can divide values into two categories: positive and negative. However, nature never judges value; therefore, in nature, there is only one sort of value, and that is usable-value. Thus, the only real criterion to recognize and measure the valuableness of a value is the value of its usability; all other measures are artificial, arbitrary, and imaginary.

PREJUDICIAL USE-VALUE FOR LABOURER AGAINST CAPITALIST

The subtitle of Marx's *Capital* is: *A Critical Analysis of Capitalist Production*. But the point is that Marx's analysis of capitalist production is not an impartial academic analysis for the sake of scientifically progressing human knowledge. In fact, Marx had a very specific goal. His analysis was supposed to achieve that goal by convincing his readers that in the frame of a capitalist mode of production, the capitalist is a bad person and the labourer is a good person. Of course, Marx's *Capital* was not designed to be a scientific book on political economy. Rather, its primary duty is to theoretically justify The Communist Manifesto, which is a blueprint for working-class revolution in human society. Indeed, Marx's *Capital*, although he never said it explicitly, and in spite of its economic name, is a military war book that promotes the necessity of physical, social warfare between labourers and capitalists.

To understand the military nature of Marx's *Capital* is very important, for we can then understand the rather religious essence of Marx's intentions. He not only wanted to explain his economic idea, he also wanted his idea to gather religiously faithful, dependent individuals (a fanatic army) who would sacrifice everything, including their lives, to carry on a technically limitless war called "class struggle." In fact, the religious and military essence of Marx's idea has its roots in the prejudicial utilization of use-value in economic structure. Below, we will study Marx's prejudicial analysis of use-value in favour of the labourer and against the capitalist.

The most important sign of being alive, either for animals or plants, is breathing—that is, if something does not breathe, it is an object or mineral. This is how we can judge commodities, for a commodity has to have use-value to serve human want, or it is not a commodity. As Marx said, "A commodity is, in the first place, an object outside us, a thing that by its properties satisfies human wants of some sort or another."[124] Marx also said that no matter who uses the commodity, a maker of the commodity or his customer would make no

---

124 Marx, *Capital*, Vol. I, 43.

difference, and consequently, use-value always stays use-value. Marx said, "Anyhow, whether the coat be worn by the tailor or his customer, in either case it operates as a use-value."[125]

Moreover, Marx said that the reason for which a human uses a commodity is not important. He said, "The nature of such wants, whether, for instance, they spring from the stomach or from fancy, makes no difference."[126] He added: "Neither are we concerned to know how the object satisfies these wants, whether directly as means of subsistence, or indirectly as means of production."[127] The conclusion here is that Marx accepted and explained that from one side a commodity can have use-value for human wants, and from the other side, humans can have wants for the use-value of commodity.

Thus, regarding the usefulness of commodity as use-value and serving human wants, Marx said:

> A commodity is, in the first place, an object outside us, a thing that by its properties satisfies human wants of some sort or another. The nature of such wants, whether, for instance, they spring from the stomach or from fancy, makes no difference. Neither are we here concerned to know how the object satisfies these wants, whether directly as means of subsistence, or indirectly as means of production.[128]

It did not take that much for Marx to start discrimination against capitalists as he said, "As use-values, commodities are, above all, of different qualities, but as exchange-values they are merely different quantities, and consequently do not contain an atom of use-value."[129] Here, Marx was telling us that because the capitalist is exchanging the commodity, the commodity does not carry use-value for him. In fact, it is quite obvious that making a profit is the human want of the

---

125 Marx, *Capital,* Vol. I, 50.

126 Marx, *Capital,* Vol. I, 43.

127 *Ibid.*

128 Marx, *Capital,* Vol. I, 43.

129 Marx, *Capital,* Vol. I, 45.

capitalist, and exchanging commodity will bring profit; therefore, the use-value of a commodity for a capitalist's want is exactly embodied in the exchange of a commodity. And since we learned from Marx that the use-value of commodity can, in absolute limitless form, serve absolute limitless human want, the use-value of a commodity for bringing profit to a capitalist, therefore, passes through the exchange of commodity. Marx knew very well why he was rejecting the use-value of commodity for a capitalist; that is, he did not want to recognize the want of a capitalist as a legitimate human want. Marx's attention toward capitalists is a racist attention. For, by refusing the human want of the capitalist, first, the human right of the capitalist for having want has been violated. And, second, a capitalist as a natural human who could have want has been rejected. Even though the rejection of a capitalist's humanity is not expressed explicitly, it nevertheless opens the road for the fanatic Marxist partisans to believe that a capitalist person deserves to be removed by all means, regardless of kind or severity.

The situation for the labourer in the Marxist political economy is different. We start our investigation by looking at Marx's obsession with labour. He said, "If then we leave out of consideration the use-value of commodities, they have only one common property left, that of being products of labour."[130] This statement by Marx is definitely the result of his obsession with labour; otherwise, it is total nonsense, for commodity without use-value is equal to zero or nothing. A use-valueless commodity cannot exist. Marx understood that what he said was absurd because he then very quickly said, "If we make abstraction from its use-value, we make abstraction at the same time from the material elements and shapes that make the product a use-value. . . . Its existing as material thing is put out of sight. Neither can it any longer be regarded as the product of the labour."[131]

Indeed, Marx is very clearly confirming that a commodity abstracted from its use-value does not exist. Thus, in any circumstance, a commodity is not separable from its use-value. In the previous section, we

---

130 *Ibid.*

131 Marx, *Capital*, Vol. I, 45–46.

explained that any commodity is a product of a combination of use-values, and labour is included among them as one of these use-values. We also explained that all the use-values that make a commodity are equal, and among them does not exist superiority or inferiority, for without any of those use-values, the given commodity would disappear. Marx correctly said, "In the use-value of each commodity there is contained useful labour."[132] Although, on different occasions, Marx confirmed that use-value is the most important element for determining the existence of a commodity, his priority nevertheless remained always for his agenda. In other words, since *The Communist Manifesto*, his mind never changed. Marx, in his politico-philosophical life, never grew up; i.e., he never succeeded in freeing himself from prejudice. Therefore, at all costs, he could bypass the use-value as he said, "As values, all commodities are only definite masses of congealed labour-time."[133] This statement is absolutely irresponsible and a prejudicial way of denying all other components of commodities and attributing the existence of a commodity to only one thing.

The culmination of Marx's prejudice is his declaration of labour as the pivot for political economy. He was very proud to say that he was the first who came to this understanding. The first point to be noticed in Marx's fanaticism regarding labour is that he presented labour as "a creator of use-value" and not as one of the creators. Then he said:

> At first sight a commodity presented itself to us as a complex of two things—use-value and exchange-value. Later on, we saw also that labour, too, possesses the same two-fold nature . . . I was the first to point out and to examine critically this two-fold nature of the labour contained in commodity. As this point is the pivot on which a clear comprehension of Political Economy turns.[134]

---

132 Marx, *Capital,* Vol. I, 49.

133 Marx, *Capital,* Vol. I, 47.

134 Marx, *Capital,* Vol. I, 48–9.

Definitely, here, Marx forgot to tell us that he means the "Political Economy of Karl Marx" and not political economy as a science. We remember that in the Marxist political economy, Marx told us that human labour could bring things from the dead to life: "In so far then as labour is such specific productive activity. . . . by mere contact, the means of production from the dead, makes them living factors of the labour process, and combines with them to form the new products."[135]

We have already explained that in nature and in the human environment and society, human labour is a use-value. Use-values as natural phenomena, related to each other, are not superior or inferior. Human labour as a natural use-value is not sacred, and it does not have any celestial quality or aspect.

POLITICAL ECONOMY AND USE-VALUE

Etymologically, political economy is a combination of the Greek words Polity + Economy, which has its roots in the ancient Greek word *oikonomos* that means "household manager." The pioneers of political economy are Adam Smith, David Ricardo, and Thomas Malthus. However, we are not interested in spending too much time on these details.

Karl Marx's mother tongue and his academic language, which he studied at school and university, was German. He wrote his book *Capital* in his mother tongue. In 1867, the first edition of Marx's *Capital* was published in Hamburg, Germany. The full original title of Marx's book, on the cover of the first German edition of *Capital*, Vol. I was: *Das Kapital, Kritik der Politischen Oekonomie* (*Capital, A Critique of Political Economy*).

Political economy is the interdisciplinary study of how economically, politically, and socially human individuals interact with each other in society. Political economy is also the study of how, through a particular social structure, economic and political systems in human society are linked. In fact, in our time, in a society in which the capitalist mode of production prevails, political economy studies the

---

135 Marx, *Capital,* Vol. I, 194.

mechanism through which some human individuals (employees and consumers) make their living and the price called profit (surplus-value) that they pay for their requirements. It also shows that some human individuals (capitalists) collect the profit (the paid price). And finally, it shows how the organs of social anatomy function and administer the mechanisms of the society.

Let us now take a look at the details of the efforts whereby human individuals make their living. The basic and indispensable elements that accommodate and assure human life with its requirements are commodity and service, which are produced by employees and bought by consumers. Its profit is collected by capitalists. Hence, the conclusion is that the commodity and service are the fundamental entities of political economy, which, without commodity and service, would become meaningless and disappear.

As we have already seen, the existence of every commodity and service is conditioned by its use-value, for in order to be able to satisfy any human need and want, a commodity or service must be useful and usable; therefore, it must have a particular use-value. Thus, any denial of the use-value of any commodity or service is equal to the denial of the existence of that commodity or service. Consequentially, denial of use-value in general will result in the denial of commodity and service as the fundamental elements of political economy, and political economy will hence become meaningless and useless.

Let us now examine the relation between the fundamental element in every category of science and the specialist individuals whose role is to apply that science for the common well-being in human society.

In medicine, medical doctors study and learn medical science to protect and restore human life. Thus, in medicine, human life is a central point and the fundamental element that gives meaning and justification for the existence of medicine and medical doctors. Therefore, if, in any manner, a doctor denies the existence or importance of human life, consequentially, this denial would become a reason for the denial of medicine all together. For if human life does not exist, how or for what will medicine exist?

In accounting, accountants learn how to make financial transactions measurable and explicable through numbers. Therefore, the fundamental element in accounting is numbers. If an accountant denies the existence of numbers, how could accounting exist?

Now, we will get back to Marx. As we have already seen, Marx denied the use-value for capitalists when he said, "As use-values, commodities are, above all, of different quantities, but as exchange-values they are merely different quantities, and consequently do not contain an atom of use-value."[136] We examined above that without use-value, which is a fundamental element of political economy, political economy itself becomes meaningless. Hence, we will find ourselves in front of the question that if use-value does not exist, how could Marx apply political economy in the capitalist mode of production? By denying the use-value, Marx is in fact denying himself as a political economist and philosopher who is willing to critically analyze the capitalist mode of production. This is how Marxism—by denying use-value—makes itself void and inefficient. Therefore, since Marx's understanding of the capitalist mode of production is wrong, his solution for any modification or change becomes wrong and harmful.

---

136 Marx, *Capital*, Vol. I, 45.

FETISHISM AND PROPHECY

A s we have seen, the starting point for Marx is the commodity because, for him, the commodity pre-supposes the wealth of those societies in which the capitalist mode of production prevails. Then the same commodity pre-supposes to understand the use-value, and since, in a capitalist society, the commodity circulates between individuals, use-value is denied and the exchange-value takes its place. From the other side, though, Marx said that the commodity is a congelation of human labour. Therefore, human labour pre-supposes the commodity. Thus, the value (that, consequently, is not use-value) of the commodity belongs to the labour, which has created it. At this point, Marx attributes a metaphysical identity to commodity, brings it out of the material sphere and puts it into the mystical sphere, and says it is fathomable in the religious world. This is where dialectical materialism vanishes and the mysterious theological life of commodity for rabbi-priest-mullah Marx starts. In this position, Marx choreographs a theo-logical dance for commodity and labour and calls it **"the fetishism of commodities."** Below, we will dissect the waltz of fetishism.

Under the title of fetishism, Marx wrote 4,426 words, from which I take only the first 821 as these tell us everything that we need to know. But before going into the details of Marx's fetishism, we need to remember that in 1843, when Marx was twenty-five years old, he wrote that "religion is the opium of the masses" in his *Critique of Hegel's Philosophy of Right*. Then, in 1867, when he was forty-nine years old, he published *Das Kapital*, where he wrote about the fetishism of commodities. There, in order to find an analogy that could help the understanding of a commodity's complexity, he said we must have recourse to the religious world. It appears that the use-value of opium has imposed itself on Karl Marx.

Near the beginning of part I of this book, in the chapter on Wealth and Commodity, I mentioned that Marx starts *Capital* with a prophetical attention that never goes away. I also said that I would later analyze this mater extensively. Here is where we will study the question of fetishism and the prophetical intention of Marx that is part and parcel of it.

Marx, in his book *Capital*, writes about "The Fetishism of Commodities and the Secret Thereof." The first and second sentences are: "A commodity appears, at first sight, a very trivial thing, and easily understood. Its analysis shows that it is, in reality, a very queer thing, abounding in metaphysical subtleties and theological niceties."[137] As we know, commodity is the most important entity in Marx's theory of capitalism. According to Marx, fetishism is not about studying the simple and trivial appearance of commodities. Rather, fetishism is about articulating the important subtleties and niceties hidden in the very core of a commodity. As we know, Marx was a trained philosopher, and as such was aware that there are four main branches (metaphysics, epistemology, axiology, logic) in philosophy for considering our world. So why did Marx choose the main branch of metaphysics and the subfield of religion and theology to teach us the complexity of commodities? It is crucial to find out why Marx, who did not believe in God, needed theology (the study of the nature of God and religion) to teach his believers the complexity of the most important entity in his subject matter.

---

137 Marx, Capital, Vol. I, 76.

Before moving further, let us look at the choices that Marx had. For instance, among the four main branches of philosophy, why did Marx not choose logic? And among the subfields, instead of religion, why did he not choose the philosophy of science or language or politics? Marx was a brilliant great writer. And most importantly he was writing his book in his academic and mother tongue, therefore, he did not choose his methods and subjects innocently or accidentally. Thus, we need to dig further into this vital issue.

Marx, as a philosopher, knew very well that through metaphysical discourse, a metaphysical reflection can be implanted within an individual's consideration of objective existence and subjective understanding. We will soon come back to this issue to study it further. He also knew very well that religious discourse can create an addictive belief among those who are willing to be convinced by an account. Therefore, they become an ardent, faithful, permanent, loyal army of believers ready to sacrifice and work hard for their faith. This is how all religions create followers, and once the believers get into the cult, they don't get out. This was the reason that Karl Marx himself called religion "the opium of the masses." As an expert on this concept, he applied it to create his own everlasting army. Although Marx never explicitly claimed that he had an intention to create a new religion, he very effectively created a well-structured fetishistic ideology of commodity (religion) that was professionally sold as a materialist ideology for the emancipation of the working class. As we have seen, those who become addicted Marxist believers never cease to believe in Marxist ideology. In the medical community, it is known that opiate withdrawal is almost impossible to achieve, although some exceptional cases exist. This is the secret thereof to understand why Marx said to his son-in-law Paul Lafargue that: *"Ce qu'il y a de certain c'est que moi, je ne suis pas Marxiste"* – "That which is certain, it is that I am not Marxist."[138] For, while he was making others addicted, he was keeping himself clean.

---

138 Frederick Engels to Eduard Bernstein, November 3, 1882: 3; also, *MECW* 46, Moscow, 1924: 353.

Let us go deeper into fetishism. The *Oxford Dictionary* says a fetish is an inanimate object worshipped for its supposed magical power or it is considered to be inhabited by a spirit. In Latin, *facticius* means artificial and *facere* means to make; it is believed to be a human-made object that has supernatural powers. It is possible to imagine that by creating a fetishistic appearance, Marx was willing to demonize the commodity as a negative basic element of the capitalist mode of production. This could make sense, as commodities are produced to make profit when exchanged, and profit means not paying the working class their fair share for making the commodity. But this interpretation is too naïve of a simplification of the subject for the genius of Marx. In the fetishism of commodity, Marx did highly sophisticated work that we will have to analyze in detail.

Let us start with religions in general. Although most religions encourage their followers to pay more attention to the spiritual side of life and not be materialistic, nevertheless certain clothing and sacred objects are important for different reasons. In some cases, religions expect their followers in daily life or in religious rituals to dress up in special clothes or to carry certain pieces of fabric, metal, wood, etc.; although, in reality these are just objects—human-made commodities. Even though none of these human-made commodity objects are made in or imported from the celestial divine world, religions have their reasons and descriptions to explain and justify the metaphysical subtleties and theological niceties of their use.

Let us examine, in a more tangible manner, the religious consumption of human-made commodity objects. The human body (both male and female) is a highly concerning matter for all religions. Every religion has its own methods and techniques for covering the human head and/or body for different rites and occasions. To simplify our example, we will consider only one form of head cover or head cap.

Imagine in a fabric shop that customer A buys a piece of fabric to sew a vest. In the same fabric shop, from the same bolt of fabric, customer B buys a piece of fabric to sew a religious head cap. Then, customer C goes to the same fabric shop and from the same bolt of fabric buys a piece to sew a fancy seat cover for a chair. And finally, the remaining short piece of fabric at the end of the fabric bolt ends up as a rag in the hands of a mechanic in a garage. Thus, the same bolt of fabric has become a vest, a religious head cap, a fancy seat cover, and a rag.

Now we will study each customer's need for the fabric and the sources from which those needs spring:

- Customer A needs the fabric to sew a vest to cover his body, which is a very natural and material human need.

- Customer B needs the fabric because of his religious beliefs. He has accepted to be convinced by a religious leader that a supernatural power has been planted in the head cap he will make so that he will be blessed by wearing it. Whereas, in reality, the head cap will never do or cause anything objective and tangible for customer B.

- The case for customer C is also simple. He needs the fabric to sew a chair seat cover, which is an extraneous, material human want. It is true that even without a cover, one can sit on a chair. But if one can afford it, a fancy, comfortable, covered chair seat can provide the consumer with more comfort and pleasure.

- The case for user D is quite straightforward. To be able to clean one's hands in a messy workplace is a material, professional human need.

Now let us come back to customer B and his need. Customer B is aware that the head cap is not doing anything material for him, but he believes that it is his duty to put the head cap (a piece of fabric) on his head. The crucial issue here is to **believe**. Customers A, C, and D don't need to believe in anything for the tangible service that will come from using the fabric. The use-value of the fabric is enough reason for these three customers to buy the fabric and use it. But for customer B, the use-value is not simple and materialistic; rather, the use-value of the fabric is a human-made, imaginary need of the customer.

Here we will focus on the human-made imaginary need to see how this works. In order to believe in metaphysical and theological issues, a person must be convinced in the truth of something that does not exist tangibly in reality. In this situation, somebody (a social subject) tells a metaphysically theological account, which another person (a social object) hears. This is a social relation between two or more individuals, and among them, the subject (storyteller) presents or produces one or more idealistic points. To make these points convincing and accept-able, the storyteller metaphysically posits that they are connected to theological sources that are celestial and divine and, therefore, not tan-gible to humans or understandable for the ordinary mind. In order to benefit from the subtleties and niceties of a theological phenomenon, one should believe in their secrecy and mystery. This is how religious clothing, objects, and artifacts become meaningful and have mysteri-ous use-values that satisfy the idealistic needs of believers.

The storytellers (subjects) connect individual believers to their claimed theological points through consumption of sacred material commodities. The starting point of this trajectory is verbal, human-made theological points that end up in the consumption of human-made material commodities made of minerals. More simply, it goes from the metaphysico-theological to a commodity. And, by reverse engineering, our genius prophet Marx taught his believers this trajec-tory in the opposite direction. He went from mineral-made commodi-ties to the metaphysico-theological niceties.

Still ,we are not finished and must go back to customer B to further examine the religious consumption of sacred things. Customer B will wear his head cap because of his religious beliefs. But even though customer B is a religious person, one day he might decide to store his head cap in a drawer and continue his natural human life without wearing it. However, we know that there are some other individuals that believe in the same religion as customer B, but who never practise their religion rigorously and never wear any sacred or religious cloth-ing. Still nothing here prevents them from living their full, natural human life. Furthermore, there are definitely some individuals who do not believe in any religion at all, and they live their natural human life without any problem or deficiency. The point is that sacred objects—and for that matter, all metaphysically and theologically mysterious commodities—are ineffective in affecting natural human life. Without them, humans can live a full, natural, and completely constructive life. Nevertheless, it is legitimate to ask why, in spite of uselessness, these metaphysico-theological objects exist. Even more importantly, we must ask why Karl Marx needed to make a metaphysico-theological argument for describing the role of commodity under the capitalist mode of production in human society.

To study this question, we must return to religion and the mechanism by which storytellers (social subjects) sell their ideas to believers (social objects). Before all, it must be said that all politicians, philosophers, rabbis, priests, mullahs, imams, celebrities, journalists, writers, business leaders, artists, etc., are storytellers and, therefore, social subjects. On the opposite side, average people, listeners, voters, readers, employees, consumers, spectators, ticket buyers and membership payers are all social objects. It is crucial to know about social subjects. Some social subjects are independent individuals without any connection to a group, community, corporation, institution, or political party. Some other social subjects are connected to certain groups, communities, corporations, institutions, and political parties—some legal and some illegal. Another point is that there are three categories of individuals among both independent and dependent social subjects. One category is made up of honest and sincere individuals whose actions and activities are based on their hope to improve human life and civilization. The second category is made up of dishonest and charlatan individuals whose activities are based on manipulation and misleading others for their own private and personal interests, no matter the price. And, finally, the third category is made up of individuals who are looking for social opportunities and possibilities to make their living, and are neither good nor bad.

Social subjects need the long-lasting, and even everlasting, permanent loyalty of their social objects. In certain spheres—such as art, literature, music, entertainment, and science—this can be achieved quickly and easily. But in areas in which offered benefits are just an illusion, social subjects require high intellectual capacities, financial resources, and perseverance and patience. These areas often necessitate a mechanism that establishes the adherence of the objects to the subjects. In metaphysico-theological spheres, in which everything is imaginary, the adherence mechanism (some might call it brain-washing) must engage objects' brains in a paralyzing preoccupation with rules and regulations that dictate a series of musts and duties. In effect, this deprives objects of sane thought by creating a yoke of guilt and fear that attaches the objects to the subjects for a long time.

Following these rules, regulations, musts, and duties turns an object's brain into hard concrete and creates everlasting worries and stress that they have not respected the protocols correctly. In the long run, an object's mind becomes dependent and narrow, although an object will think (believe) that they are doing good for themselves and their community and, therefore, they will be forgiven and blessed. As Marx said, "Religion is the opium of the masses." There are abundant scientific and philosophical documents on this topic, so we will return to Marx and his adherent mechanism.

We know that Marx liked to deny use-value. But he also denied labour, when he wrote: "The mystical character of commodities does not originate, therefore, in their use value."[139] He explained that:

> So far as it is a value in use, there is nothing mysterious about it, whether we consider it from the point of view that by its properties it is capable of satisfying human wants, or the point that those properties are the product of human labour.[140]

We will study this situation step by step. As we have already described, any commodity is a total sum of several use-values, such as raw materials, administration, labour, and a means of production that have been gathered and modified in a certain composition for creating a new particular use-value that can satisfy a human need or want. Therefore, in any given circumstances, if a use-value is denied, consequentially, the labour embodied in it is denied. But, since Marx had an agenda, he emphatically cleared the state of labour in relation

---

139 Marx, *Capital*, Vol. I, 76.
140 Ibid.

to the mysteriousness of the commodity. Therefore, he clearly said that the mystical character of the commodity does not come from the labour that created it. This point is very delicate. This is the starting point of a voyage from the real, material object (commodity) toward metaphysico-theological emptiness through the mechanism of verbalizing the objective functions of humans into an imaginary expressed value. We will accompany Marx in this voyage.

So, now, we will listen to Marx tell us what the rules and protocols are. There are three steps to the method that Marx uses to tell his story. These are amazingly similar to the method for flying a passenger airplane. The three steps in flying are: 1. Take-off roll, which is a preparation process, during which the airplane accelerates to reach flying speed; 2. Lift-off, which is the moment the airplane leaves the ground and becomes airborne; and, 3. cruising altitude, which is the relaxing period of flying toward the destination. Finally, at the end of every flight is a safe landing. However, this part does not exist in Marx's story, for Marxism never lands.

Let us now learn, in more detail, the rules and protocols of Marx's story. The take-off roll for Marx is statement that: "The equality of all sorts of human labour is expressed objectively by their products all being equally values; the measure of the expenditure of labour power by the duration of that expenditure, takes the form of the quantity of value of the products of labour."[141] This brings Marx to his flying speed.

As we remember from above, Marx said that the mystical character of commodity does not originate in the use-value. So he is asking the question: "Whence, then, arises the enigmatic character of the product of labour, so soon as it assumes the form of commodities?"[142] He answers this right away: "Clearly from this form itself,"[143] in which "itself" means "commodity." Marx said it is not coming from use-value and then he clearly stated that it is coming from commodity. Therefore, we must understand that the use-value and commodity are two different

---

141 Marx, *Capital*, Vol. I, 77.
142 Marx, *Capital*, Vol. I, 76.
143 Ibid.

things. Okay, we will accept this, for now. However, we are in front of a commodity, which is a real object, and the non-palpable, mysterious character is supposed to be originating from this commodity object. Marx continued the story toward the mysteriousness when he said, "The mutual relations of the producers, within which the social character of their labour affirms itself, take the form of a social relation between the products."[144] This is the lift-off and exactly the moment that Marx's feet leave the ground. Here he becomes airborne and starts the ascension from Earth to Heaven.

This satisfaction provides him with sufficient energy to issue a prophetical statement as such:

> A commodity is therefore a mysterious thing simply because in it the social character of men's labour appears to them as an objective character stamped upon the product of that labour; because the relation of the producers to the sum total of their own labour is presented to them as a social relation, existing not between themselves, but between the products of their labour. This is the reason why the product of labour becomes commodity.[145]

Thus, so far as Marxism is concerned, the mission is accomplished; therefore, the Working Men of All Countries Can Unite.

For us, however, this is the starting point. We have to find out why Marx has done all these metaphysico-theological efforts and why he had to have recourse to the religious world.

In human society, all that concerns social relations—both between individuals and between individuals and society—are based on the laws and regulations that are all made and enforced by the authorities of the society. From the other side, all that concerns production relations are human-made, material objects that consist of raw materials, administration, labour, means of production, and means of commodity circulation between the capitalists, employees, and consumers.

---

144 Marx, *Capital*, Vol. I, 77.
145 Ibid.

Therefore, since all that concerns both social relations and production relations that are human-made or human-thought material things so why we need recourse to the religious world to understand the material thing (commodity). However, this need does not exist for real. This need is definitely an illusion, which is a mere fabrication of an imaginary social relation between products—exactly as imaginary as is God and saints in religions.

In fact, Marx knew this, and he himself said it:

> The existence of things qua commodities, and the value-relation between the products of labour which stamps them as commodities, have absolutely no connection with their physical properties and with the material arising there from. There it is a definite social relation between men that assumes, in their eyes, the fantastic form of a relation between things.[146]

Relations between things happen either in nature or in human society. Those relations between things that occur in nature—such as water running into the rivers, snow falling on the mountains, or sun shining on the sea—are all natural events that happen by natural forces. Humans have no control over these, except in certain cases, when people will try to consume it wherever they might become available, such as skiing on the snow in the mountains or taking sun bath on the seaside. Moreover, the relations between things of any kind that occur in human society are all controlled by human individuals. Therefore, they absolutely do not have any dependency on or rapport with the metaphysico-theological sphere or religious world. Marx knew this and said, "It is plain that commodity cannot go to market and make exchanges of their own account. We must, therefore, have recourse to their guardians, who are also their owners. Commodities are things, and therefore without power of resistance against man."[147]

---

146 Ibid.

147 Marx, *Capital*, Vol. I, 88.

Still, we have not finished with Marx. However, when we see him conjuring so hard, we must determine his ultimate goal. Marx told us that:

> There is a physical relation between physical things. But it is different with commodity... In order, therefore, to find an analogy, we must have recourse to the mist-enveloped region of the religious world. In that world the productions of the human brain appear as independent being endowed with life, and entering into relation both with one another and the human race. So it is in the world of commodities with the products of men's hands. This I call the Fetishism which attaches itself to the products of labour, as soon as they are produced as commodities.[148]

Here, Marx was saying that there is a physical relation between physical things, but it is different with commodities. Thus, while he is telling us that a commodity is a physical thing, at the same time, he wants us to believe that a commodity is not a physical thing. We will walk step by step through the details that Marx provided. He said that a commodity is different, and in order to find an analogy that can help us understand this particularity, we need a recourse from the religious world. This is quite amazing. In order to understand a commodity, which is a hard, solid, physical thing, we need help from religion that itself is an imaginary and illusionary phenomenon. Marx was trying to convince us to believe in a void illusion, in so far as he says that in the religious world "the productions of the human brain appear as independent beings endowed with life, and entering into relation both with one another and the human race."[149]

This statement is totally absurd. **Marx knew very well that human products of any kind will never be independent, and consequentially, will never be endowed with life.** We have already heard him say that "Commodities are things, and therefore without power of

148 Marx, *Capital*, Vol. I, 77.
149 Ibid.

resistance against man."[150] But still we are far from the ultimate goal, and hence, the tale continues. Once entering into the religious world of Karl Marx, in which a commodity is endowed with life, he added that: "A commodity is therefore a mysterious thing simply because in it the social character of men's labour appears to them as an objective character stamped upon the product of that labour."[151] This is the moment of the ascension of labour into the sky. Here, we are left with no choice, but to believe in the sacredness of labour in the hands of working men, who are the creators of physical things (commodities) that are endowed with life. Thus, in the religious world of a holy working class, which has been metaphysically and theologically very well constructed by our prophet Marx, there remains nothing to do except prostrate and wish that a state of the working class will emerge to bring redemption and emancipation for humankind. Amen.

Our task now is to draw lessons from our analysis of Marx's fetishism. The first point is technical: Under the title of fetishism, Marx is very skillfully playing with words. The magical key words used by the magician Marx are social character, objective character, and social relation, along with claiming that a commodity, which is a material object, has life. In fact, the nature of these words, used in the context of political economy, is nothing but a void meaning, tinted theologically in order to become an elusive absurdity. Human civilization, through other religions, has several thousand years of experience in using these fooling techniques. The second point is a political matter: Under the title of fetishism, Marx was creating a holy image for the working class in order to legitimize its role and to establish a working-class state verses a nation state in human society.

Since the publication of *Das Kapital,* over 150 years of history has shown humans that the working class does not have the competence, legitimacy, and right to create its own class state and impose it upon humans.

---

150 Marx, *Capital,* Vol. I, p. 88.

151 Marx, *Capital,* Vol. I, p. 77.

BIRD'S-EYE VIEW AND CAPITALISM

Although it is true that I have buried Marxism, the spectre of Marx is nevertheless still alive. But first, though, we will go through the details of our bird's-eye-view observation before coming back to Karl Marx.

On a beautiful sunny day with a nice, clear visibility, we are on the twenty-seventh floor of a high-rise building. From the window, we are watching a downtown neighbourhood in a metropolis. There we see nine streets and four intersections. People and cars (similar to ants) are going in all directions. Traffic for the cars is straightforward and simple. Cars are only on the streets, and they are moving forward along the lines on the right side of the road. Ongoing cars pass only from the left side of the oncoming traffic. They follow the traffic lights for going through intersections or turning left or right. Cars calculate their position on the street and watch the situation of other cars in front or behind and on the sides. But for the pedestrians, the story is not the same or simple. Pedestrians are everywhere on the streets and sidewalks. They walk according to their own judgment of how fast or slow they go, the best way to get to their destination (their own benefit), or simple carelessness (their own comfort). Some walk on the sidewalks, some walk on the street, and some jaywalk. The oncoming and ongoing pedestrians do not care on which side they are passing each other; they do so according to their own benefit and comfort. The pedestrians, according to their own benefit or comfort, bump into each other or push their way through the crowd. The pedestrians, according only to their own benefit, watch their situation on the streets and sidewalks. And, according to their own comfort, they ignore the situations of others. In short, the pedestrians follow neither laws nor orders; indeed, they enjoy their total benefit and comfort, which is free from any restriction in a jungle, chaotic kind of situation.

Human life naturally and socially necessitates myriad efforts and activities of all kinds, some simple and easy, while some others are complicated and difficult. Human life with benefit and comfort is definitely more exciting and agreeable. Thus, the desire of individuals to seek their own benefit and comfort is as natural as blood and skin in human biology. It has co-existed with humans ever since humans existed and, indeed, will exist as long as humans do and will never go away. This desire is the same motivation that made humans into hunter gatherers, and that today is inspiring humans to go into space. The more humans use their brains, the more their benefit and comfort seeking desires become diverse and complex. Thus, when humans crave benefit and comfort, it is neither bad nor a defect nor fault; it is just the natural biological matter of human need and want. Nevertheless, in a capitalist society, this issue is different. In fact, a capitalist society is a discriminatory system that limits and sometimes deprives only one part of the population from freely seeking benefit and comfort as they may wish. The same discriminatory system helps and even provides the necessary legal means for another part of the population to excessively pursue their benefit and comfort seeking desires, even in a chaotic fashion.

As we have already learned, the capitalist mode of production is a network system made of employees, capitalists, and consumers. According to our bird's-eye-view observation, the situation for employees and consumers is very similar to that of the cars. Based on laws and regulations, employees and consumers are trapped in a net of legal and social mechanisms in which every cent of their income and expenditures is registered and controlled in advance. But the situation for the capitalists is very similar to that of the pedestrians; it is a jungle-like, chaotic kind of situation.

First, we will look at the situation that the employees are trapped in. The employees must work first before their money is paid. But before the employees receive their money, a considerable amount of money in the form of taxes and duties are already taken off their pay. At the same time, their full income, up to the last cent, will be registered and reported to the tax office for complete year-end verification. Indeed, as a norm, the employees pay their income taxes completely and on time every year. Therefore, law and order are in full control.

Second are the consumers. For every single commodity or service they purchase, they have to follow the rules and conditions that have been established by the market. For every item the consumers wish to buy, they must first pay the price and the related taxes and duties as they are asked. Then, after the payment has been made, the consumers will receive the demanded commodity or services. Hence, here, too, law and order are in full control.

Third are the capitalists. No matter what, when, and where, they enjoy absolute freedom and even assistance for seeking their desired benefit and comfort in all their activities to ceaselessly accumulate more and more money and wealth in a categorical *sans souci* environment. For capitalists, a capitalist society is not a legally, politically, and geographically bordered place. Quite to the contrary, a capitalist society provides capitalists with a cost-free society furnished with all kinds of inland or offshore haven. In fact, for capitalists, capitalist society is an infinitely dimensionless space, free from laws, restrictions, and duties. It is also equipped with myriad loopholes for any unpredicted, messy events. Thus, for capitalists, the jungle society is paradise.

Our bird's-eye-view observation teaches us that a capitalist society is inherently an unjust and unequal society. On one side, the employees and the consumers are handcuffed and thrown into the ocean of a capitalist, free market economy, which means the capitalists will devour their money, no matter what. And on the other side, the capitalists and their associates enjoy apartheid superiority, which is secured and warranted by the law of the jungle.

In our modern time, whenever and wherever the question of justice and equality is raised, the spectre of Marx will start flying. This is because all his life, Marx was a very ardent advocate of justice and equality, to the point that he sacrificed his family and his life. Marx said that instead of interpreting the world, the point is to change it. This is still very true, and it will always remain fresh. Marx also said that capitalism is unjust and unequal; this too is still true. Nevertheless, his understanding of the class structure of capitalism was wrong, and his solution for changing it was wrong. It is my job to repair his mistakes and I will do it in the second part of this book. But there remains one other point we must look at quite carefully, and that is historical materialism.

HISTORICAL MATERIALISM

Although Marx did not write comprehensively about historical materialism, he has written enough to be used by Marxist partisans and scholars to draw the specific conclusion that specific historical epochs are the result of variations in the modes of production that humans have experienced over the centuries. Thus, according to this methodology of analyzing and understanding the structure of the history of human society, they have come to the conclusion that under certain methods and modifications in human composition in the capitalist mode of production, human society will turn into socialism and communism. Thus, the problems and injustices created by capitalism could be solved and, as has been prophesied in *The Communist Manifesto*, the ultimate redemption and emancipation of human beings will be achieved.

Let us examine this issue in more detail. As we said earlier, Marx's writings on historical materialism are brief and sporadic. Among them, one that is significant is *A Contribution to the Critique of Political Economy*, which was published in January 1859 in German, with the original title *Zur Kritik der politischen Ökonomie*. Another significant document on historical materialism is Friedrich Engels's book, *Mr. Eugen Dühring's Revolution in Science*, which was published in 1878 in German, with the original title *Herrn Eugen Dührings Umwälzung der Wissenschaft*. This book is better known as *Anti-Dühring*. It is also worth mentioning that Eugen Dühring started a campaign against Marxist socialism by publishing his own version of socialism. At that time, Marx was too busy writing the second and third volumes of *Das Kapital*, so he left it to his friend, Friedrich Engels, to write a response to Eugen Dühring. It is known that *Anti-Dühring* was written under Karl Marx's supervision and approval. But as is the intention of this book, I will not focus on sources that do not come immediately and directly from Karl Marx. Therefore, I will not base my analysis on Friedrich Engels' *Anti-Dühring*.

I will return now to the first source above, *A Contribution to the Critique of Political Economy*, and more specifically, I will focus on the preface of this writing, which as *cheminement of his pensée* Marx called it "the course of my study of political economy". The starting phrase of Marx at the beginning of the course of his study is: "Although I studied jurisprudence, I pursued it as a subject subordinated to philosophy and history." Marx finished his preface by saying: "This sketch of the course of my studies in the domain of political economy is intended merely to show that my views . . . are the outcome of conscientious research carried on over many years."[152] Of course, no one would or could doubt that Marx conscientiously did his research and writing. Here, we will examine in detail the essence of what Marx said between the first and last phrase of his preface. In this preface Marx started sketching his parcours from 1842, when he was twenty-four years old, until 1859, when he was forty-one years old. This means this period consists of almost seventeen years of Marx's life. Here it is useful to remember that Jacques Derrida in his *Specters of Marx* wrote, *"Kant qui genuit Hegel qui genuit Marx."*[153] Thus, to understand what Marx is saying, it is indispensable to know the roots of Hegelian thoughts in Marx's ideas.

---

152 Karl Marx, "Preface," *A Contribution to the Critique of Political Economy* (Moscow: Progress Publishers, 1977): 1–4.

153 Jacques Derrida, *Specters of Marx*, 9.

As we saw above in his preface, Marx begins by telling us that he started with jurisprudence and, from there he went to philosophy and history. Young Marx "as editor of the *Rheinische Zeitung*" starts to learn about factual issues such as "material interests" or "the division of landed property," and then, while he is still a young editor, he gets involved in "the debates on free trade and protective tariffs." This becomes a magical time of parturition when the economist Marx is born. As he himself said, it "caused me in the first instance to turn my attention to economic questions."[154] His very keen and super active brain did not stop monitoring and scanning all kinds of intellectual, social, economic, and political activities and movements, not only in the country where he was residing, but also in the neighbouring countries in Europe and even around the world. We can see Marx's sensitivity toward the events happening in his environment as he wrote that the "echo of French socialism and communism, slightly tinged by philosophy, was noticeable in the Rheinische Zeitung."[155] He also honestly said that in the beginning, the French theories appeared to be worthless ideas. Therefore, he was rejecting this echo as he wrote, "I objected to this dilettantism."[156] In the meantime, Marx avowed that "at the same time frankly admitted in a controversy with the Allgemeine Augsburger Zeitung that my previous studies did not allow me to express any opinion on the content of the French theories."[157]

At this moment, young Marx as an editor realized that his knowledge for understanding the complicated social and political issues is not enough. Thus, as a sincere and responsible intellectual, he decided to withdraw from public activities in order to attain the necessary knowledge that would equip him for his social and political struggles.

---

154 Karl Marx, "Preface," *A Contribution to the Critique of Political Economy* (Moscow: Progress Publishers, 1977): 1–4.

155 Ibid.

156 Ibid.

157 Ibid.

Thus, he wrote, "I eagerly grasped the opportunity to withdraw from the public stage to my study."[158]

At this point, we wish to know the details of Marx's studies and its effects on Marx's understanding of history and thereon his understanding of the role that he could play in history. In this regard, first we will listen to Marx to see what he tells us about his studies and conclusions. Then we will verify Marx's studies with Hegel's principals.

In his preface, Marx mentions Hegel three times by name. He said, "The first work which I undertook to dispel the doubts assailing me was a critical re-examination of the Hegelian philosophy of law; the introduction to this work being published in the *Deutsch-Franzosische Jahrbucher* issued in Paris in 1844."[159] Thereof, he comes to the conclusion that the legal relations and political forms in human society are not comprehendible by themselves and/or by general development of the human mind. Quite to the contrary, he comes to believe that they originated in the material conditions of life. This is the point when Marx discovers that the defect "of which Hegel, following the example of English and French thinkers of the eighteenth century, embraces within the term 'civil society'."[160] And the solution that he finds is "that the anatomy of this civil society, however, has to be sought in political economy."[161] Here, Marx wants us to understand that detecting the defect and finding the solution, as he explained it above, in fact, served him as a springboard for going to political economy and developing his own theories. He wrote: "The general conclusion at which I arrive . . . became the guiding principle of my studies."[162]

As we remember above, Marx confirmed that his discovery was "that the anatomy of this civil society, however, has to be sought in political economy."[163] Thus, we are interested here to find out, first:

---

158 Ibid.

159 Ibid.

160 Ibid.

161 Ibid.

162 Ibid.

163 Ibid.

how he seeks the anatomy of the civil society in political economy. And second: what conclusion he drew from his studies, which he then used as the basis to create his own theory of Marxism and a working class revolution.

Marx started by saying that:

> In the social production of their existence, men inevitably enter into definite relations, which are independent of their will, namely relations of production appropriate to a given stage in the development of their material forces of production. The totality of these relations of production constitutes the economic structure of society, the real foundation, on which arises a legal and political superstructure and to which correspond definite forms of social consciousness.[164]

Generally speaking, what Marx says is correct, but for the sake of facilitating our investigation, we will accept this statement of Marx.

Moreover, still talking about the anatomy of civil society, Marx said, "The mode of production of material life conditions the general process of social, political, and intellectual life. It is not the consciousness of men that determines their existence, but their social existence that determines their consciousness."[165] The point here is that, based on this statement, in today's highly developed capitalist world, there are a lot of political, intellectual, and cultural issues that remain inexplicable. For instance: Why, in our extremely developed, capitalist world, can a stone-age phenomenon like ISIS exist? Or why Japan, which is one of the highest industrially developed capitalist countries of our time, remains culturally, traditionally, and legally one of the surprisingly backward countries of modern time? For example, in Japan women are under represented in politics and higher education. Or, in the Japanese legal system even for minor offences, they can keep a person in prison for long time, even a year or more just for investigation. However, for

---

164 Ibid.
165 Ibid.

the sake of facilitating our investigation, we will forget our questions and ignore this statement by Marx.

Here the matter becomes critical, for Marx starts to talk about changing from one mode of production to another—in other words, changing from one historical epoch to another—as he says:

> At a certain stage of development, the material productive forces of society come into conflict with the existing relations of production or . . . with the property relations within the framework of which they have operated hitherto. From forms of development of the productive forces these relations turn into their fetters. Then begins an era of social revolution."[166]

In this statement, there are two significant points that must be addressed separately. The first point is that Marx says every mode of production, at a certain stage of its development, will develop conflicts with its existing relations of production, which will bring the function of those particular production forces to their end and will eventually replace it with a new mode of production. This statement by Marx is simple and clear. Things come and go in the world; therefore, generally speaking, one can say that Marx is effectively right about this. On Earth, some animals, such as the mayfly, live only 24 hours, and on the other end of the scale, we know that our Earth is almost 4.5 billion years old and no one knows how many thousands, millions, or billions years more it will survive.

The second point is how this dying process will occur and, most importantly, what mechanisms or forces will create or determine the details of the new mode of production that will replace the old one. This is a very important issue for us, and we will explore this point further a bit later. But here we need to say that, although Marx and some others have talked in great detail about elements of change in the pre-capitalist modes of production, Marx and others have not provided us with an explanation on how the capitalist mode of production will come to an end and what exactly will replace it. We will come back to

---

166 Ibid.

this matter and examine it very deeply. But for now, we will continue learning about Marx's inquiry and explore Marx's view of historical development and changes in human society.

To help us to understand the historical change in human society, Marx tells us that:

> In studying such transformations, it is always necessary to distinguish between the material transformation of the economic conditions of production . . . and the legal, political, religious, artistic, or philosophic . . . in which men become conscious of this conflict and fight it out.[167]

In order to make sure that his point will be understood correctly, Marx adds:

> One cannot judge such a period of transformation by its consciousness, but, on the contrary, this consciousness must be explained from the contradictions of material life, from the conflict existing between the social forces of production and the relations of production.[168]

But still I am not satisfied with Marx's explanation, for he just repeated the general aspect and does not talk about the mechanism for and detailed elements of change. All he added is that conflict arise from the contradictions between the social forces of production and the relations of production will cause the beginning of an era of social revolution. He further emphasized that: "The changes in the economic foundation lead sooner or later to the transformation of the whole immense superstructure."[169] But, still, these are all generally speaking and do not provide details.

There is one extremely important point from Marx's statement that he very emphatically repeats and wants to make sure does not go unnoticed. He said:

---

167 Ibid.

168 Ibid.

169 Ibid.

In the spring of 1845 [when Marx was 27 years old] . . . we [Marx and his friend Frederick Engels] decided to set forth together our conception as opposed to the ideological one of German philosophy, in fact to settle accounts with our former philosophical conscience. The intention was carried out in the form of a critique of post-Hegelian philosophy.[170]

In talking about historical developments in human society, Marx has kept repeating from the beginning that the causes of change from one epoch to another are not due to human consciousness; rather, they "originate in the material conditions of life." Yet here he said that he and his friend had reached this understanding through a critical study of post-Hegelian philosophy. We will try to examine this issue more closely to make sure that we understand it as Marx is expecting us to understand it. Later, when we start our serious examination of this issue, we will examine Hegel's ideas on this matter, too.

First, we must ensure that we understand Marx's definition for the word "consciousness." As we have seen earlier, Marx said: "The totality of these relations of production constitutes the economic structure of society, the real foundation, on which arises a legal and political superstructure and to which correspond definite forms of social consciousness."[171] Here in this preface is the first time that Marx used the word "consciousness" in his writing, and he presents it as being equal to the legal and political superstructure of human society. Then, regarding the transformation from one epoch to another, he said: "It is always necessary to distinguish between the material transformation of the economic conditions of production . . . and the legal, political, religious, artistic, or philosophic."[172] He then added: "One cannot judge such a period of transformation by its consciousness, but, on the contrary, this consciousness must be explained from the contradictions of material life."[173]

---

170 Ibid.
171 Ibid.
172 Ibid.
173 Ibid.

Here we see clearly that Marx put the economic conditions of production as the infrastructure versus the legal, political, religious, artistic, and philosophic as the superstructure. He then said that it is material life that explains the consciousness and not vice versa. In fact, Marx was telling us that the legal, political, religious, artistic, and philosophic forms of human society are human consciousness. We also remember that, earlier, Marx said: "My inquiry led me to the conclusion that neither legal relations nor political forms could be comprehended whether by themselves or on the basis of a so-called general development of the human mind."[174] Although not directly here, but in a different composition, Marx used another word for consciousness, which he called the human mind. In order to understand Marx, we will accept his definition as he used it.

The last thing that we will remind ourselves of before starting our detailed examination is that Marx very clearly named four different modes of production, historically, in the economic development of human society. He wrote: "In broad outline, the Asiatic, ancient (tribal), feudal and modern bourgeois of production may be designated as epochs marking progress in the economic development of society."[175] These four epochs are consistent with the four epochs that, eleven years earlier, in 1848, Marx mentioned in *The Communist Manifesto*. There he wrote:

> In the earlier epochs of history, we find almost everywhere a complicated arrangement of society into various orders, a manifold gradation of social rank. In ancient Rome we have patricians, knights, plebeians, slaves; in the Middle Ages, feudal lords, vassals, guild-masters, journeymen, apprentices, serfs; in almost all of these classes, again, subordinate gradations. . . . The modern bourgeois society that has sprouted from the ruins of feudal society.[176]

---

174 Ibid.
175 Ibid.
176 Friedrich Engels and Karl Marx, *The Communist Manifesto*, Section l. 41

Here we can clearly see four distinguished periods: 1. a complicated arrangement of society, 2. Ancient Rome, 3. feudal lords, and 4. modern bourgeois society. Later we will further examine these four epochs of world history. Here, though, as we remember, Marx told us that a significant part of his study was a critical re-examination of Hegelian and post-Hegelian philosophy. Therefore, we will acquaint ourselves with Hegelian ideas about history, or as Hegel calls it: "The Philosophical History of the World."

HEGEL

In talking of history, very correctly Hegel calls it the philosophy of history, for history inherently is a conditional matter, which first depends on who is describing it. And second, most importantly, it is essential to know which method has been used to describe the so-claimed history. Thus, Hegel said: "The various methods may be ranged under three heads: I, Original History, II, Reflective History, III, Philosophical History."[177] Hegel said Original History is told by those:

> . . . whose descriptions are for the most part limited to deeds, events, and states of society, which they had before their eyes, and whose spirit they shared. They simply transferred what was passing in the world around them, to the realm of re-presentative intellect. An external phenomenon is thus translated into an internal conception.[178]

---

177 Georg Wilhelm Friedrich Hegel, *The Philosophy of History*, 1.
178 Ibid.

Hegel said Reflective History is told by those "whose mode of representation is not really confined by the limits of the time to which it relates, but whose spirit transcends the present."[179]

In this range, Hegel distinguishes the four categories, such as:

1. It is the aim of the investigator to gain a view of the entire history of a people or a country, or of the world, in short, what we call Universal History. In this case . . . the workman approaches his task with his own spirit; a spirit distinct from that of the element he is to manipulate.[180]

2. A second species of Reflective History is what we may call the pragmatical. Pragmatical (didactic) reflections, though in their nature decidedly abstract, are truly and indefeasibly of the Present, and quicken the annals of the dead Past with the life of today. Whether, indeed, such reflections are truly interesting and enlivening, depends on the writer's own spirit.[181]

3. The third form of Reflective History is the Critical . . . We might more properly designate it as a History of History; a criticism of historical narratives and an investigation of their truth and credibility. Its peculiarity in point of fact and of intention, consist in the acuteness with which the writer extorts something from the records which was not in the matters recorded.[182]

4. The last species of Reflective History announces its fragmentary character on the very face of it. It adopts an abstract position; yet, since it takes general points of view (e.g., as the History of Art, of Law, of Religion), it forms a transition to the Philosophical History of the World.[183]

---

179 Hegel, *The Philosophy*, 4.

180 Ibid.

181 Hegel, *Philosophy*, 5–6.

182 Hegel, *Philosophy*, 7.

183 Hegel, *Philosophy*, 7–8.

Although Hegel generously spends time to describe the first two kinds, Original and Reflective History, when he comes to the third kind of history, Philosophical History, he very clearly distinguishes it from the two previous ones. In comparison, he said, "No explanation was needed of the two previous classes; their nature was self-evident. It is otherwise with this last, which certainly seems to require an exposition or justification."[184] For Philosophical History, Hegel said, "Philosophy of History means nothing but the thoughtful consideration of it. . . . It is this that distinguishes us from brutes."[185] It appears to Hegel that world history is a rational process, in which reason rules the world. He said, "Reason is the substance of the Universe; that by which and in which all reality has its being and subsistence. . . . It is only an inference from the history of the world that its development has been rational process."[186] For Hegel, the rational process of history means a gradual emergence of Spirit (*geist*, in Hegel's mother tongue) in the world as freedom. That is, the history of the world is a gradual increase of freedom and self-consciousness of human beings. In other words, world history is the unfolding of spirit in time, thus the spirit is the engine (driving force) of history.

Moreover, in Hegelian history, things are constantly changing with an inner motivation for self-consciousness and knowing itself toward freedom, which is a principle of spirit (i.e., the reason that drives things forward to certain aim). Thus, history for Hegel is teleological, which means the rational process of history is a purposeful movement that always moves toward a reasonable or certain direction. Therefore, spirit always goes toward freedom. As a result, more people are self-aware of the spirit of people (*volksgeist*). Consequently, they can better govern themselves. Therefore, humans play a crucial role in the self-development of spirit. Hence, with regards to Reason or Idea of self-consciousness, Hegel said, "It is its own material which it commits to its own Active Energy to work up; . . . It supplies its

---

184 Hegel, *Philosophy*, 8.

185 Ibid.

186 Hegel, *Philosophy*, 9–10.

own nourishment, and is the object of its own operation."[187] In a more accurate understanding, Idea itself is a result of a rational process, for Idea is a synthesis of subjectivity and objectivity or matter and spirit.

For, in a rational process, Hegel said:

> The history . . . has constituted the rational necessary course of the World-Spirit—that Spirit whose nature is always one and the same, but which unfolds its one nature in the phenomena of the World's existence . . . this "Idea" or "Reason" is the True, the Eternal, the absolutely powerful essence; that it reveals itself in the world.[188]

He also said, "We have examined the Idea embodied in the Greek Spirit; and is nothing else than this Idea made objective as essence of being."[189] Hegel writes from his compatriot, the great German savant, Schiller, "While the gods remained more human, the men were more divine."[190] The point here is that in Hegel's understanding of spirit, within his Germanic abstraction, he engineers a dancing movement between matter and concept to create an illusory, tangible, but idealistic sense of Spirit God, "now hidden, now open,"[191] as he writes:

> But the Greek gods must not be regarded as more human than the Christian God. Christ is much more a Man: he lives, dies—suffers death on the cross—which is infinitely more human than the humanity of the Greek Idea of the Beautiful. But in referring to this common element of the Greek and the Christian religions, it must be said of both, that if a manifestation of God is to be supposed at all, his natural form must be that of Spirit.[192]

---

187 Hegel, *Philosophy*, 9.

188 Hegel, *Philosophy*, 10.

189 Hegel, *Philosophy*, 244.

190 Hegel, *Philosophy*, 249.

191 Engels and Marx, *Manifesto*, 41.

192 Hegel, *Philosophy*, 249.

And Hegel, obviously and definitely, introduced to us the pure Germanic root of Spirit when he said:

> The German Spirit is the Spirit of the new World. Its aim is the realization of absolute Truth as the unlimited self-determination of Freedom—that Freedom which has its own absolute form itself as its purport. The destiny of the German peoples is, to be the bearers of the Christian principle. The principle of Spiritual Freedom—of reconciliation (of the Objective and Subjective).[193]

Since the phenomenon of Reason in the Hegelian understanding of history is quite a special issue, let us examine Hegelian Reason in more detail. Hegel never hides that he has a very special attention to Reason and he said clearly and emphatically that:

> In those of my hearers . . . I may fairly presume, at least, the existence of a belief in Reason . . . we should at least have the firm, unconquerable faith that Reason does exist there; and that the World of intelligence and conscious volition is not abandoned to chance, but must show itself in the light of the self-cognizant Idea.[194]

As Hegel said unequivocally, the point is that only in a very particular context, which is a clear state of independence and self-cognizant that is free from arbitrary controlled relations, the Hegelian Reason can justify itself. As he told us that:

> It is not intelligence as self-conscious Reason—not a Spirit as such that is meant; and we must clearly distinguish these from each other. The movement of the solar system takes place according to unchangeable laws. These laws are Reason, implicit in the phenomena in question. But neither the sun

---

193 Hegel, *Philosophy,* 341.
194 Hegel, *Philosophy,* 20.

nor the planets, which revolve around it according to these laws, can be said to have any consciousness of them.[195]

In short, Hegel said that his Reason is an independent principle, which is a suitable base for creating a rational process. Therefore, the amalgamation of social events or "passions of mankind," being processed through certain actions and reactions, will form history. In fact, what Hegel was trying to imbue in us, although not explicitly, was that the history of the world has a certain mechanism, which functions with certain disciplines and is fuelled by certain factors. This aspect of the Hegelian theory of history could be misleading, and it could cause misinterpretation in historical analysis. It seems Hegel was aware of this predicament. Therefore, in examining the Greek Anaxagoras as a pretext, we can see how hard Hegel endeavoured to prevent his readers from misunderstanding. He said:

> We have next to notice the rise of this idea—that Reason directs the World—in connection with a further application of it, well known to us—in the form, viz., of the religious truth, that the world is not abandoned to chance and external contingent causes, but that a Providence controls it.[196]

We can also clearly see that Hegel took this matter very seriously. He said:

> Yet I might appeal to your belief in it, in this religious aspect, if, as a general rule, the nature of philosophical science allowed it to attach authority to presuppositions. To put it in another shape—this appeal is forbidden, because the science of which we have to treat, proposes itself to furnish the proof (not indeed of the abstract Truth of the doctrine, but) of its correctness as compared with facts.[197]

---

195 Hegel, *Philosophy*, 11.
196 Hegel, *Philosophy*, 12–13.
197 Hegel, *Philosophy*, 13.

Hegel clearly was not shy in trying to involve the divinity with the events of the world and eventually with his Reason as said:

> The truth, then, that a Providence (that of God) presides over the events of the World—consorts with the proposition in question; for Divine Providence is Wisdom, endowed with an infinite Power, which realizes its aim, viz., the absolute rational design of the World.[198]

Nevertheless, Hegel did not neglect to warn us that, despite what he asserted above, it still remains that: "Reason is Thought conditioning itself with perfect freedom. But a difference—rather a contradiction—will manifest itself, between this belief and our principle."[199]

In spite of all said above, it is certain that Hegel's philosophical structure for understanding history lies in his dialectic. Thus, we need to briefly examine the Hegelian dialectic in order to grasp the real sense of Hegelian history. Dialectic is a process during which contradictory things, ideas, or phenomena collide and, as a result of being eliminated in each other, create something new. Hegel explains the three steps of this process as thesis, antithesis, and synthesis. The roots of dialectic go back to the ancient Greek, and Hegel admitted that: "Dialectic, it may be added, is no novelty in philosophy. Among the ancients Plato is termed the inventor of Dialectic."[200] In fact, Socrates was the one who used the dialectical method to debate with his interlocutors. As Hegel wrote:

> Socrates . . . used to turn Dialectic, first against ordinary consciousness . . . he used to simulate the wish for some clearer knowledge about the subject under discussion, and after putting all sorts of questions with that intent, he drew

---

198 Ibid.
199 Ibid.
200 Hegel, *Encyclopaedia of the Philosophical Sciences,* Note to § 81-1.

those with whom he conversed to opposite of what their first impression had pronounced correct.[201]

Hegel also told us that: "Plato employs the dialectical method to show the finitude of all hard and fast term of understanding."[202] But Hegel distinguished his dialectic from that of Plato's, for he believed that dialectic actually goes beyond the realm of philosophy or merely affecting the exchanged ideas discussed between the interlocutors. More specifically for Hegel, dialectic does not mean that certain ideas or elements being conditioned by, or if they come in contact by some external entities therefore can cause changes or improvements. Thus, to explain his own dialectic, he said, "Dialectic gives expression to a law which is felt in all other grades of consciousness. . . . Everything that surrounds us may be viewed as an instance of Dialectic."[203] He even said that: "Apart from this general objectivity of Dialectic, we find traces of its presence in each of the particular provinces and phases of the natural and spiritual World."[204] The point for Hegel was that everything has an inner force of self-estrangement, which means everything is alienating itself from itself. He explained:

> The true view of the matter is that life as life, involves the germ of death, and that the finite, being radically self-contradictory, involves its own self-suppression. . . .We are aware that everything finite, instead of being stable and ultimate, is rather changeable and transient; and this is exactly what we mean by that Dialectic of the finite, by which . . . it is forced beyond its immediate or natural being to turn suddenly into its opposite.[205]

---

201 Ibid.

202 Ibid.

203 Ibid.

204 Ibid.

205 Ibid.

As we know in Hegelian theory, the spirit (Hegelian God) is the driving force of history. For teleological determination resulting from the development of the self-consciousness of spirit, which is the result of the necessity for reconciliation between divine providence and evil events, he told us: "Man above all things becomes aware of the reasonable order of things when he knows of God, and knows him to be the completely self-determined."[206] Spirit naturally, by its inner self-suppression force or the capacity of alienating itself from itself, consequently, creates a hindrance to its existence. This means that spirit inevitably brings itself to a state of self-sublation, in other words, a state of self-destruction and re-emergence. In German, Hegel calls this *aufheben,* which has a dual meaning: both to cancel and to preserve. Thus, to summarize, the Hegelian philosophy of history is that everything finite (thesis), natural, or spiritual carries an inner contradiction or its opposite (antithesis). As a result of the incompatibility between these opposing sides, it will collapse as self-alienated and, consequently, a new thing (synthesis) will emerge. What must not be forgotten is that, in the process from thesis to synthesis, things improve from the less sophisticated to the more sophisticated state.

---

206 Georg Wilhelm Friedrich Hegel, *Encyclopaedia of the Philosophical Sciences,* Note to § 8ß2.

MARX VERSUS HEGEL

Here now, our task is to find out two things. First, what did Karl Marx learn from the Hegelian philosophy of history and dialectic? And second, how did Karl Marx apply his Hegelian learning to his own theory (ideology) of Marxism? Regarding Hegel, we know that he was a pious man who repeated affirmatively the words God, religion, and Christianity in his writings. Regarding Marx, we know that he said religion is the opium of the masses, and he was not a believer in God. Nevertheless, in their writings, we can see that the origin of their thought is almost 100% identical. Yet, amazingly, we witness that the outcomes of their analyses are 100% opposite. We know that Hegel taught his philosophy of history in Berlin University between 1822 and 1830. These lectures eventually became a book, which means, in the starting year, he was fifty-two years old. Marx wrote his preface for *A Contribution to the Critique of Political Economy* in 1859, which means he was forty-one years old. We also know that when Hegel died in 1831, Marx was a high-school boy and only thirteen years old. He had probably never heard Hegel's name. Now, we will look at their writings.

Hegel wrote:

> Man with his necessities sustains a practical relation to external Nature, and in making it satisfy his desires, and thus using it up, has recourse to a system of means. For natural objects are powerful, and offer resistance in various ways. In order to subdue them, man introduces other natural agents; thus turns Nature against itself, and invents instruments for this purpose. These human inventions belong to Spirit, and such an instrument is to be respected more than a mere natural object.[207]

Thirty-seven years later, Marx wrote:

> In the social production of their existence, men inevitably enter into definite relations, which are independent of their will, namely relations of production appropriate to a given stage in the development of their material forces of production. The totality of these relations of production constitutes the economic structure of society, the real foundation, on which arises a legal and political superstructure and to which correspond definite forms of social consciousness. The mode of production of material life conditions the general process of social, political, and intellectual life.[208]

It is very clear that, as a method and logic, Marx accepted Hegelian dialectic, and he adapted it in his theory of the capitalist mode of production. In Marxist ideology, the capitalist society is a class society consisting of capitalist and workers (thesis). And Marx explicitly acknowledged the inherent interest contradiction between the capitalist class and working class (antithesis). He also accepted that this contradiction would eventually end in a clash in the form of a class struggle. He also believed that as a result of class struggle (in the form of a working class revolution), a new social order would emerge (synthesis). Marx also

---

207 Georg Wilhelm Friedrich Hegel, *The Philosophy of History*, 241.
208 Karl Marx, "Preface," *A Contribution to the Critique of Political Economy*, 2.

agreed that history has a clear direction, which is going from a less sophisticated to a more sophisticated structure and function. But the crucial point is that Hegel, as a man of God, believed that the whole universal order and its changes and developments in nature, the world, and society are a necessity that is controlled and directed according to the determination of divine providence. Whereas, Marx believed that all the necessities in human society are determined by the relations of production that are imposed by the kind of the established mode of production in society. Here we come to the very vital point that separates Hegel from Marx: Hegel, as a God believer, surrendered himself to divine determination.

However, Marx, as a revolutionary believer and materialist, thought that in the role of a decision-maker or as an engineer of a historical epoch (communism), he could take the whole business of history in his own hands. He wanted to order a specific historical epoch with a particular social structure, within which certain economic relations tailored in certain fashion (socialism or communism) that he deemed appropriate for humans. In fact, he believed *The Communist Manifesto* would provide humanity with redemption and emancipation. We can believe in Karl Marx's *bonne foi* and that he wished all the best for humanity. But recorded history tells us that so far humans have never seen a human-made or handmade historical epoch, based on one person or one generation or one nation's demand or preference. Nobody has ever decided or planned that the hunter-gather society become a slavery society or then a few centuries later turn to feudalism. What we can understand from historical epochs is that a historical epoch is much larger than a human individual, generation, or country, and that it cannot be planned in advance. In other words, a historical epoch is not a pizza that a philosopher can order and have delivered. Although we admire Karl Marx's good faith in humanity, his theory for building a communist society seems more like the order of a philosopher who is expecting the working class to deliver it. Karl Marx dared to act as an engineer for communism, and of course its outcome was regrettable.

Here, we need to understand the difference between Hegel, who acted as a philosopher for progressing human knowledge about human life, human society, and the nature surrounding humans, and Marx as an engineer whose goal was to build a historical epoch.

Hegel, as a philosopher, represented his theories as abstract ideas that were designed to create an imaginative belief and understanding about the good and evil that can happen in nature and society by the divine will of Spirit God. Therefore, as members of human society, the role of individuals in social and historical events becomes secondary and passive. In Hegelian thought, Spirit is the decision-making power and human individuals are merely obeying followers of the divine reason. Hence, the role of Hegel in this intellectual structure becomes merely as a verbal encourager who preaches to convince members of society to remain faithful and appreciate all the changes that Spirit God offers them.

But the case is very different for Marx, and the reason for this difference must be sought in Marx's understanding of human society and its individual members. Marx, contrary to Hegel, believed that the social existence of humans determines their consciousness. Again, contrary to Hegel, Marx believed that although all human individuals in society are part of the totality of the social relations created by the material forces of production, all individual members in society are not the ones to determine a new historical epoch. In fact, Marx's theory for human society is a selective theory based on one of two groups of individuals (capitalists and labourers) being the main role player in a capitalist society.

However, the Marxist definition for capitalists is quite simple and straightforward; in short, a capitalist is equal to capital, which means money invested in commodity production. But the definition for a labourer is different. The labourer is a person who sells labour-power against money called a wage. For Marx, it was very crucial that labourers "inevitably enter into definite relations, which are independent of their will, namely relations of production."[209] Here, Marxist theory

---

209 Ibid.

enters into a different composition. When we talk of production, the means of production automatically are part of the production process. Certainly, the relation between means of production and capital will raise the matter of private property. Having all these ingredients in hand as the principle elements of the social existence of humans and having a theory was essential. Marx said, "The totality of these relations of production constitutes the economic structure of society, the real foundation, on which arises a legal and political superstructure and to which correspond definite form of social consciousness."[210] This spurred Marx to initiate the idea of making a historical epoch by reverse engineering.

Of course, Marx has never explicitly said or written that he personally had the intention to fabricate a historical epoch, even as a justification for the proletarian revolution. He introduces the working class as a historically legitimate power to establish the new social order, but his goal was to fabricate a new historical epoch. For instance, in Marx's last paragraph (the 11) of the *Theses on Feuerbach* (1845), he said, "The philosophers have only interpreted the world in various ways; the point is to change it."[211] In addition, he co-wrote *The Communist Manifesto* (1848) as a blueprint for a proletarian revolution and the preface for *A Contribution to the Critique of Political Economy* (1859) can confirm for us his real intentions.

Let us now get back to Karl Marx's reverse engineering to fabricate a new historical epoch. As we remember, he told us that in real natural history, everything starts from social existence and eventually ends up in legal, political, and social consciousness superstructure. In the reverse engineering, Marx starts with the working class political party, guided by the communist ideology as its social consciousness that will justify the establishing of socialism or communism. He saw this legal and political superstructure as a solution for the social injustice of capitalism. He believed justice would prevail by organizing the labourers in a revolutionary army to abolish private property and pave the way

---

210 Ibid.
211 Karl Marx, *Theses on Feuerbach. Paragraph 11.*

for a socialist or communist means of production. However, in this scheme, the proletariat would be King and the owner of the society above all other citizens. This was Marx's recipe for his handmade historical epoch, which he promised in *The Communist Manifesto.* In the meantime, the past 175 years of human history have confirmed that Marx's handmade historical epoch is not realizable. Therefore, we need to focus in on the magnitude of this job.

In order to understand this, we can imagine that in today's society, humans have a great deal of knowledge about water, aquatic science, oceanic science, and minerals. But nevertheless, humans cannot build or move an ocean just because we have a great deal of knowledge about oceans. By the same token, human cannot order or build a historical epoch just because humans have a great deal of knowledge in economics, sociology, political science, etc. A historical epoch is an outcome of a very complicated and long process that happens over several centuries and as a result of the sum total of the work and life of at least several hundred generations.

Thus, although Hegelian philosophy of history conditioned by the divine providence was not really beneficial for humanity in general and, particularly for modern human society, we can say it was less harmful than the scars left on human civilization over the past 175 years by Marxism.

Let us now examine some details of the historical epochs. According to recorded history, we know there does not exist a clean surgical cut separating historical epochs. Nevertheless, certain particular changes are decisively determinant in changing from one outgoing historical epoch to the next in-coming historical epoch. For instance, the typical characteristic of the historical epoch known as slavery was the master and slave. When slavery was abolished, and feudalism was established instead, both masters and slaves disappeared. Although the process of the old system disappearing and establishing the new one was long and slow, nonetheless, neither masters nor slaves ever had any major role or significant effect in the establishing of the new feudal system. The situation was also the same in the appearance of capitalism in that neither the landlords nor the peasants (determining elements of feudalism) had any major role or significant effect in the establishing of the new capitalist system. Hence, why in changing from capitalism to whatever next historical epoch labourer (proletariat) that belongs to the outgoing epoch should or could play a major or determining role.

Moreover, the effects of the elements of an old, abolished system on a newly established system have always been considered as negative and harmful. For instance, in changing from feudalism to capitalism, Marx himself calls reactionary the effect of the peasants for the new coming bourgeois society as he wrote in *The Communist Manifesto*:

> The peasant, all these fight against the bourgeoisie, to save from extinction their existence as fractions of middle class. They are therefore not revolutionary, but conservative. Nay more, they are reactionary, for they try to roll back the wheel of history.[212]

Thus, human social history has proven that the principle for changing from one old historical epoch to another is that in the old historical epoch, new elements with different technical capacities and functions emerge. They then grow up to the point that, after gaining enough economic and political strength, they overthrow the old social classes and old system in order to establish their new ones.

Surprisingly, Marx knew this principle well, for when talking about the change from feudalism to capitalism, he said, "In one word, the feudal relations of property became no longer compatible with the already developed production forces; they became so many fetters. They had to be burst asunder; they were burst asunder."[213] But in the Marxist prescription for overthrowing capitalism and establishing communism, this principle has been violated. For, according to Marxist theory, through the working-class revolution, the labourers, which are one of the principle elements of the old system, are supposed to overthrow the capitalist system and replace it with the new system of communism under the workers dictatorship. In *The Communist*

---

212 Engels and Marx, *Manifesto,* Section I, 54.
213 Engels and Marx, *Manifesto,* Section I, 47ß.

Manifesto, Marx said, "The immediate aim of the Communist is the same as that of all the other proletarian parties: formation of the proletariat into a class, overthrow of the bourgeois supremacy, conquest of political power by the proletariat."[214] Marx has repeated this point several thousand times in different occasions.

The point is that Marx rejected Hegel because Hegel believed that the determining law for changing history comes from the Spirit God, whereas Marx believed that the determining law for changing history comes from material life conditions. But what we see in reality is that Marx arbitrarily and prophetically applied his own fabricated thought, in fact, his own communistic consciousness (Marxist theory) as the determining law for changing history. This is in contradiction with Marx's statement that: "It is not the consciousness of men that determines their existence, but their social existence that determines their consciousness."[215] Very specifically, regarding thought and consciousness, which indeed were a determining issue for Hegel in understanding the relation between humans and their environment, Marx said, even many years earlier than in his preface, that: "It depends not on consciousness, but on being; not on thought, but on life; it depends on the individual's empirical development and manifestation of life, which in turn depends on the conditions obtaining in the world."[216] But all of Karl Marx's "obtaining" was always pure, theoretical, and bookish, and he himself names it as a vital requirement. Therefore, in all his life, Marx never had any empirical obtaining or practical experience from the world. Therefore, all that his brain knew was nothing but nonpractical consciousness, although *par excellence.*

Marx was a genius, who with his *langue de vipère,* slaughtered many very important German philosophers, such as Hegel, Feuerbach, Bauer, Stirner, and others. He accused them of being lost in abstract consciousness, being arbitrary, and not having their feet on the ground. Also. Marx wrote several thousands of pages about the determinism

---

214 Engels and Marx, *The Communist Manifesto,* Sec. II, 60.
215 Karl Marx, *A Contribution to the Critique of Political Economy,* Preface: 2.
216 Karl Marx, *The German Ideology,* 280.

of the material condition of life in history and about what capitalism is and the necessity of proletariats overthrowing it for a better life. Therefore, this contradiction between his points in criticizing the other philosophers and the revolutionary idea that he expected the working class to deliver is not a simple or innocent mistake. In the meantime, regarding the contradiction between what Marx condemned and what he promoted, the title of the second volume on German ideology must not be underestimated or ignored. Let us below examine this title more closely.

The above mentioned title is *Critique of German Socialism According to Its Various Prophets*. The crucial word here is "Prophets." Indeed, Marx knew very well what prophets are and what prophets do. In fact, regardless of the name or kind of any religion, ideology, or sect, the thing that prophets (the owner of the business) do is that they develop an empty original idea (an ideology) and involve it into a collection of real material things and relations gathered from the real human environment. They then create a comprehensive method of thinking that can modify the intellectual wiring of the human brain. As a result, the trapped individuals in the ideology, as the convinced masses, become ardent believers in those imagined principles and powers as effective means for healing and emancipating them from their difficulties. It is quite fascinating to see how Marx so brilliantly explained the role of the ideologists and prophets in real social life. He wrote:

> Why the ideologists turn everything upside-down, clerics, jurists, politicians, statesmen in general, moralists. . . . Everyone believes his craft to be the true one. Illusions regarding the connection between their craft and reality are the more likely to be cherished by them because of the very nature of the craft. In consciousness—in jurisprudence, politics, etc. —relations become concepts; since they do not go beyond these relations, the concepts of the relations also become fixed concepts in their mind.[217]

---

217 Marx, *The German Ideology*, 101–102.

And in talking of the German philosophers as prophets, Marx said:

> They attempt to clarify them by invoking the German ideology and notably that of Hegel and Feuerbach. They detach the communist system, critical and polemical writings from the real movement of which they are but the expression, and force them into an arbitrary connection with German philosophy. They detach the consciousness of certain historically conditioned spheres of life from these spheres and evaluate it in terms of true, absolute, i.e., German philosophical consciousness.[218]

Let us examine the phenomenology of the historical epoch and the process of its advent and deterioration. It must be stated that the historical epoch, as every other thing in the universe for that matter, is not an exception to the rule of use-value. Thus, as we have already discussed, as a general principle, use-value by its nature is inherently an independent phenomenon. As a result, whatever is tangible or conceivable in any manner, that carries use-value in one way or another, will also carry its natural wish of survival and its resistance to harm and death. Historical epochs are the legal, political, and moral setups that, according to general understanding, support and administer human societies by either freewill or by coercion. As long as the use-values of the consisting elements of every historical epoch are still functional and capable of satisfying the requirements of that given historical epoch, that historical epoch will survive and continue functioning—even though Karl Marx or whomever else might wish otherwise. It is useful to remember that Karl Marx lived all his life with oil lamps and he never saw an electric bulb—never mind a smart phone or space shuttle. This means he had absolutely no idea of the dimensions of the function and capacity of the use-value of the capitalist system to progress human civilization. Nevertheless, 175 years ago, Karl Marx dared to say:

---

218 Marx, *The German Ideology,* 482.

And here it becomes evident, that the bourgeoisie is unfit any longer to be the ruling class in society, and impose its conditions of existence upon society as an over-riding law. . . . Society can no longer live under this bourgeoisie, in other words, its existence is no longer compatible with society."[219]

219 Engels and Marx, *Manifesto,* sec.I, 56–57.

CONCLUSION TO PART I

We have explored several errors in Marx's theory, including the three gravest flaws, which we will recap here. Our plan then is to close the file on Marxism and send it to the archives of history.

We must remember that the pivotal element in Marx's analysis is the commodity, and the most important attribute of the commodity is its use-value. Thus, a commodity without use-value cannot and will never exist. Therefore, Marx's first grave mistake was denying the use-value of a commodity for the capitalist because of exchange-value. Exchange-value does not and cannot exist by itself. However, Marx said, "As use-value, commodities are, above all, of different qualities, but as exchange-values they are merely different quantities, and consequently do not contain an atom of use-value."[220] However, Marx knew that this was not true, for he said, "Use-values. . . . In the form of society we are about to consider, they are, in addition, the material depositories of exchange-value."[221] Therefore, even exchange-value cannot exist if the use-value does not exist. Furthermore, he said, "If then we leave

---

220 Marx, *Capital,* 45.
221 Marx, *Capital,* 44.

out of consideration the use-value of commodities, they have only one common property left, that of being a product of labour."[222]

A denial of use-value automatically ends up as a denial of labour as well, as Marx confirmed: "If we make abstraction from its use-value, we make abstraction at the same time from the material elements and shapes that make the product a use-value; we see in it no longer a table, a house, yarn, or any other useful thing."[223] Consequently, the denial of use-value becomes the denial of commodity and labour all together and, therefore, a denial of the existence of everything. Marx told us this clearly: "Its existence as a material thing is put out of sight. Neither can it any longer be regarded as the product of the labour of the joiner, the mason, the spinner, or of any other definite kind of productive labour."[224] Based on the exchange-value, which is merely an imaginary agreement between two individuals, Marx denied the use-value, which is really a material, useful thing. Hence, the denial of use-value is equal to the nullity of the whole capitalist (or any) mode of production. Marx himself confirmed that use-value is not peculiar to capitalism when he wrote: "Anyhow, whether the coat be worn by the tailor or by his customer, in either case it operates as a use-value."[225] Indeed, by denying the use-value of commodity, the whole theory of Marx becomes based on emptiness and a void. Thus, Marxism, based on emptiness, is a stillborn theory. For the defect is right at its beginning, in its foundation. As a fundamental defect in its core, the denial of the use-value of commodity for the capitalist makes Marxism a stillborn ideology. Therefore, inevitably, any social structure based on Marxism will rot and collapse.

Moreover, in the universe, everything exists because of its use-value, and everything has meaning because of its use-value. In the human eye, some use-value is good and some use-value is bad. But nature does not care about human opinion; thus, in nature, the use-value of everything

---

222 Marx, *Capital*, 45.

223 Ibid.

224 Marx, *Capital*, 45–6.

225 Max, *Capital*, 50.

is just a use-value. Therefore, denying the use-value of something is equal to denying the existence of that thing definitely. Hence, denying the use-value in general is equal to denying the whole universe.

Marx's second grave mistake was believing that capitalist society, similar to slavery and feudal societies, is made up of two social classes. This would mean a binary society, which consists of capitalists and the proletariat. As Marx wrote in *The Communist Manifesto*, "The modern bourgeois society that has sprouted from the ruins of feudal society has not done away with class antagonisms. It has but established new classes. . . . Society as a whole is more and more splitting up into two great hostile camp, into two great classes, directly facing each other: Bourgeoisie and Proletariat."[226] Whereas, we have shown that capitalist society has a network structure that consists of three classes: employee, capitalist, and consumer.

Marx's third grave mistake was that he believed the capitalist mode of production must be vanquished and be replaced by a completely different—socialist or communist—mode of production.

We know that injustice and inequality are inherent in the capitalist mode of production. Marx struggled against both of these; therefore, his solution was to suggest that capitalism be eradicated. Of course, injustice is wrong and severely harmful to human beings. Injustice is a cancer to human society, and thus, any effort to prevent or eradicate injustice is noble and laudable. Nevertheless, although the capitalist system has inequality in the financial context of human society, it has an immense social kinetic energy that has an enormous capacity for doing good. If used in the proper way, it will be tremendously beneficial for human society in both the short and long term. Thus, capitalist financial and income inequality is an asset to our modern society that we must recognize, appreciate, and use in a smart way for our common well-being. It is unfortunate to say that this energy is presently burning like a wildfire in front of our very eyes.

The other point is that one or a few defects in the capitalist mode of production should not be considered enough reason to destroy and

---

226 Engels and Marx, *Manifesto*, 41–42.

eradicate the whole system. It is true that if a major defect in a system makes it completely non-functional or harmful; the whole mechanism must be destroyed. But if a mechanism, besides its defects, has considerable potential for doing good, it should be repaired or modified. In Part II, I will examine the social kinetic energy of inequality and human labour. But the crucial point here is that Marx intended to change a historical epoch by replacing it with an artificial, hand-made plan through reverse engineering.

Over the centuries, philosophers, historians, and economists—Karl Marx included—have taught us that historical epochs eventually die with all their old components and are replaced by new components, means, methods, and relations. Karl Marx dreamed of reanimating (recycling) the working class with his home-made ideology in order to fabricate a new historical epoch based on socialism or communism. Perhaps Marx was ahead of his time based on the matter of rate upon which he developed his theory of surplus-value. As we know, surplus-value is the rate of profit to the variable capital. Marx believed his ideals for a reanimated old social class (working class) could bypass human history with light speed and jump two or three centuries ahead. He hoped to advance human civilization with a shortcut that would result in a new historical epoch. Even today, after 175 years, space shuttles are not able to travel at light speed, never mind historical epoch. Thus, Karl Marx's attempt to artificially fabricate a historical epoch was a naïve solution for trying to fix the social problems arising from the capitalist mode of production. Although social problems in our capitalist society are real and serious, nevertheless discriminative and racially tinted ideologies can never solve any problem in human society. In addition, state and nobody, for that matter, has the right to determine the kind of use-value of commodity for an individual (i.e., nobody can say who can use what and how). This is against human right and this is tyranny.

Moreover, it is too early to predict or judge the social and political impacts of artificial intelligence (AI) in human life or the changes that it might cause in the structure of society. Just recently we saw the panic that AI caused among screenwriters in Hollywood because film production companies have started to replace human script writers with AI writers. As a result, human writers will lose their jobs and all the devastating impact that it will have on their family and futures. To contest this professional insecurity, more than 11,000 writers went on strike for 148 days. This strike was organized by the Writers Guild of America (WGA). Eventually, WGA signed an agreement with Alliance of Motion Picture and Television Producers (AMPTP) for three years' job protection and the strike ended. Although Hollywood writers got back to work, but the menace of AI tossing people into unemployment and misery is far from being over.[227]

AI is replacing writers, accountants, cashiers, workers in assembly lines, even doctors and nurses. AI will definitely be in every household before long, but whether or not it could be a social class in a new mode of production remains to be seen. Thus, humans—either individually or socially—have to start the necessary adaptations to welcome AI and other technological advancements at home and in society. Our plan in Part II is to repair Karl Marx's mistakes and to draw a blueprint for smart life.

227 Alissa Wilkinson and Emily Stewart, "The Hollywood Writers's Strike is Over – And They Won Big," *Vox*, September 28, 2023, https://www.vox.com/culture/2023/9/24/23888673/wga-strike-end-sag-aftra-contract.

MANIFESTO

PART II:

MODERN HUMAN
SMART LIFE

AN INQUIRY INTO HUMAN SOCIETY

NIMA MAZHARI

MONTREAL
2024

SMART CIVILIZATION IN MODERN HUMAN SOCIETY

In Part I, I promised to repair Marx's mistakes. In Part II, I will honour my pledge. One thing that I criticized Marx for was that he first wrote *The Communist Manifesto* as the prescription for a cure. Then, nineteen years later, he wrote *Capital* as the diagnosis, whereas, the logical sequence is the other way around, as doctors first examine and diagnose, then prescribe the cure. Hence, in Part I of this book, first I critically analyzed Marxism, through which I examined capitalism, and in Part II, I am presenting the solution. Another thing that I criticized Marx for was that his theory was based on illusory entities, such as exchange-value, surplus-value, and an artificially handmade historical epoch. Thus, to avoid this mistake, my theory is based on the facts, starting with human nature and going to social institutions and the smart social structure that can serve modern human. So let me start with human society.

Today's society is a very complex and old phenomenon. It has been built over several thousand years, during which our ancestors—some wise and others not, some gentle and others not—made many decisions. The sum total of all those decisions eventually transferred to us, with all the history of good and evil, to make the society that we live in today. However, in this investigation, we will not focus much on history, but rather on what exactly our present human society is today. We want to know how we can design our society in a smart way in order to extract maximum benefit and pleasure from its really available use-values.

A modern human society must be determined and judged by the quality of life of its citizens and the way animals and the environment are provided for and protected under the control and supervision of modern humans. In the frame of a collective responsibility between a society and its citizens—regardless of geographical limits and free from ideological, racial, ethnic, and gender constraints—a smart civilization is one in which the social order and institutions are structured to prepare healthy human individuals for their fair participation in a just environment in order to satisfy their needs and wants. A smart civilization is a matter of an updated culture and social structure that has the capacity to provide modern humans with the modern necessities for a smart life.

A smart life is a life that meets the requirements of modern humans according to the knowledge and intelligence of humans today. In political economy today, knowledge and intelligence are not based on religious or illusory divine providence that will imbue in us all those artificial, old, false, superstitious, obsolete, fabricated counts and principles. It, rather, is based on the fresh and most importantly tangible and measurable real facts, far from miserably prying in front of commodity objects or ideas made of minerals or tales by some humans in the near or far past, preached by hypocrite preachers.

However, social structure is a human-made mechanism and, therefore, it cannot be updated by people who believe in outdated ideas and who have old-fashion mentalities. Updating the culture and social structure for an emergence of a smart civilization requires a serious and radically modernized mentality, both generally in society and particularly among the decision-making authorities who are in the position to make the needed social changes. Nevertheless, modern humans definitely deserve a smart life.

But first we must understand the main fundamental components and mechanisms of our present human society. During our critical inquiry, we will examine what elements need to be changed, modified, or even eliminated. We also must determine what is missing and what must be added in order to make a modern human society that can provide us with the best possible smart life—for a smart life is our goal.

NUMBER OF COUNTRIES IN THE WORLD

The number of the countries in the world is ephemeral because it is constantly changing. Instead of being preoccupied with looking for a peaceful, high-quality smart life, humans of the twenty-first century are busy following ideologies and competing for resources, which leads to stupid wars and attempts to change borders and create new countries. Once in a while, these efforts succeed, and the number of countries in the world changes. However, all attempts to separate people, and thus increase the number of the countries in the world, are not smart and goes against modern human interest; i.e., it is reactionary. To the contrary, all attempts to bring more people together and thus decrease the number of countries in the world are progressive and good for a smart civilization.

However, for our analysis, it will suffice to mention that, according to the United Nations, our world today is comprised of 206 countries, which are grouped in three categories. There are 193 countries, which are full member states of the United Nation. There are also two countries, the states of Palestine and the Holy See, which are non-member and called observer states, and eleven other countries, which are in the third category, called self-governing territories or de facto states.

STRUCTURE OF HUMAN SOCIETY

The structure of human society consists of four fundamental sections:

1. Social structure
2. Political structure
3. Cultural structure
4. Economic structure

Like everything else in human life, from primitive cave people to modern humans, different structures of society have been developed, from the simple to the complex. On the way, there are always some sincere and intelligent individuals who welcome changes and developments. They embrace the achievements of progress and enjoy what the new developments can offer them. However, there are also those idiots or charlatans who not only resist progress and its benefits, but also encourage others to join them in denying the positive effect of the development in favour of keeping an old and outdated way of living. Unfortunately, this enthusiasm to look for greatness in the obsolete past still strongly exists in our present human society, even though it will result in loss and failure for anyone who believes in it, and it will harm human society in general. Therefore, the focus of a smart civilization must look forward and not backward, and a culture of embracing the achievements of modern developments must be promoted and encouraged.

Another significant point is that capitalism and Marxism both stress that the economy and means of production are infrastructures, and all other activities are superstructures. Therefore, the economy is the most important issue and every other thing in society should be conditioned and measured by it. Both are wrong. We have made the list above of the sections in the structure of human society. In each section, there are infrastructural components that play a determining role. The sum total of all those functions is what determines well-being and quality of life in a society.

Thus, in the frame of our investigation, we will continue our analysis by studying these structures of human society.

THE RULE OF FOUR

We remember, above, the structure of human society consists of four fundamental sections. These four sections are based on a principle that is called the rule of four. As all medical doctors know, in human life the four main vital signs are: 1 – body temperature, 2 – blood pressure, 3 – pulse (heart rate), and 4 – respiratory rate. Below we will explore this principle more in detail through examples.

High-school math teachers use a method called the rule of four to teach mathematics to students. The rule of four consists of: 1. numeric,

2. symbolic, 3. graphical, 4. words. As a representative from a school district that uses this method explained, "The Rule of Four is a way to think about math both at the entry point of a task and in the representation of math thinking. Showing our thinking through multiple representations helps us have a stronger and deeper understanding of the mathematics. It also allows us to see connections across concepts and topics."[228]

We do not intend to teach high-school math here. Rather, our goal is to focus on the idea of the rule of four as a principle and, more particularly as a natural principle, as we can see that it exists repeatedly in other areas. Therefore, it can merely be a guide for us to use in our analysis. To begin, we will quickly look at some examples of the rule of four in different spheres.

- In accounting, there is the rule of four for financial statements. Professional accountants know that financial statements are very important tools to determine and control the financial status of a company because the financial statements show where a company's money came from, where it went, and where it is now. There are four main financial statements: 1. Balance sheet, 2. Income statement, 3. Cash flow statement, and 4. Statement of shareholders' equity.[229]

- Biochemistry and molecular biology study biomolecules and their reactions. Most biomolecules are organic compounds, and just four elements make up 96% of the human body's mass: 1. oxygen, 2. carbon, 3. hydrogen, and 4. nitrogen.[230]

228 "Rule of Four," Mathematics Department, San Francisco Unified School District (SFUSD), https://www.sfusdmath.org/ruleoffour.html; and, "SFUSD Core Curriculum," Mathematics Department, San Francisco Unified School District (SFUSD), https://www.sfusd.edu/departments/mathematics-department-page/sfusd-math-core-curriculum.

229 "Beginner's Guide to Financial Statement," U.S. Securities and Exchange Commission, February 5, 2007, https://www.sec.gov/reportspubs/investor-publications/investorpubsbegfinstmtguidehtm.html.

230 Wikipedia, s.v. "Biomolecule," last edited January 6, 2024, https://en.wikipedia.org/wiki/Biomolecule.

- In biology, cells are the smallest common denominator of life. All cells are made from the same four major classes of intracellular organic molecules include: 1. nucleic acids, 2. proteins, 3. carbohydrates, and 4. lipids.[231]

- In biology again, the analysis of the components of a prokaryotic cell, which is a simple single-celled (unicellular) organism, shows that, "All cells share four common components: 1. plasma membrane, an outer covering that separates the cell's interior from surrounding environment, 2. cytoplasm, consisting of a jelly-like region within the cell in which other cellular components are found, 3. DNA, the genetic material of the cell, and 4. ribosomes, particles that synthesize proteins."[232]

- In physics: "At the most fundamental level, all the forces in the universe come from only four forces (as currently understood): 1. the gravitational force, 2. the electromagnetic force, 3. the weak nuclear force, 4. the strong nuclear force. These forces are known as the **fundamental forces**."[233]

- In philosophy, four main branches of philosophical and sub-philosophical issues are studied. The four main branches of philosophy are: 1. metaphysics, 2. epistemology, 3. axiology, and 4. logic.[234]

- And finally, the Rule of Four that most people are aware of is the four basic mathematical functions: 1. addition, 2. subtraction, 3.

---

231 C.M. O'Connor and J.U. Adam, *Essentials of Cell Biology* (Cambridge: NPG Education, 2010).

232 "Comparing Prokaryotic and Eukaryotic Cells," *Biology for Majors I*, Lumen, https://courses.lumenlearning.com/wm-biology1/chapter/reading-comparing-prokaryotic-and-eukaryotic-cells-2/.

233 "Fundamental Force," Energy Education (2014), https://energyeducation.ca/encyclopedia/Fundamental_force.

234 Matthew Lynch, "Need to Know Education: Understanding the 4 Main Branches of Philosophy," *The Edvocate*, August 5, 2016,

multiplication, and 4. division. These have application even in the most advanced mathematical theories.[235]

Insofar as we have explored the rule of four, it is evident that it exists in many different fields. Assuming this phenomenon is real, it is an independent natural matter that is out of human control. Yet more can be learned from the rule of four. Through study and research, it is up to humans to learn and discover the four fundamental entities wherever they exist. Further, with the discovery of every new package of four fundamental elements in any domain, we must learn to use this knowledge in the best possible manner in order to extract the maximum use-value embodied in it. This is a serious challenge that requires a high quality of human wisdom and intelligence. The failure to discover and use the rule of four, wherever it exists, could mean great loss and suffering.

---

235 "The Four Basic Mathematical Operations," Universal Class, https://www.universalclass.com/articles/math/pre-algebra/the-four-basic-mathematical-operations.htm.

THE SOCIAL STRUCTURE OF HUMAN SOCIETY

Since the basic element of human society is humankind, our study must begin with an analysis of a human individual. We will examine the four fundamental things in the existence of human nature and the best methods to deal with them in society's socio-economic life in order to serve society's collective well-being.

A human is a mortal biological machine that is made by nature. Its existence is totally dependent on four fundamental requirements:

1. Breathing
2. Eating
3. Defecating
4. Sleeping

These are the four basic works of our animal-human existence. Any absence or shortage of any of these four basic operations can cause a serious health disorder in a human or even death. So let us examine each of these fundamental requirements more closely.

BREATHING

Breathing is a type of work. It is the first work that a human being must do in their direct interaction with the real material world at birth until death. As we read in the article titled "Baby's First Breath," published online in 2009 by SickKids Hospital, about kids' health,

> Your baby will need to work very hard to take her first breath. . . . The first few breaths after birth may be the most difficult breaths your baby will take for the rest of her life. . . . The most profound change at birth is the baby's first breath. At this point, your baby's lungs, which were filled with fluid during pregnancy, must suddenly fill with oxygen from the air. The fluid in the lungs is removed through the blood and lymph system, and is replaced by air. Your baby's lungs must be able to exchange oxygen for carbon dioxide. With each breath after birth, more air will accumulate in her lungs, which will make it easier for them to breath. After a few breaths, the baby will be able to breathe more easily, and their breaths will start to become deeper and more regular.[236]

Breathing is a complex process, which, through the respiratory system, brings oxygen to the body and carries out carbon dioxide and water. The main parts of the respiratory system are the airways, lungs and linked blood vessels, and muscles that enable breathing.

A respiratory centre at the base of the brain controls breathing. The centre sends ongoing signals down the spine and to the muscles involved in breathing. These signals ensure the breathing muscles contract and relax regularly. Sensors in the brain and in two major blood vessels (the carotid artery and the aorta) detect carbon dioxide or oxygen levels in the blood and change the breathing rate as needed.[237]

Human beings cannot exist without breathing. A human body that does not breathe is a cadaver, which decays and disappears. Every time a person breathes, ten muscles are used for inspiration and eight muscles are used for forced expiration. An adult person breaths twelve to eighteen times per minute, which, over the course of a day, adds up

---

236 "Baby's First Breath," SickKids Hospital, https://www.aboutkidshealth.ca/articl e?contentid=420&language=english#.

237 Ibid.

to 17,000 to 25,000 breaths per day. Breathing is a permanent labour that assures the continuity of life.[238]

EATING

Eating is a type of work. It is the second type of work that a human being has to do in their direct interaction with the real material world at birth until death. In fact, the American Academy of Pediatrics (AAP) states that healthy and full-term infants be placed and remain in direct skin-to-skin contact with their mothers immediately after delivery until the first feeding is accomplished.

Humans must eat in order to survive. Eating is the ingestion of food to provide a human being with energy and to stimulate growth and cell repair. Eating is a complex process that happens through the digestive system. The human digestive system is made up of the gastrointestinal tract (GI tract). This is a long, twisting tube of about 9 metres (30 feet), which consists of the mouth, esophagus, stomach, duodenums, small intestine, and the large intestine that ends at the rectum and anus. The liver, pancreas, and gallbladder are the solid organs of the digestive system. Parts of the nervous and circulatory system also play roles in the digestive process. Together, a combination of nerves, hormones, bacteria, blood, and organs of the digestive system complete the complex task (labour) of digesting the food and liquids that a person consumes each day.[239]

DEFECATING

Defecation is a type of work. It is the third type of work that a human being has to do in their very direct interaction with the real material world from birth until death. Defecation is the final act of digestion, by which organisms eliminate solid, semi-solid, and/or liquid waste material from the digestive tract via the anus.

---

238 Google search, "adult human breath."

239 Raylene Phillips, "Uninterrupted Skin-to-Skin Contact Immediately After Birth!" **Newborn and Infant Nursing Reviews**, Vol. 13(2), 2013: 67-72.

SLEEPING

Sleeping is a type of work. It is the fourth type of work that a human being has to do in their very direct interaction with the real material world from birth until death. Generally speaking, everything that is alive needs sleep to survive.

Sleep is an important part of your body routine-you spend about one-third of you time doing it. . . . Sleep affects almost every type of tissue and system in the body – from the brain, heart, and lungs to metabolism, immune function, mood, and disease resistance. Research shows that a chronic lack of sleep, or getting poor quality sleep, increases the risk of disorders including high blood pressure, cardiovascular disease, diabetes, depression, and obesity.[240]

Without sleep, a human individual will die.

---

240 "Brain Basics: Understanding Sleep," National Institute of Neurological Disorders and Stroke, https://www.ninds.nih.gov/health-information/public-education/brain-basics/brain-basics-understanding-sleep.

LABOUR

In societies where the capitalist mode of production prevails, every employee is a natural person that sells his labour-power. As soon as an individual accepts to deprive himself from his personal and private wishes and make himself available during a certain period of time to be employed for compensation (wage or salary) by a capitalist person (or by an institution, either capitalist or government), this individual is an employee. As long as an employee is alive and possesses labour-power, they can sell it; a dead human does not have any power, including labour-power, to sell. We have seen that there are four basic life requirements that must be fulfilled in order for a human to live. In other words, the four basic life requirements are prerequisite labour for an individual to be able to offer usable labour to the economic market. Hence, in a civilized society that distinguishes itself from savagery, an employee not only must be paid for their labour on the site of employment, but must also be compensated (paid) for the labour that has been already required for the four basic life functions. We will examine this issue more closely.

First of all, we must distinguish the difference between the wages that are paid for the labour used for production or service at the workplace and the compensation that must cover the labour used for the four basic life requirements. To clarify the situation, let us take a look at this issue through an example. If we consider, for instance, a person who works as a machine operator in a car factory or a person who works in an office of the revenue agency of a given government. It is obvious that either of these individuals is paid whatever their salary might be for the time that they work at the workplace. With the money that these individuals earn, they can purchase food and furniture and pay for a dwelling place. Everything is clear as far as it concerns the labour in the workplace for an earned salary. But what about the labour that is needed to assure that these employees will return to their work the next day? Let us imagine that we have food on the table, but until that food is eaten, it will not contribute to saving a person's life. In the meantime, we know that eating is a work that requires labour (actions done by muscles), and this is the same kind of labour that one will use to operate a machine or to do office work. Human labour is labour (use-value), regardless of where it occurs or what it is used to do. The required labour for the four basic life requirements is not compensated by a worker's salary. Hence, it is obvious that someone owes this missing compensation to employees, and that person is the one who is profiting from the labour: the employer.

Let us look closer at this issue and continue our analysis with the same individuals above—the machine operator and the office worker. The first point about these individuals is that both are members of the same human society, regardless of their specific jobs. The prerequisite labour for the four basic life requirements is the same for both of them. Therefore, the prerequisite labour is not only an economic matter but also a social and collective issue that concerns all members of society. Without adequate fulfillment of the prerequisite labour, not only is the healthy participation of individuals in socio-economic activities harmed but also the health and security of the society itself as a whole. This point that the four basic life requirements require labour is important.

From this angle, we see that it is the growth level of modern human society that is called into question. The question is: How can a mature, civilized society accept that a fellow member offers prerequisite labour without fair and rightful compensation? Moreover, we can ask this question in a different manner: Why should a truly civilized society allow or tolerate that some of its members (employees) unjustly remain deprived of their fair and rightful compensation for work that they have to do in order to make themselves available to other members (employers) of the same society? At the end of the day, both employees and employers are living in the same city, just a few blocks away from each other.

The social aspect of the four basic requirements can be seen from another angle. Human society needs citizens; otherwise, it would not be a society. Human individuals as citizens of human society have a duty to remain alive and fulfill the four basic requirements of life. Thus, human individuals must work in order to remain citizens in their society. In return, society has to compensate these citizens for the work that they do for the four basic requirements.

Talking about the four basic life requirements and the labour that it necessitates might seem out of context. But once we get used to talking about it, we will be ashamed of ourselves and ask why we did not think of this earlier. For, our modern civilization today is filled with innovation and technology, such as AI. In order to expand our analysis of human labour, we must clarify what kind of civilization is fit for the modern human society of today.

Before moving to the next section, it is relevant to state that there is another aspect from which human labour must be considered. Since human labour is offered in the economic market, it is not a natural thing that happens by itself in the natural environment involuntarily. Human labour is a completely controlled and volitional activity that a human individual consciously and purposefully puts into action. Thus, it is important to consider in what social circumstances the human labour has been prepared, offered, and received (consumed).

ELEMENTS OF A SMART CIVILIZATION

C lose analysis of a smart civilization shows us that, based on the rule of four, there are four fundamental entities in the social structure of modern human society that are directly and decisively related to the quality of human life. These are:

1. Health
2. Education
3. Justice
4. Communication

These four entities are infrastructural pillars of a smart civilization that can provide a smart life within modern human society and, therefore, they are every human individual's concern in any human society on Earth. These four pillars mean that in a modern human society, healthy and adequately educated individuals can live in an equitable environment and be equally protected legally by a genuine rule of law and, therefore, can communicate with each other freely as they need or want in order to live a peaceful, decent, and fair life. We will study each of these four infrastructural necessities in more detail.

HEALTH

Every society needs to have a healthy population because unhealthy people are not productive. In addition, it is expensive to have unhealthy people because: the treatment of unhealthy people costs a lot of money; the time of related individuals is wasted as they have to take care of their unhealthy relatives or friends; and, unhealthy people diminish the progress of society. Healthy individuals can offer complete and more adequate labour to their society; hence, health is a collective concern of society. Further, and most importantly, health is not a luxury in a smart civilization. It is a survival need and, therefore, it is human right. Every individual is entitled to live, in the limit of human knowledge, a healthy life free of suffering. But since health is a complex matter and often involves expensive professional help, individuals cannot provide themselves with healthcare necessities without help. Therefore, a smart, civilized society cannot and must not ignore or abandon its citizens in pain and suffering. Providing free health care to its members is the collective responsibility and duty of a modern society.

EDUCATION

Members of a modern human society must know how to speak, listen, read, and write in order to communicate with other members of society and become active members with the necessary qualifications to participate in society's social, economic, and political activities. Therefore, education, which is totally free from ideology and religion, is an indispensable human need. Educated individuals can offer complete and more adequate labour to society; hence, education is a collective concern of society. In modern human society, education is not a luxury; rather, it is a survival need. A lack of or inadequate education can reduce and even severely harm an individual's quality of life. Therefore, education is a human right. But since education is a complicated matter and often involves expensive professional help, individuals cannot provide themselves with the requirements of education by themselves. Providing free education to its members is the collective responsibility and duty of a modern society.

In the past fifty years, despite corruption, mismanagement, and mistakes, there have been significant improvement in the spheres of health and education, especially in Western Europe, North America, Australia, and New Zealand. Therefore, we will not spend too much time on these issues now, although we will come back to them later. But after introducing the next two pillars of justice and communications, we have serious work to do in examining them further.

JUSTICE

Human society cannot exist if two or more individuals do not interact. In all interactions of any nature, individuals share or exchange human labour—either mentally or physically or both. Therefore, an accepted and respected justice system is the one and only thing that can ensure the benefits of human interaction, which are progress, peace, and pleasure among human individuals. Justice, by definition, means not causing harm; as a result, causing harm of any nature is a violation of justice, and human nature and the violation of justice are not compatible. Hence, a natural human reaction physically, mentally, and psychologically to injustice of any kind and measure is hostile, antagonistic, and destructive, regardless of being introvert, extrovert, obvious, or hidden.

COMMUNICATION

A society that provides its citizens with free and complete communication is the only place that a modern human's physical and mental potential can flourish. Further, modern humans cannot freely and completely communicate with old, backward, and obsolete means and methods. Communication is an infrastructure matter for a smart civilization, and without free and complete communication, human labour cannot be adequately used and appreciated. All that can be used, in any form and way, to help two or more individuals share and exchange ideas or objects of any nature is an instrument or tool of communication, and these are all humanly sacred. In the twenty-first century, human individuals are entitled to be in communication with each other absolutely free from any restriction, control, limitation, or obstacle. Thus, the quality and extent of communication is a very crucial matter and directly dependent on and conditioned by the means of communication. The kind and efficiency of instruments play an important role in the quality and extent of communication. Hence, later on in this book, we will investigate the instruments of communication in more detail.

JUSTICE AND HUMAN NATURE

Now, let us return to justice as a pillar of a smart civilization. As mentioned earlier, injustice and human nature are not compatible. As it is known, the nature of human personality is a spectrum between positive and negative personal attributes. Positive attributes include being friendly, honest, loyal, trustworthy, reliable, caring, hard-working, generous, empathetic, ethical, frank, etc. Negative human character traits include being lazy, arrogant, irresponsible, egotistical, deceptive, greedy, dishonest, immoral, untruthful, violent, unreliable, selfish, etc.

In our investigation, we will not be concerned about the roots of and reasons for human traits, as this is a subject for psychology rather than political economy. What we will examine is when social relations between individuals, in which one or both sides act upon their negative personal traits, cause a violation of justice. And, of course, history has shown that in every aspect of human activity around the globe, malevolent actions based on negative personal traits occur regularly and cause traumatizing effects on people's life.

The issue of positive or negative personal traits of people in a social sense is a complicated subject, which we will explore further. Since everything in human society is done, controlled, and decided by human individuals, the whole structure of society (administration, politics, and economy) is exposed to the personal traits of those who are politically and economically running society and making decisions about the everyday collective life of its members. From the other side, in the social relations between individuals, the parameters of financial and/or political interests play an important role in determining if an individual is going to act based on positive or negative personal traits. Some individuals come to the conclusion that they are rightfully entitled in certain situations to act or react based on either their positive or negative personal traits. Hence, a correct and corruption-free justice system, with correct and corruption-free checks and balances, is required so that the citizens of a society are not exposed to the law and order of a society that is contaminated by the negative personal traits of those decision-makers and executers. The sad news is that in our life in the twenty-first century, many awful, inhuman, and ferocious experiences are happening to innocent and defenceless people of all ages, sexes, and race every day around the globe. This is the reason why providing justice for human individuals based on a genuine rule of law and a correct and corruption-free justice system is a necessary infrastructural entity of a smart civilization.

We will continue our investigation through a question: In today's world, does a justice system exist that provides adequate justice to the needs of modern humans? The answer is definitely negative. While some countries are better than others, today's modern human is living socially, politically, and economically in communities that do not serve adequate justice.

The lack of adequate justice in today's societies is not due to a lack of knowledge about law or interest about human rights. To the contrary, knowledge about law and legality has been well studied and researched since a very long time ago. From Socrates and his students, Plato and Aristotle (about 2,500 years ago), up to the Renaissance and, more specifically, closer to our time in the seventeenth and eighteenth centuries, there have been many great philosophers and thinkers concerned with this issue. These include Voltaire, John Locke, Montesquieu, Thomas Hobbes, and Mary Wollstonecraft, and modern human rights activists like Martin Luther King and Nelson Mandela. They have taught law and order and the principles of decent human life. We have been exposed to events such as George Floyd's death, which caused the Black Life Matters movement, and Harvey Weinstein's affairs that created the Me Too movement. Yet, still, human society does not seem to be learning needed lessons quickly enough.

Why has human society not learned its lessons in order to create and establish an adequate, modern justice system? These lessons would help humans to live a better life with more peace, honour, and dignity! Should we doubt modern human intelligence for learning? The answer to this is definitely negative. Modern humans are so intelligent that we have landed and walked on the Moon (384,400 kilometres from Earth) and even landed robots on the planet Mars (88,602,789 kilometres from Earth) to remotely analyze the materials and weather there. Thanks to modern human intelligence, hospital doctors can do very complicated surgeries to save people's lives, and from the other side, we have created sophisticated military equipment that can effectively kill others around the world. Even in very remote regions of some very underdeveloped countries, people (some of whom don't even know how to read and write) are using cars, computers, and wireless smart phones. All these achievements do not leave any room to doubt the intelligence of modern humans.

Nevertheless, we still do not have the answer to the question that we asked above. As we have already stated, the problem is not a lack of human intelligence or knowledge. Even in some countries ruled by dictators, there are advanced, humanist, and equitable codification and good laws written in their constitutions and books. But the point, however, is the mechanism of the application of the law and the apparatuses through which law and order become implemented in society. As Francis Fukuyama (an American political scientist, political economist scholar) explains, there are significant differences between societies that function based on the rule of law and those that are controlled by the method of rule by law.[241] For example, the terrorist criminal mullahs in Iran rule society with fascist laws. The point is that, according to the

---

241 Francis Fukuyama, *The Origins of Political Order* (2012).

social structures that determine the legal method—either the rule of law or the rule by law—the justice system and political texture are two mechanisms that control the social institutions and people in society. In fact, in order to understand this issue, we will need to study the mechanism of the justice system in present human society.

THE FUNCTION OF A JUSTICE SYSTEM

French philosopher Montesquieu (1689–1755) published his book, *De l'esprit des lois* (*The Spirit of the Laws*), in 1748. He was the first person who explained that the governing powers in human society— executive, legislative, and judicial—must be separated. Montesquieu believed the governing structure of human society could appear in three forms: republic, monarchy, or despotic. And for him, a republic could have two forms: a democratic republic, which would be the ideal, with the highest degree of freedom and rights for its citizens; and a aristocratic republic, with a lesser degree of freedom and rights for its citizens. The point for Montesquieu, in the separation of the governing powers, was that it controlled and limited an individual's influence and, therefore, corruption. His intention was to cut the bridge between the powerful people of society, who can act as implicitly organized gangs (like a hidden mafia) in social institutions and impose their wishes and interests upon society. This is a kind of social situation within which economically and politically powerful people can infringe upon the rights and freedoms of average and powerless individuals, without any accountability and consequences.

Above, although we have compressed the beliefs of Montesquieu, it gives us a clear image of his ideas for the separation of powers in human society and the function of the justice system. Next, we will examine if the governing powers in contemporary society are really separated and if the justice system functions independently.

THE CONTEMPORARY JUSTICE SYSTEM

In contemporary occidental countries, the social structure is influenced by the concept of nation-states, which was born following the two peace treaties of Westphalia in 1648, which ended the Thirty Years' War in the Roman Empire. The idea of nation-states, which, briefly, means a society of unified people under the strong effects of the achievements of the Age of Enlightenment (such as scientific and industrial revolutions and intellectual movements), could create more advanced and complicated social structures and political and economic institutions. Today, one of the most important social institutions in Western countries is the justice system, which they proudly claim is an independent social institution.

First, Western societies tell the world that their justice systems are free from political and economic influences and interferences, and therefore, the trials and judgments in their justice systems are held and rendered justly and free from prejudices. Second, occidental societies claim their societies are structured based on the rule of law and, thus, all their citizens in front of the law are equal, and no one is above the law. Insofar as the laws are written on paper, everything looks nice and right, but the experience in real life is not the same.

It is relevant to see what Francis Fukuyama says about the nature of the rule of law. "The rule of law rests on the law itself and the visible institutions that administer it—judges, lawyers, courts and the like. It also rests on the formal procedures by which those institutions operate."[242] This statement by Fukuyama is very important. Hence, we will examine the process through which the justice system in developed countries is made. But before moving further, we must consider that, if in a given society, the government, parliament, and senate are all from the same make (for example, Liberal or Democrat or Conservative or Republican) and as a whole, they are in charge of running the administration, making laws, and appointing judges—in other words, establishing justice in our society—all those powerful individuals in the key positions of the governing machine, and their friends and relatives, enjoy legal, political, and financial immunities or impunities, either officially or unofficially. Now the question is: Can this mechanism (no matter where on Earth) really provide a society with a genuine rule of law? Since the answer is definitely not, this makes it understandable why our world is boiling in trouble.

We will go through some steps to familiarize ourselves with the existing justice system in the Western world. In Western societies, judges are appointed by politicians or kings. This method of appointing judges by itself means that everything is wrong from the start. For the appointing of judges by decision-making authorities in its nature makes the appointed judges nothing but a bunch of political slaves. This gets even worse when we see that the appointed judges come from particular political ideologies or fanatic religious beliefs or have certain ties to some political parties in power. Still, this is not the end of it as the situation culminates in the structure of the supreme courts. In some Western so-called developed and democratic countries (some funnily called the G7), they appoint nine, twelve, sixteen, or how ever many political slaves and call it the Supreme Court. With this, they leave the faith of a nation in the hands of those few political slaves. They name this farce an "independent justice system," which is supposed to

---

242 Fukuyama, *Origins*, 259.

establish justice in society and protect people against the infringement of their rights. This is definitely not happening anywhere on our planet. It is needed to say that in the Supreme Court of Germany, which they call the Federal Court of Justice (*Bundesgerichtshof*—BGH), the number of judges varies, and it can go up to 120 judges. But despite the large number of judges (compared to some other countries), they are still appointed by politicians and official authorities, so the quality of the justice system cannot change, and this remains the same as other Western countries.

The other point is the application of law. In developed countries, the slogan is that every citizen is equal before the law and, therefore, no one is above the law. Obviously, nobody needs any explanation for this joke.

The conclusion is that an adequate social institution that can provide modern human individuals with genuine justice and equitability does not exist on the globe. The reason for this (although, it must be said, the secret) is the capacity of the social institution called the justice system. The justice system, insofar as it is known today in all 206 countries in the world, is a silent weapon of mass destruction in the hands of the governing powers (political and economic) that is used to control and suppress the mass of the population, in order that those in authority can do and live their lives (read corruption) as they wish. As soon as a person or a group asks serious questions about the wrongdoings of powerful people in a governing body of society, the justice system effectively silences their voice. Therefore, the more defective a justice system is, the better it will do the job as a silencing weapon. As a whistleblower since 2004, I am living the experience of a justice system being used as a suppressing weapon in Canada. (I will tell you the story of my experience with the justice system in Canada after the section on communication.)

There are further defects in the presently known justice system. As we have already learned from Montesquieu, the governing structure of human society consists of three powers, one of which is legislative. The legislative power in society is generally called the parliament and senate (although some countries have different names for their legislative power), and this is the birthplace of laws. According to the political tradition in Western developed countries, elected representatives of citizens sit in the parliament and senate. After studying the legal needs of the society, they choose and make laws that will become respected by the entire population of that society. By coordinating all the activities of the inhabitants, this establishes a social order that will offer a comfortable, peaceful, and decent life for citizens. It is useful, though, to say that, in Canada, the members of the Senate are not elected by citizens for four years; rather, they are appointed by the prime minister and can stay in office until they become seventy-five years old, which is a corrupt mechanism for a legislative institution.

However, while we have a birthplace for laws, we do not have a death place for laws. This is another defect in the social structure for justice. Why are laws born, but they do not die? This is another secret in the justice system that makes it a silent weapon of mass destruction. No matter how outdated, useless, and even harmful laws become over time, they still can serve corruption. Francis Fukuyama taught us about the secret of the rule by law. This is how and why, in the early twenty-first century, modern humans are living an unjust life, in a legally rotten and miserable world. And as a result, employees are not paid enough and too much is taken from the consumers. Therefore, unavoidably, the accumulated wealth in the hands of capitalists remains useless and thus wasted. We will look at the details of this issue later.

Today, the existing justice systems are like terrifying pit bull dogs that are chained to societies to bite vulnerable people who do wrong or those who say something that authorities and powerful people do not like. There is not an equitable justice system in our world, which is accountable for its acts or that cares for accountability at all. Cases go from one court to another, paid for with public money and people's lives. Nobody cares if a person is guilty or innocent. From the other side, political and economic corruption and wrong doings are everywhere, such as with the Panama Papers, election lies, and criminal politicians, while a genuine justice system is absent.

For my book *Les Ambassadrices* (about accomplished women in Quebec), I photographed Anne Montminy, Olympic diver and lawyer, in the winter of 2001. At the time, she was very young, only twenty-five years old. She had won her Olympic medals just a few months previously, and one year before that she had finished law school. While I was taking pictures, I asked her if she could compare her sporting competition with a lawyer's work in a courtroom. For a few moments she was silent, and then she said, they are not really very different. In a competition, the challenge is physical and you try to win against someone who is doing the same thing. You want to prove that you are doing better. In a courtroom, the work is verbal and not physical, but still you are trying to win against someone who is doing the same thing, and you want to prove that what you are saying is better. Then she added something very interesting. She said in a courtroom all depends on the number and kind of the jurisprudence that you are presenting to the court; if your jurisprudence impresses the judge, you win. In spite of her being very young and still not a practising professional lawyer, her observation was quite interesting and meaningful, especially in stressing the number and kind of jurisprudences.

The issue of jurisprudence in the courtroom means that the authorities in the justice system (as Fukuyama names them: judges and lawyers) are not looking for the truth. What matters in the courtroom is the setup, and the quality and method of presentation. According to judicial tradition, jurisprudence is one of the principal elements of the setup and presentation. In order to understand the judicial tradition and the role of jurisprudence, we must examine the two dominant judicial philosophies and methods that are practised in the world: common law and civil law. But before starting the examination of judicial philosophy, it is useful to explain an important point regarding the definition of jurisprudence. The word "jurisprudence" comes from the Latin term *juris prudentia*, which means the science or philosophy of law. Apart from the theoretical meaning, in daily legal practice, jurisprudence technically means case law on a particular subject. In practice, this legally means that the decisions rendered by the judges in legal disputes, is based on the principle of the precedent in similar cases.

JUDICIAL PHILOSOPHIES

Two judicial philosophies, common law and civil law, are presently practised in the justice systems of the Western world, as well in other parts of the world. These judicial philosophies are called transatlantic models. Charles H. Koch, professor of law at William & Mary Law School, wrote "For one thing, the two basic models already cover over 70% of the world's population in some 62% of the existing legal systems."[243] And some countries, like South Africa, use a combination of civil and common law.

In terms of the origins of these judicial philosophies, we can say that: "Common law dates to early English monarchy when courts began collecting and publishing legal decisions. Later, those published decisions were used as the basis to decide similar cases." And for the civil law, "Historians believe that the Romans developed civil law around 600 CE, when the emperor Justinian began compiling legal codes. Current civil law codes developed around that Justinian tradition of codifying laws as opposed to legal rulings."[244]

In the case of common law, rendered judgments (jurisprudences) have been collected for several centuries (since the early English monarchy), and the sum total of those judgments is the law for the justice systems to work with (common law). Written law does not exist in the common law category. Furthermore, in the common law system, the judges have the authority to evolve (make) the law. This is important because, based on this authority, the judges in the courtroom can, regarding the circumstances and sometimes the availability of the jurisprudences, make a kind of judgment that will make a precedent for a new law. This is why in courtrooms, it is the setup and presentation that make the case and not the truth and justice.

---

243 Charles H. Koch Jr (2004) "The Advantages of the Civil Law Judicial Design as the Model for Emerging Legal Systems," *Indiana Journal of Global Legal Studies* 11, No. 1 (2004): 139. https://www.repository.law.indiana.edu/ijgls/vol11/iss1/6).

244 "Civil Law vs. Common Law," *Diffen*, https://www.diffen.com/difference/Civil_Law_vs_Common_Law.

Later on, when I share the story of my experience with the Canadian justice system, it will show why jurisprudence and the function of common law is a concerning issue for modern human society. Out of absolutely nothing, the Canadian justice system created a criminal case for me. And since, by the logic of common law, a precedent in a similar situation becomes law, a prosecutor can use this precedent against another whistle-blower, and it will be totally legal and correct. We have also learned that the common law method had been practised for many centuries. Therefore, we can imagine how many thousands of corrupt judges, like Judge Wilbrod Claude Décarie, in my case, have served justice systems around the world with rendering corrupt and false judgments in criminal or civil cases and making them precedent. Lawyers know quite well the Latin expression *stare decisis*, which literally means "let decisions stand" or, more precisely in a legal sense, it means the principle of determining points in litigation according to precedent. Thus, common law judicial philosophy is definitely too old and outdated and can never provide modern humans with a fair and equitable life.

Although civil law philosophy has a better grip on reality than common law, it is not sufficient for modern human society either. Nevertheless, compared to common law, civil law has a few strong points that make it more reliable. For one thing, "Its core principles are codified into a referable system which serves as the primary source of law."[245] Second, it is not a strongly precedent-oriented system.

But what is concerning about civil law is the role of judges in the trial process. We will examine this point more closely. In civil law, a judge is "Chief investigator. . . . Though the judge often brings the formal charge." And in an inquisitorial position, "judges ask question and demand evidence."[246] There is no doubt that, up to certain point, this is good because it will make the role of judge more active in scrutinizing the points of the case—especially compared to the role of judge in common law, which is a quite passive, observant role. Those

---

245 Ibid.
246 Ibid.

who are familiar with legal procedures know that legal trials are a very stressful experience for both the professionals and citizens who, for whatever reason, go through that experience. Therefore, if, during a trial, the judge develops an emotional, psychological, or intellectual problem with the defendant, this defect can affect the fairness of the trial and eventually the judgment. The question is how a justice system can make sure that the role of a judge will not change to the level of a police detective or a lawyer. More precisely, the question is how a judge in civil law court can remain totally impartial until the end of trial, and therefore render a just judgment.

These are just a few points to show briefly that the two dominant judicial philosophies are too old and outdated to provide modern human society with adequate smart justice.

JUSTICE SYSTEM FOR MODERN HUMANS

Now we will talk about the method of justice that we care about. In fact, the justice system of modern humans does not work with appointed pieces. Rather, it functions with elected representatives, who receive their legitimacy from the citizens of their society and, therefore, do not owe their seat to a specific person. Thus, judges must be elected by the citizens with complete and voluntary transparency. This means that at the time of the nomination for election, the nominees, without hesitation, must reveal all their financial, tax, education, legal, and social records. Citizens are fully entitled to have complete knowledge about the person for whom they will vote. Indeed, nothing is more ridiculous than hearing that individuals who wish to be elected and honoured with very significant public power to make decisions that will affect the lives of a mass of people expect to remain hidden behind the excuse of private life. This expectation should include all elected decision-making authorities in modern human society.

One of the constant duties of the Supreme Court should be to scrutinize laws according to their age and function, and therefore, euthanize laws that are outdated or have somehow become harmful. Social laws are not celestial and divine; they are human-made and, therefore, must have an expiry date according to time and social circumstances.

Further, the number of judges who serve the Supreme Court must be equal to the number of the Members of the Parliament, with one judge from every constituency. The reason for this is that a genuine Supreme Court is not an auxiliary component in the complex structure of society. To the contrary, a real Supreme Court is an infrastructural institution that should watchdog the genuine practice of justice and affairs in every section of society and government. It should ensure that the machinery of justice has been adequately structured and maintained for delivering its original duty. In the case of some malfunction or corruption, it will intervene on time to prevent harm to society and its citizens. In addition, the Supreme Court must create a system for hiring and training judges for the local courts.

One of the extremely shameful and unforgivable experiences that occurs every day in Western countries is that innocent and defenceless people spend weeks, months, and even sometimes years behind bars without having access to real justice, while some well-connected, corrupt authorities break laws and get away with it. A smart civilization cannot and should never tolerate such an awful encroachment against its citizens.

All judges are employees hired by society, and they are paid salaries for their labour. The commodity that judges have to sell to society is their knowledge, experience, and thought. They must assume responsibility for the quality of their work, and therefore, be held accountable in the case of wrongdoings, as are architects, doctors, engineers, accountants, teachers, etc. If a judge, as one of the highest and most powerful functions in society, cannot assume responsibility for what they do, how can society expect other professionals with much less power and protection to assume responsibility for what they do?

The justice system is a humanly sacred institution in human society and, therefore, it must remain under permanent transparency and scrutiny. The accountability of the justice system must never be compromised or conditioned by time or anything else, for it is eternal.

COMMUNICATION AND MODERN HUMAN

We will now return to our exploration of communication, the fourth pillar of a smart civilization. Communication is a door and window between the inner and outer worlds of human beings. All that humans can achieve, know, and learn is seldom accessible through communication. In fact, means of communication are tools that connect human individuals with nature, society, and each other. Without communication with the outer world, the human brain and body cannot live. Communication is also the managing system that organizes and administers all human exchanges of all kinds and natures with the outer world. The first and basic human communication with the external world starts with the first breathing (receiving oxygen from nature) of a baby at the first independent connection with nature at the moment of birth. And the first human communication in life starts when a baby receives her first breast feeding from her mother. Thus, communication in human life is not a luxury thing; rather, it is a fundamentally nature-imposed, indispensable human need.

In a human society in which the capitalist mode of production prevails, communication is a very vital and complicated matter. Human beings, physically, are small creatures who live on an Earth that is immensely huge and vast compared to the human body. To have a smart life, in our present capitalist society, modern human has no choice but to stay in constant communication with every corner of the earthly globe, which is only possible through advanced and sophisticated means of communication. Thus, communication that provides modern human with life requirement necessities is a human right. For a smart life, modern humans must be equipped with the strongest and fastest means of communication. Below, we will have a closer look at the means of communication.

LANGUAGE AND COMMUNICATION

Language is a pivotal instrument in human communication, and one of the basic tools of communication that human babies start to learn at about ten months of age. According to statistics, there are about 7,100 languages spoken in today's world. And in the 206 countries in the world today, about 125 languages are practised as the official, governmental, or educational language. Economically and politically in international relations, there are about twelve languages that are widely practised, but the United Nations has six official languages: English, French, Russian, Arabic, Chinese, and Spanish. But, in today's world, there is only one language that is unequivocally and indisputably accepted by everybody around the globe as the lingua franca of the world, and that is the English language. The English language's uniqueness and importance has been studied and scrutinized in detail by linguists and experts with academic and technical interest in language. However, the only significant point for our analysis is that the English language is the richest, most powerful, and most developed language in human possession, which does not have an owner. The English language is a world asset, which belongs to and is part of human civilization, regardless of geography.

Real democracy and justice for humans on Earth will only be achievable if all individuals, regardless of their race, gender, and geographical location, can communicate directly with each other, free from any limit or restriction. Of course, for direct communication between individuals, English is the only instrument that can penetrate all obstacles and connect people around the globe. People have to know what others say, and they have to tell others what they have to share, without any intervention or barrier.

The English language is also the sun in the centre of the galaxy of all human knowledge and technology that can brighten human society. The light of science and knowledge is the most powerful disinfectant for ignorance and backwardness, while ignorance and backwardness are the plagues to the development of human civilization. Once society adopts the English language, combined with free healthcare and education, and coupled with genuine justice, it will experience the ultimate development and prosperity because, in this situation, every drop of human labour will be used to its maximum effectiveness and result.

One day, all languages in the world should disappear in the face of the English language. Of course, this will not happen overnight or even in just a few decades. But, sooner or later, it will eventually happen. The smarter societies are, the faster they will adopt English. Thus, 7,099 out of 7,100 existing languages should go in to the trash bin of history, leaving modern humans with the benefit and luxury of the powerful English language. It is a civilized duty for modern humans to learn English and help others to learn it. Every attempt to encourage or enforce that a group of people be divided between more variations of languages is a reactionary, anti-human effort, and therefore, harmful to a smart civilization. However, all attempts to encourage and facilitate people to unite under the umbrella of English language is progressive and, therefore, useful for a smart civilization.

OTHER MEANS OF COMMUNICATION

Today, the significance of mass communication has been widely recognized, and they are even teaching the theory and practice of it in colleges and universities around the world as an academic program called Communication Studies or Communication Science. Wilbur Schramm (1907–1987) is known as the founding authority of mass communications. Since 1947, Schramm was the pioneer figure in founding departments of communication studies across universities in the United States. In 1954, he published *The Process and Effects of Mass Communication*. Communication tools are varied and, since the beginning of the twentieth century, they are mesmerizingly developed. Telephone, radio, television, roads, railways, seaways, and airways are all mass communication tools that every day, globally, bring huge numbers of individuals together.

The technology of virtual communication and social media, although very recent, has grown very quickly. It is everywhere, and it is in almost everybody's hand. However, since communication is a social infrastructure matter for human society, its accessibility for all inhabitants of the whole society at all times is a very crucial matter. Moreover, communication means are industrial and professional objects, which are very expensive commodities. As a result, it would be impossible for human individuals to provide themselves with adequate necessary communication tools on their own. Thus, it is a collective responsibility of society to make sure that its citizens have access at all times to the required communication tools, just as they must have access to potable running water.

Although communication means are super beneficial for modern humans, they can be used abusively by corrupt authorities, nasty individuals, or both. As we have already seen, the justice system can be used as a weapon against individuals if their actions or words are not pleasing to power holders in the higher positions of society. Communication tools have the same capacity to be used as weapons to harm those considered as a threat to powerful politicians or business authorities. Since 2004, I have been a victim that the mass media in Canada have written and pronounced millions of words against me over the radio, on television, in newspapers, and on social media across Canada.

Some communication systems and communication institutions are possessed by private owners. Therefore, if the capitalist owners, for whatever reason, decide to punish trouble-making politicians or individuals, they can use the communication tools (the infrastructural installations of the society), which are their private property, as the means to impose their wishes. Consequently, modern human society will become a hostage, manipulated by capitalists who are in search of private interests. No matter what, modern human society cannot tolerate leaving its social infrastructural installations at the mercy of one or more individuals (natural or legal persons). For instance, a super-rich capitalist owner—a little Citizen Kane (in social scale, he is only a human)—no matter how big the number in his bank account, should never have permission to use or abuse the communication system to play a power game against individuals or society (with a bow to Orson Welles). Hence, modern human society has to have mechanisms, which are in a permanent, full-time alertness, to scrutinize all its infrastructural components to make sure that they are all in healthy and functioning condition to serve society. There must also be a watchdog to make sure that social institutions (healthcare system, education system, justice system, and communication system) are not being abusively used as weapons of character assassination to harm innocent citizens—for this is state terrorism. I, as a victim, am the very proof of state terrorism in Canada.

Apart from the real accidents, because of abuse and negligence, we can all remember examples such as: bridges, which have collapsed on the cars; roads, which have been washed away; trains, which have been derailed; and telephone and internet lines, which have been interrupted. In addition, there have been qualified professional people who have lost their jobs; intelligent, hard-working people who lost their chance for a good education; and innocent, honest people who wasted their lives in prisons, all because of the misuse of social power against vulnerable, innocent individuals.

Before starting the next section, as I had promised, I will share my own personal story to reveal how the Government of Canada used Canada's justice and communication systems as a weapon of character assassination against my family and me. The following is the account of my own real experience with the justice system in Quebec and Canada, which was first published in 2013.

I LIVE THROUGH THE BIGGEST SCANDAL IN QUEBEC, CANADA

Wednesday, March 24, 2004. It was a beautiful sunny day. Myriam, Maude (my family), and I drove from Montreal to Ottawa. We arrived on Parliament Hill. The security officers showed us toward a small door behind the old stone building of Parliament, through which we entered the building. Beside the door, before going into the building, I parked the car in a place that had been kept available for us.

The first person we met as we entered the building was Liberal MP Marlene Jennings. Smiling and polite, she welcomed us. We had already met her in the preliminary hearing just a couple of days before. With no delay, Marlene took Maude's hand; at the time, she was nine years old. In her first sentence to Maude, she said, "Your mom is a hero, and everybody loves her." Marlene told us that she would take care of Maude, so we didn't need to worry about her. Marlene and Maude left us. (Marlene joined us later in the hearing room.) Myriam and I were directed to the place where Myriam had to answer the same questions that she had already answered a couple of days before. Only this time it was public, with more people to question, contrary to the first time, which had taken place behind closed doors, without journalists and without publications.

Yes, that beautiful sunny day, Wednesday, March 24, 2004, in front of the public accounts committee in the Parliament of Canada, Myriam testified. In fact, she fulminated against the rotten Liberals who corrupted the sponsorship system. In other words, she bombed the mafia, terrorist, robber Liberals. From there on, the war between terrorist Liberals and my family had started.

In order to discredit us, first Via Rail Canada hired a lawyer called Michel G. Picher to fabricate a report saying that Myriam had resigned from her work at Via Rail because she was passing illegal contracts to me. Responding to this, Myriam and I wrote a full complete report with documents and photographs showing precisely that everything Michel G. Picher had gathered in his report was nothing but lies and fabrications. The first Liberal plot to hurt our reputation not only failed to cause significant damage to us, but it also became even more evident that the Liberals were working hard to mislead public attention.

After the first plot failed, the mafia, terrorist Liberals thought that if they could buy Myriam's family and fabricate an accusation from her father that said that Myriam had stolen paintings (after so many years I still don't know which or what paintings and no one else knows), it could make for an easily believable criminal drama to destroy Myriam and I. So that is why all those James-Bond types of police activities, with the participation of Radio Canada (the French section of CBC), took place in June 2004. That was when the police searched our commercial and residential buildings in Levis, Quebec, and media all across Canada wrote and pronounced millions and millions of words, hoping to cause real serious damage to Myriam and I.

But after the dust had finally settled, everything about this accusation became beyond ridiculous because there were no paintings and nobody knew what these so-called paintings looked like. There was absolutely no description of these alleged paintings. The mafia, terrorist Liberals had to do something. They found the solution in creating witnesses, which meant that some paid people would come to court to say this or that. So that is why all statements gathered by the police concerning this case were dated from after June 2004, with only one exception: Myriam's father. Well, the script was written after shooting the film.

Although, through media, the mafia, terrorist Liberals made a huge storm against Myriam and I, nothing legally happened before July 2005. On July 6, 2005, the police arrested me for stealing paintings, an accusation which had initially been made against Myriam. Then, it took a horrible and devastating year until we had the preliminary inquiry.

Running the preliminary inquiry was quite an experience. I did not have a lawyer because I had fired him, so I had to take care of the hearing and represent myself. From the very beginning, I had asked all witnesses (twenty) to be heard in the preliminary inquiry. From the very start, the prosecutor, Mario Dufresne, did everything to prevent the witnesses from being heard in court. Nevertheless, I fought very hard and eventually I got to interrogate about ten witnesses. As a result, I raised a couple of extremely important questions that changed the setup of the game. Here are some of those questions:

- The sender of the anonymous letter (Pierre Bédard, Myriam's father) said under oath that he alone wrote and had put the letter with four photographs in the envelope and mailed it to the receiver without absolutely ever talking to anybody about it. But the receiver (witness Kathe Roth) of the envelope said under oath that Catherine Kovacs (the journalist of Radio Canada) had called her and talked to her about the anonymous letter.

- We also learned that the four photographs sent, along with the anonymous letter in the envelope, were not the same four photographs that were received by the receiver (witness).

On this question, even Judge Claude Parent was shocked, and himself asked Chief Detective Jean-François Talbot, the officer of Sûreté du Québec: "Did you know before that there are two different sets of photographs, or are you learning about this at the same time as us, here in this courtroom?" Chief Detective Jean-François Talbot responded that he did not know about this before, and he was learning about the two different sets of photographs right here in the courtroom.

Above all, this confirmed that the sender of the anonymous letter (Pierre Bédard) was lying.

From the very beginning of the prosecution, I asked the prosecutors to provide me with the statement of Catherine Kovacs. At any cost, they refused. Even during the preliminary inquiry, I wanted to hear Catherine Kovacs, and again at any cost, Judge Claude Parent refused.

As we can see, in this case, Catherine Kovacs was not a journalist or even a simple witness. Catherine Kovacs was one of the suspects who played a very important role in the creation of this terrorist case against Myriam and I.

Another important question was where the stamp of Canada Post had been forged on the envelope of the anonymous letter. Was it in Radio Canada? Was it in the Heenan Blaikie law firm? Was it in Montreal? Was it in Quebec? Or...

While we were busy in the preliminary inquiry and being accused of having stolen the paintings, a website belonging to the Canadian Government called CNC showed one of those allegedly stolen paintings and claimed that they had it in stock for sale. So, I printed the website page and presented it in the court. In return, rather than dropping the charges against me, the website of CNC became smoke and disappeared.

Of course, I did not give up. I continued the pressure. I interrogated Jean-Claude Bergeron, a gallery owner in Ottawa, who was later placed as an expert witness for the prosecutor. Throughout the interrogation, I showed the court that Jean-Claude Bergeron had this very painting in his inventory. Jean-Claude Bergeron also confirmed under oath that he was buying and selling paintings through the government website (CNC).

I said the questions raised in the preliminary inquiry changed the setup of the game. What that means is that the Liberals made terrorists plan to destroy Myriam and I. They created a family problem in which family members hurt each other. It was predicted that the role of the justice system would be a neutral observer. But the story did not go as planned. Even providing the fake witnesses did not help. So, with the very serious questions raised in the preliminary inquiry, the justice system had a huge responsibility. In order to reach a guilty verdict, the justice system had to break a lot of laws, principles, and rules. So the mafia, terrorist Liberals again had to do something. Here came the meeting between the lawyer Marcel Aubut and Myriam Bédard in a restaurant called Decca 77. This restaurant is located on the ground floor of the same building in which the law firm Heenan Blaikie has its office; the same law firm with which Marcel Aubut is associated. The main door of the restaurant is at 1077 Drummond, on the corner of René-Levesque. The meeting took place on the evening of June 22, 2006. That was the last time Myriam and Marcel met.

Since the mafia, terrorist Liberals had already been successful in buying Myriam's family, they had a brilliant idea: why not buy Myriam, herself? Just imagine if Myriam would agree to come forward and lie just like her father did. She could talk as a victim, an abused woman beaten and manipulated by a guru monster, abuser, smuggler, criminal man called Nima . . . Bingo! Mission accomplished for the mafia, terrorist Liberals!

Therein lies the importance of this meeting on June 22, during which Marcel Aubut tried to convince (threaten) Myriam Bédard to leave me; if not, her life would become hell until she was eighty-five years old.

The Liberals' plan did not work. I asked Myriam how she had answered Marcel's demand, and she told me that it was not up to that piece of shit to tell her with whom she had to live. She also added that she does not have any talent for terrorism. She said she is not a bitch either.

I have to mention that in different occasions, businesswise, Marcel Aubut was both Myriam's lawyer and mine, so he had a pretty close and private knowledge of and access to our lives. He is one of the terrorist team leaders who played a very important role in the creation of this terrorist case against Myriam and I. Marcel Aubut is also the president of the Canadian Olympic Committee.

From here on, the mafia, terrorist Liberals, instead of backing away, decided to control everything that would ensure the trial would come up with a guilty verdict. To do this, they had to control lawyers, judges, witnesses, jury members, and all the proof presented in the courtroom. There is no doubt that they did.

For a justice system, no matter where on Earth, it is a huge, huge, huge responsibility to accept this type of control and influence over itself. Alas, alas, alas, the justice system in Quebec and Canada allowed the mafia, terrorist Liberals to impose such corruption upon it. It is an inerasable stigma on the history of Quebec and Canada.

We had about four weeks to start the trial. I presented sixteen motions, asking for the information and documents that were missing for me to proceed with the trial. We went before Judge Sophie Bourque with my sixteen motions. She had brought me one of her schoolbooks. She said that she knew I was representing myself and consequently, there were certain things I needed to know about the criminal court. I thanked her and assured her that I would read the book. Then, she said that she was the judge chosen for the trial, so see you in four weeks. Before dismissing us, she looked at the sixteen motions and asked the prosecutor to provide me with all I was asking for. The last thing I told Judge Sophie Bourque was my desire to have Catherine Kovacs as a witness, and she said, "No problem, it is your right. We will send her a subpoena to Radio Canada, and I am sure she will come."

When we walked out of the courtroom, I could not believe what had just happened in those few minutes. Compared to all my previous experiences, this one was very smooth, correct, and logical. I said to myself, either Sophie Bourque is playing a game to fool me, or she will be removed from this case. I had never seen Sophie Bourque before, and I never saw her again.

Before the trial, I decided to leave the case to a professional lawyer. I told my lawyer about the sixteen motions for which the prosecutor, as usual, had never responded. I also mentioned that the judge for the trial was Sophie Bourque, and my lawyer confirmed that he already knew that.

On May 7, 2007, the trial started, and I learned that the judge had been changed. Judge Sophie Bourque was replaced by Judge Wilbrod Claude Décarie. I was not surprised, for I knew that the mafia, terrorist Liberals had decided that, at any cost, the trial needed to render a guilty verdict. So, they needed a judge fit to accomplish such a task.

I had already seen the preliminary inquiry. I had seen how Judge Claude Parent had delivered the order, so I could feel and understand how the invisible hands were pulling the strings of the puppets in the courtroom. The anonymous letter and photographs passed as if they were completely admissible proof. The question of Catherine Kovacs coming to court as a witness took some time. Radio Canada sent a lawyer who was working for the same law firm that Judge Wilbrod Claude Décarie had worked for, so they could communicate with each other very well. The lawyer argued that Catherine Kovacs had nothing to do with this case, and it is *no wonder* that Judge Décarie understood and accepted the lawyer's argument. He ruled that the testimony of Catherine Kovacs was not necessary.

But the big potatoes in the trial were different than those in the preliminary inquiry. Just a few examples of them;

- The prosecutor, very generous with public money, had prepared a huge, very rich, and colourful book of all the paintings that Kathe Roth (the daughter of Ghitta Caiserman Roth) had at home. They gave a copy of this book to everybody except me. The witnesses were coming to the courtroom and, under oath, looking at the pictures in the book and saying, "Oh yes, yes, this is one of the paintings that Nima has stolen." Whereas Kathe Roth had already said to the court that none of them had ever moved; she had all of them at home. But it didn't matter; Judge Wilbrod Claude Décarie accepted the proof and the testimonies anyways.

- The prosecutor called Myriam to the court as a witness. In my trial, the prosecutor forced Myriam to sit in front of the judge and jury, and they brought a witness to testify against her without telling her that she was accused. She was there as a witness, not as an accused. In my trial, they made it her trial, and Judge Wilbrod Claude Décarie accepted and ordered Myriam to sit in the courtroom in front of the jury. He did not tell her, and he did not give her a chance to have a lawyer. I asked whether this was my trial or Myriam's trial, because if it was my trial, Myriam could not defend herself, and if this was her trial, I could not defend myself. Nobody ever told us that this was a trial for two accused persons. In the courtroom, the judge, the prosecutor, and the lawyer violated Myriam's and my constitutional rights. But no surprise, nobody had an ear for me or for Myriam. Judge Wilbrod Claude Décarie had an agenda. Once, I blamed my lawyer, Yves Gratton, because I wanted to push him to become tougher against the prosecutor. He told me, "Mr. Mazhari, you are not the only preoccupation in my life. I must also think of my wife and my children." I understood his message.

The trial ended with a guilty verdict, just as I had expected, *of course, beyond all reasonable doubt*. At the very last moment, Judge Wilbrod Claude Décarie himself said that there was no proof for anything, so he would see us on June 29. On Friday, June 29, 2007, Judge Wilbrod Claude Décarie came to the courtroom and condemned me to six months in prison, with no proof whatsoever as he had pronounced earlier.

I knew I would not give up. The case was sent to the Appeal Court. Again, the mafia, terrorist Liberals were in trouble. In order to confirm the guilty verdict, they had to corrupt and control the Appeal Court. This was again another complicated stage. Well, the mafia, terrorists Liberals again had an idea.

One day, on my way to my studio on St-Laurent Boulevard, somebody stopped me and said he admired Myriam Bédard because she was a great Olympic Athlete who made history with two gold medals, and that he understood what we were going through. He invited me for a coffee. In a very modest café on the corner of St-Dominique and Pine, behind the same building in which I had my studio on the third floor, we sat to have a coffee. This man started talking to me about the beauty of life and the injustice of what had happened to us. It did not take very long before he reached his point. He told me I should stop wasting my life because going to the Appeal Court was useless. He came to the conclusion that if I pled guilty and stopped the case in the Appeal Court, he could manage to provide me with $5 million, and that I should remain quiet for a couple of years and then he could make me a brand-new person. Then, Myriam and I would live our lives happily ever after. There, I understood why the Appeal Court was not rendering the judgment. They were buying time, hoping something might happen.

I did not touch my coffee on the table; I just left the coffee shop. When I talked to my landlady about the offer that I had got, she got very excited. She advised me to accept the deal. I knew why she was happy: I owed her money for the rent of the last several months and she wanted her money. The $5-million man caught me on my way another time. He was standing on the sidewalk. He only said, "Bonjour, M. Mazhari," and I replied, "Have a nice day." I then continued on my way to the studio.

The mafia, terrorist Liberals' plan to buy me did not work. They had to corrupt and control the Appeal Court. On October 7, 2009, after 322 days, the Appeal Court confirmed the guilty verdict and six months of imprisonment.

On Friday, October 9, 2009, I went to the Bordeaux prison. October, November, December, and January, I was in prison. I came out of prison on Monday, February 1, 2010. Since I was insisting on bringing my case to the Supreme Court of Canada, they kept me in prison four times longer than they usually keep real criminals in similar cases. They put me in a cell with a broken window in those cold months of the year. Along with these torturing conditions, my probation officer (tutor) Sylvie Tessier worked very hard to convince me to plead guilty. I just thanked her for her advice. At any cost, I wanted my case to go to the Supreme Court of Canada, for which I even did a hunger strike. I wanted to know if the mafia, terrorist Liberals would go that far to corrupt even the Supreme Court of their country. For sure they did. On April 15, 2010, the Supreme Court of Canada refused to hear my case, for they knew what was in it.

In a society, when a citizen is exposed to harm or injustice, the state and social institutions are supposed to come forward and provide the individual with the necessary protection. In our case, my family and I were attacked by the state. We were exposed to injustice by the justice system. So where could we go to seek justice and protection?

The mafia, terrorist Liberals tried very hard and seriously to employ any available individual who could get close to us and cause harm and damage. Whoever around us tried to hurt us in serving the mafia, terrorist Liberals became professionally successful. Those who did not have a job magically found a decent, well-paid job. And those who already had a job magically received very generous and well-awarded promotions. All this was thanks to the hidden hands of the mafia, terrorist Liberals, who were very well connected to public money.

I found my family and I attacked by the powerful state terrorism here in Quebec, Canada. I understood that mafia, terrorist Liberals are more mafia than mafia, and more terrorist than terrorists. I learned that they are mafia, terrorist Liberals without any principles, dignity, or honour whatsoever. They can rob their country without absolutely any limit or hesitation. They can corrupt the justice system of their country from top to bottom. They can destroy their national heroes. They can pay family members to tear each other apart. I had to defend and protect my family and myself. My self-defence started from the moment that the war between the mafia, terrorist Liberals and us started. I was hoping that somewhere, this stupid situation would stop before it went too far.

I am an artist. To defend my family and myself, I used my artwork as my ammunition. I believe art is an extremely powerful and effective weapon. Through my artwork, the more I blamed them, the more I spat on them, the more I urinated on them, the more I shat on them, rather than backing away and stopping their terrorist acts, the mafia, terrorist Liberals surprised me by proving to me that they are shameless and valueless. They become even more mafia and more terrorist.

My family and I are living with state terrorism here in Quebec, Canada. I continue to write and create my artworks, which are my self-defence and my battle in this imposed war against the mafia, terrorist Liberals in Quebec, Canada. I have lived through the biggest scandal in the history of Quebec, Canada.

Nima Mazhari
Montreal, August 25, 2013

GOVERNING STRUCTURE OF MODERN HUMAN SOCIETY

To investigate the governing structure of modern human society, we will need a quick return to Montesquieu. As we learned earlier, Montesquieu was the first one who talked about the three governing powers—executive, legislative, and judicial—in the structure of human society and the importance of the separation of powers to avoid or reduce the misuse of power by corrupt, influential individuals in the high positions of society. There is no doubt that the idea of Montesquieu was a noble idea, but . . .

Although we said that the idea of the separation of powers is a positive point, a legitimate concern is if there are any real mechanisms to make this separation really happen. We have already asked this question, and we also stressed our suspicion about the genuine occurrence of the separation of powers. Here, we will talk about this issue extensively. As usual, our survey field (*lieux d'enquête*) is the Western countries. We will start by creating an imaginary idea and slowly bring it to the real world. So let us imagine a political party; let us call it the "Conservative Party of Mars" (CPM). Then some members of CPM form the government (executive power), and some other members of the CPM become the majority in taking care of the parliament and senate (legislative power). Next, some direct or indirect members of the CPM become appointed by the head of the executive power (the president or prime minister) as judges sitting in the supreme court (judicial power). In the end, the inhabitants of this Martian society can celebrate the decision of the majority of their fellow citizens in their society that, through a genuine election in a fully democratic system, all three separated powers will run the society for the well-being of all citizens. Yet all people of the same gang (party) are dividing the powers between themselves and proudly calling it a separation of powers. The funniest point of this farce is that each member of the CPM keeps their jobs, although rotating from one power to another, for thirty to forty years. For instance, Jean Chretien, once Prime Minister of Canada, was a Liberal politician for forty years (1963–2003), rotating from one building to another or even from one office to another—from downstairs to upstairs.

Let us try to imagine this story in a different example. We will suppose in a city there is only one water purification centre, which distributes water to all households in town. Then, if every household believes that their water is different from the water of their neighbours, while the source of water is the same, wouldn't this belief sound like they are talking with a mental impairment?

We will start now analyzing the components of the governing structure for modern human society.

COMPONENTS OF THE GOVERNING STRUCTURE

The governing structure of modern human society, as in contemporary political science, is known as a representative democracy, but it must consist of four infrastructural power institutions rather than three. These power institutions would represent the power and will of a nation for self-government and protection. The duties of these institutions are to make decisions for the necessities of society, while providing the society with protection and all its requirements. These four power institutions are:

1. Executive
2. Legislative
3. Judicial
4. Treasurial

These four power institutions are separated from each other. They have only one goal and that is the full protection of the interest of the nation. Therefore, their only raison d'être is to serve and safeguard the country and the nation in their totality in every sense of it. These institutions do not owe anything to each other, while they owe their entire existence to their nation. Every single decision-maker sitting in these power institutions will receive their legitimacy and their title from the nation through an election. An election is the only power transferring means that will determine a seat for an elected decision-maker member of the power institution. Therefore, every elected decision-maker member will owe total loyalty and responsibility to the well-being of the nation. But before discussing the detail of each power institution, there are four general points that need clarification in order to help us understand the function of each institution better.

These four points are:

1. Voting method
2. Age prerequisite and serving time
3. Election method
4. Cameral structure

VOTING METHOD

In the power institution, at the time of making a decision, an elected member must vote while faithfully considering the interests of the nation and absolutely not their personal interests or the interests of any political party or other entity. Therefore, every elected member must vote independently and openly, while remaining accountable for their decisions; the elected members should be proud of serving their nation independently and responsibly.

It is relevant here to examine an example. The tradition in Canada's parliament system is that at the time of voting for a motion, the elected Members of Parliament vote according to the directive of their political party and not according to what they believe is in the interest of their constituents. This tradition is called "the practice of party discipline." This is how they officially explain it: "the practice of party discipline means that members of the same party vote together in Parliament. Since the emergence of structured political parties in the late nineteenth century, party discipline in some form has been an essential feature of the Canadian political landscape."[247] The reason that they

---

247 Lucie Lecomte, Legal and Social Affairs Division, Library of Parliament of Canada, Publication No. 2018-26-E. 1.

have adopted this method is that "the practice of party discipline serves two purposes: it ensures that the government and opposition sides in Parliament are clearly demarcated; and it provides a degree of ideological certainty on which the voter can rely."[248]

By this clarification, we are supposed to understand that the demarcation of the differences of the political parties and ideological faithfulness are more important than the well-being and interest of the citizens who elected the Members of Parliament to make decisions to protect their interest. Well, isn't that nonsense?

AGE PREREQUISITE AND SERVING TIME

Another point, apart from the question of voting, is the age of the elected members for the power institutions in a modern human society. Once in a while, we hear big noise from certain political parties or their journalist friends that among their elected members they have broken the record for having the youngest Member of Parliament or the youngest minister of this or that. Sometimes they go even further in announcing that they have chosen or elected the youngest-ever president or prime minister in this or that country. But the very simple question is: What is all this rejoicing for? What is the big deal about having a very young and, therefore, inexperienced person in charge of an extremely important job? When we are talking of the power institutions or highest administrative position, as president or prime minister of a country, we understand very well that we are talking about a position that will make decisions that will affect the life of several million people in the society. A decision by a president or prime minister can very significantly affect the life of every single citizen in a country. It can even go beyond borders and cause very serious international problems for quite a long time, such as in the case of a war or pandemic. Once, a person fifty years or older was considered an old person. But in our time, hearing of people over one hundred years old is not surprising any more. We know very well that sincere and responsible political work, in spite of its appearance, is hard work that requires solid, social

---

248 Lecomte, Publication No. 2018-26-E. 1.

maturity and a very strong commitment to serve the public. For any citizen to serve as a member of a power institution is an honour and highly respected work. It is also a very serious responsibility for an individual to ensure they will serve society with full honesty, dignity, and sacrifice. Therefore, there must be a proper age prerequisite for the individuals who will be elected for the jobs in the power institutions. Further in this discussion, when we argue the power institutions separately, we have some suggestions for the issue of an age prerequisite.

The serving time for elected members of the power institutions is another crucial point that needs to be addressed. Over a very long time, human history has shown that politics and power make a mixture that by its very nature is highly perishable and toxic. Therefore, nobody should stay in it for too long, for it can destroy human integrity and make an individual corrupt and crooked. Hence, a powerful political life for individuals must be limited.

ELECTION METHOD

The first thing that must be clarified is that an election is a mechanism through which candidates present their sincere readiness for doing honourable public work for the well-being of their society and nation. From the other side, people must believe in the sincere intention and true competence of the candidates by giving them the opportunity to serve society. The elected members of a power institution will have quite significant power and prestige as the people's power is transferred to them as authorities who will serve society. Nevertheless, the public is the boss, and the elected members are the hired employees to serve the public, and certainly not the other way around. The situation is the same for the head of state as the highest position in the administration of a country (either called president or prime minister). We will examine why this is important with an example.

We will take the United States, as an example. In the US, over centuries, they have developed a culture, within which they have created a God-like image for the President of the United States. The United States is a superpower country, and the president of such a country has huge military, economic, and political power. Nevertheless, the primary job of the President of the United States is to serve Americans as a nation. Thus, the President of the United States is an employee hired by Americans to serve them, and he should remain a fully accountable servant of his nation. But the reality is different. In fact, the reality is that the president does not see himself as a servant of the nation. To the contrary, the president has become a phenomenon far above and beyond the nation and, therefore, has taken on an untouchable, nonhuman persona. The president can say or do whatever, right or wrong, and he can get away with it, without any consequences or accountability.

Over decades and centuries, this culture has become a solid political belief that also covers other very powerful politicians and their friends and families. As an example, I will quote Donald Trump, after the election in 2020, once he was talking to a group of journalists. Instead of just answering a question, he said to the CNN reporter, "I am the President of the United States, and you cannot talk to the President of United States like that."[249] Although we have chosen the United States as an example, we know very well that the situation is not very different in other Western countries. We can remember Silvio Berlusconi in Italy, Tony Blair in England, Jacques Chirac in France, etc. We also know that when there is a fight between powerful political parties, they talk about accountability to tear each other apart and destroy one another, but they just care about the interests of their gang and not their nation.

Let us get back to our election method, its mechanism, and effects on the function of power institutions. For our analysis, as a model, we will take the election of government and parliament in Canada. In Canada the country chooses the Members of Parliament through one election. Then the leader of the party that has the majority of the elected members in parliament will become the prime minister to form the government. This means people have not chosen the prime minister. In fact, through this mechanism, they have chosen to put everything in the control of one political party. In this method of election, even

---

249 CNN, November 26, 2020.

from the beginning, the parliament and government are not separated; quite the opposite, they are very deliberately combined together. They have knowingly chosen this method of election because it makes the parliament a photocopy machine of law making for the government, especially when the government is in full majority. Further, in Canada, the prime minister chooses the judges of the Supreme Court. In this system of combined election, all three power institutions become one large ruling body, perfectly prone to all kinds of infection and corruption. In the case of Canada, corruption is the most natural characteristic of the whole political system. Hence, the conclusion is that the form and mechanism of election is a crucial issue for the separation of the power institutions.

Therefore, in a modern human society, as we have seen earlier, we have four power institutions, for which there must be two elections. The elections must be two and half years apart from each other, which makes every election valid for five years. In one election, the members of the executive and treasurial institutions will be elected, and in the other election, the Members of Parliament and the judges of the Supreme Court will be chosen by the entire nation.

Concerning the election for the four power institutions, modern human society needs to develop a very clear social culture of transparency. The culture of transparency means that every individual who is seeking opportunity to become a member in one of the four power institution should voluntarily divulge to society his or her political, social, and financial life, in order to tell openly and honestly who he or she really is that deserves the people's trust. But apart from a general social *culture* of transparency, a modern human society needs also to have very clear *laws* for transparency so that the candidates know in advance that under the legal criteria for being a candidate of a power institution, they must disclose the records of their political, social, and financial lives. One of the horrible experiences of the very obvious and malicious violations of transparency was the resistance and then refusal of Donald Trump to reveal his tax records. Even two years after he has left the office, his tax records have not been disclosed. This kind of stupid and malevolent attitude must be illegal and absolutely should not happen in a modern human society.

CAMERAL STRUCTURE

To make its laws, a modern human society needs only one place, a parliament or whatever name they may call it, as unicameral legislative system. To study this issue, we will look at the existing legislative in Western countries. Mostly, Western countries have a bicameral legislative system. Those who praise the bicameral system believe that in the bicameral system every law, before being implemented, will automatically be double-checked because it becomes verified by two different representatives in two different institutions. Although in appearance it looks quite convincing, the reality in the political world is different. In fact, the bitter truth is that the existence of two legislative institutions provides a battlefield on which political parties can fight each other, not in the interest of the nation, but for their own political interests and rivalry. It also creates more opportunity and time for lobbying groups and foreign entities to influence and manipulate legislative system.

In a modern human society, since there will be an elected Supreme Court with enough judges to act as watchdogs for the legality and constitutionality of all laws in every step of their birth and death, the unicameral legislative system is safer and more practical for the function of the society and also more straightforward for being scrutinized by observing eyes.

THE GOVERNING STRUCTURE

EXECUTIVE

The executive power institution is the governing office to provide a society with all immediate, long or short-term needs. It establishes and entertains international relations with other nations. It also provides its nation with a qualified, well-trained, and well-equipped military army for defending the nation against foreign harm. In human history, despite of all past corruption and malfeasance, the functions and duties of government in general are well known. Therefore, we will not spend too much time on the functioning components. We will pay more attention to the issues that we deem crucial to the executive power institution in a modern human society.

An important subject for us is the head of state (let us call it president), and the individuals that must work with the head of state (let us call them ministers) to run the executive power. Regarding this matter, our concern is how and under which conditions the head of state and the ministers in a modern human society are given the authority to be in charge of their offices.

We will study an example to clarify the function and position of the executive power as a power institution in regard to the other power institutions in a modern human society. Our example is the

Government of Canada. In Canada, as we have already seen it, the head of state (called prime minister) is the leader of the party that has won the majority of the Members of Parliament. This means the head of state is already connected to the parliament (executive power + legislative power). The prime minister chooses the ministers from the seating Members of Parliament. This means the same individuals, the prime minister and ministers, will make decisions for the executive power of the country while they are in their offices as government, and they will make decisions for the legislative power of the country when they are sitting in parliament. We have also seen that the prime minister appoints the judges of the Supreme Court. And of course, Hallelujah, the governing powers in Canada are all separated.

In our example what we have seen is that the governing power institutions in Canada are nothing but a circus. Therefore, the Canadian model of power institutions does not have a real and effective capacity to serve the requirements of modern human society. Here, our task is to explain a real, effective mechanism that will reasonably and efficiently provide modern human society with its modern requirements.

Thus, in modern human society, the head of state is the most important person in the running of the administration of the society. This person must be elected directly by a nation. The elected head of state will have permission from society to hire and bring together highly qualified and trustworthy individuals to run the executive power offices (ministries). There are certain conditions that must be met by the head of state and the ministers. To be blessed by a nation to have the honour to become a head of state in a modern human society is a once-in-a-lifetime opportunity for an individual to shine. Hence, a head of state in a modern human society will be elected only one time for five years. They will come to serve and go. It is crucial for a head of state to have enough professional and life experience. Therefore, in a modern human society, the minimum age prerequisite is forty-five years for an individual who is interested in serving the nation as a head of state. There are also conditions for those who will serve as ministers. The minimum age prerequisite is forty years for individuals who will serve as ministers. Serving as a minister is also a once-in-a-lifetime opportunity for an individual to shine; therefore, ministers come and go with the head of state. However, they remain accountable for life for what they have done during their terms. The election for the head of state must be two and half years apart from the election for legislative and judicial powers.

A good example for the election of the head of state is the American presidential election, which is fairly a good system, although it needs some corrections to become up to date to meet modern standards. One of the very serious defects in American presidential elections is that American people vote, but it is not the people's vote that ultimately determines the winner of the election.

LEGISLATIVE

In talking about legislative power, for our convenience, we will employ the word "parliament" as a general name for the legislative power. Parliament is a place for enacting laws and also an institution that provides information, research, and advisory services, and acts as a watchdog for the executive power functions. For certain vital issues such as declaring or participating in a war or examining and hiring ministers, the executive power needs the consent of the legislative power.

The age prerequisite for individuals who are interested in serving their society in the legislative power should be thirty-five years. Serving in legislative power is a highly respected political career, which should never exceed ten years, which is equal to two terms.

JUDICIAL

Judicial power is the third governing power institution in a modern human society. The Supreme Court is the central part of the judicial power, through which the whole administration of the justice system must be formed and run. The number of judges sitting on the Supreme Court must be equal to the number of Members of Parliament, and they should be elected by the entire nation every five years at the same time with the Members of Parliament. The minimum age prerequisite is fifty years for any judge who is interested in serving a nation as a Supreme Court judge. The period of serving as a judge in the Supreme

Court should never exceed ten years, which is equal to two terms of five years.

Let us now examine the matter of the number of judges who should serve the Supreme Court of a modern human society. As we said earlier, the number of judges serving the Supreme Court in a modern human society is equal to the number of Members of Parliament. In order to understand the importance of the number of judges on the Supreme Court and the reason that this number is related to the number of Members of Parliament, we have to first examine the function and the insufficiencies of the traditional Supreme Courts. Hitherto, Supreme Courts function with very few judges, and very often they are located in buildings in capital cities, far from most of the public. In a lot of countries around the world, among the general population, big numbers of people don't even know what the Supreme Court is, where it is, and what it does.

In terms of function, in the case of dissatisfaction with the legal results of a litigation, if a citizen (natural or legal) decides to bring a case to the Supreme Court, there is only a chance that the case will be heard. The Supreme Courts do not have enough judges or the necessary administrative systems to process large numbers of files. Therefore, every year, the Supreme Courts hear very few and selected files. Thus, quite often a Supreme Court rejects files. Who can know what is really going on? Are they rejecting the files because they really deserve to be rejected, or are they doing it arbitrarily or under corrupt political influences?

Nevertheless, there is absolutely no doubt that once in a while all Supreme Courts in history do some good or important things. In human society, a Supreme Court is not a decorative office. Quite the opposite; all the credit of any modern human society depends on the quality of the function of its Supreme Court. Justice is the most important value and the most effective criteria that can establish equitable social, economic, and political relations among citizens of a modern human society. Our modern, smart civilization of the twenty-first century will definitely not have any value if its citizens are not living a just life. Humans will never have decency and dignity without justice. In today's society, people's lives and money are in the hands of three power institutions: the executive, legislative, and judicial. In a modern human society, people's lives and money will be in the hands of four power institutions: the executive, legislative, judicial, and treasurial. In every human society, these power institutions make decisions for everything and everybody. Hence, only a society that has genuine and effective social machinery for establishing real equitable relations between citizens, and between citizens and the social institutions, can provide a smart life for modern humans. Otherwise, human beings will be the victim of social gangsterism, as we are living in the present world.

Let us get back to our discussion about the number of judges for the Supreme Court of a modern human society. In fact, the number of judges is not an isolated issue; it is directly connected to the administrative mechanism of the Supreme Court. In practice, since the Supreme Court is the main and central component of the justice system, and it should run, control, and act as watchdog for everything in the justice system; it must be physically present in every corner of society, just as the legislative power, through its members, is present in every constituency. Traditionally, Supreme Courts are passive phenomena, waiting until someone knocks on their door and asks for something. Whereas, the Supreme Court of a modern human society must be an active organization and have their eyes on everything that goes on, not only in the justice system but also in all other parts of the society. For, the rule of law is a fragile and perishable issue, which needs permanent surveillance.

Therefore, it is the duty of the Supreme Court to create a social apparatus operated by competent elected experts that can constantly and automatically survey the establishment of the rule of law in the warp and weft of society among individuals and institutions, wherever it is necessary. In the meantime, since the judges of the Supreme Court have the legal expertise, experience, and professional sensitivities, the Supreme Court has to have an alarm system to inform or warn other power institutions in case of misconduct or insufficiency of their required conditions. This function of the Supreme Court could save tremendous time, energy, money, and regrettable memories for a society.

TREASURIAL

Treasurial is the fourth governing power institution in a modern human society. It is the national piggy bank that belongs to the entire society in the present and infinite future time. The origin of the idea of this power institution comes from the Norwegian Government Pension Fund Global, which was originally called the Oil Fund. Let us first, very briefly, find out what the Oil Fund is, and then we will study the details of our treasurial power.

In 1969, they discovered oil in Norway. In 1999 the government of Norway founded an institution called the Oil Fund (*Oljefondet*). The Oil Fund is a sovereign wealth fund that belongs to the government of Norway. Its aim is to collect and invest the surplus revenues of Norwegian gas and petroleum so that this wealth benefits both current and future Norwegian generations. In January 2006, the name of the Oil Fund changed to the Government Pension Fund Global (*Statens Pensjonsfond Utland*). In 2020, the fund's market value amounted to about US$1.3 trillion.[250]

Now we will get back to our main subject of treasurial power. In a modern human society, with every election for the head of state, the society would also elect the members of the treasurial power. The number of the members for this power depends on how big or small the society is; it could go from fifty to one hundred members. The minimum age prerequisite should be forty years for the individuals who will serve as a member of the treasurial power, and the members should never be elected more than two times.

In terms of the function of the treasurial power, we need to explain a few things that will help us to understand the role of this institution in a modern human society. In every human society, there are certain valuable things that timelessly belong to the entire community,

---

250 "Government Pension Fund Global: Annual Report 2021," Norges Bank, Investment Management, https://www.nbim.no/.

to all those who are already born, and all those who will be born in the future. As we can see in Norway, Norwegian people consider that their discovered oil is their national wealth, which belongs to all Norwegians now and in the future. Therefore, they decided to collect and invest the revenue from the oil and save it in a fund that will serve both current and future Norwegian generations. We can understand that Norwegian oil is a natural material that Norwegian geography has offered to the Norwegian people. But the point is that we do not really care about the source of the national wealth. What we are concerned with is the wealth that is a timeless property of a nation.

When something valuable becomes a collective property of a nation, it raises a legal responsibility for handling it because the owner is public not private. The issue becomes more complicated when that wealth becomes a timeless matter; hence, a permanent, well-equipped, and qualified office must be in charge in order to manage the national and the timeless national wealth in a modern human society. The world must thank the Norwegian people for showing humanity a very well-managed, successful example of handling national wealth. Later, we will discuss the details of the relationship between national wealth, individual labour, collective labour, and the role of the treasurial power in establishing equitability in modern human society.

Furthermore, we will examine the administration of the treasurial power. The treasurial power has very important work to do in society. In the meantime, it is different than executive power and different than a central bank.

Although we admit that the Norwegian experience is unique and very valuable in its kind, but national wealth is not only limited to oil and gas. Therefore, in a modern human society, the elected members of the treasurial power will receive authorization from the entire society to look for and protect national wealth, wherever that might be. It is easy to understand that if national wealth is in the form of money, a few financial experts could be hired who would prepare plans to invest the money so it could also bring in some revenue. But what if the national wealth is in the form of art, monuments, historic build-ings, palaces, antique objects, etc.? These valuable things should be considered timeless valuables that can be managed in a way that they will become wealth-making and wealth-accumulating sources for the current and future generations of any given society. We know that the mere presence of protected and organized wealth by its nature is not only the security and stability for a society, but it also means comfort and prosperity too. Definitely, knowing that there is US$1.3 trillion in the chest would allow a nation to sleep well.

TREASURIAL POWER VERSUS OTHER INSTITUTIONS

TREASURIAL POWER VERSUS EXECUTIVE POWER

E xecutive power is in charge of responding to the immediate and day-to-day needs of a society, such as healthcare, education, roads and transportation, and defending society against threats and harm from inside and outside. The executive power collects tax money, with which it pays all the expenses of the government, which is also used for running the administration and ministries, and which is also for fulfilling the duties of the society to international institutions and relations. But, mainly, the executive power is not a money-making or wealth-accumulating office. In fact, often because of incompetence or some other problems, executive powers end up with budget deficit and accumulating debt troubles.

In contrast to the executive power, the treasurial power has nothing to do with the immediate and daily needs of the society. The treasurial power has nothing to do with the collection of tax money, either. However, the similarity between the executive power and treasurial power is that they both function within the framework of laws, they both implement laws, and they both are responsible for delivering certain programs and services to society; although the responsibility of the executive power is much vaster and more various than the treasurial power. The treasurial power never loses money; it never gets in the red or negative. The dominant financial role of treasurial power is not to pay expenses but, rather, wealth-making and wealth-accumulating for current and future generations. Although, by paying pensions and other similar things, the treasurial power will participate in helping to raise the quality of citizens' lives, this is only a very tiny percentage of the wealth of the treasurial power. In short, the treasurial power is the wealth-producing machine of a modern human society.

TREASURIAL POWER VERSUS A CENTRAL BANK

The role of a central bank in a society is to manage monetary policies, while supervising and controlling currency circulation in the country. A central bank is also the provider and printer of notes and coins. Surveillance of market fluctuations is another main responsibility of a central bank. A central bank closely watches inflation, deflation, stagnation, and stagflation in order to prepare and adopt the necessary policies to reduce damage and increase the productivity of the economy.

In contrast to a central bank, the treasurial power will have absolutely nothing to do with the monetary policies, currency circulation, or notes and coins printing. But the treasurial power has similarities with the central bank, for it also closely watches all economic booms and recessions. This is because the treasurial power is a huge investing machine that constantly is in search of better and more profit; therefore, market fluctuations are a very serious concern.

VARIATION OF LABOURS

Today we are living in a capitalist world. No matter what a state might call itself politically —either a monarchy or republic, Islamic or Jewish, communist or democratic—there only exists one mode of production in the world, and that is the capitalist mode of production. Therefore, our duty is to investigate the labour within the capitalist mode of production. The element that connects human labour with the capitalist mode of production is goods and services, for capitalism is the dominant mode of producing and distributing goods and services in the world. This means the circulation of commodity. The only human element in the production and distribution of goods and services, directly or indirectly, is human labour. Thus, we have to examine closely human labour in the capitalist mode of production. The capitalist produces goods and services; therefore, human labour in this part is the labour of the employees who work in the production process to produce the goods and services. In the distribution, the capitalist brings the produced commodities (goods and services) to the market and offers them to consumers. The buyers of the goods and services, who are called consumers, pay money against receiving the goods and services. The important point here is that the consumers are people who have made their money by selling their labour somewhere and somehow. The money that the consumers pay in order to receive the goods and services is the result of selling their labour. This means, indirectly, the capitalist is taking the consumer's labour against the goods and services that are offered.

Let us look at a linear schema of this situation: The capitalist pays money to buy the labour from the employees. The capitalist consumes the labour of employees in the production process to produce the commodity. Therefore, this labour is commodity-producing labour (use-value, commodity). Then the consumers sell their labour to make money in order to bring and give it to the capitalist in exchange for receiving a commodity. Therefore, this labour is commodity-consuming labour (use-value, money). Thus, the sum total of the employees' labour is the first potential energy, and then, the sum total of consumers' labour is the second potential energy. These are two different level of labour (first labour and second labour). As a result, the transaction between the employees and the capitalist, and the transaction between the capitalist and consumers, combine together to create the kinetic energy of the commodity circulation (production and distribution). This is the energy that accumulates wealth in the pockets of the capitalist. Here we will be interested to see the mathematic form of this linear situation with numbers.

We already know that Marx divides capital into two parts: constant capital and variable capital. He said:

> That part of capital then, which is represented by the means of production, by the raw material, auxiliary material and the instruments of labour, does, in the process of production, undergo any quantitative alteration of value. I therefore call it the constant part of capital, or, more shortly, constant capital.
>
> On the other hand, that part of capital, represented by labour-power, does, in the process of production, undergo an alteration of value it both reproduces the equivalent of its own value, and also produces an excess, a surplus-value, which may itself vary, may be more or less according to circumstances. This part of capital is continually being transformed

from a constant into variable magnitude. I therefore call it the variable part of capital, or, shortly, variable capital.[251]

In short, it means, all materials (whatever is immovable) are constant capital, and whatever is alive as human labour-power is variable capital. We accept Marx's definition, and for our analysis we borrow it from him.

Let us take a pair of shoes as an example. A capitalist will spend $10 constant capital (CC) for materials, plus $10 variable capital (VC) as the wage for the employee's labour-power to produce a pair of shoes. The total cost of producing a pair of shoes will become $20. Then the capitalist will sell this pair of shoes for a market price (MP) of $40. The profit (surplus-value) of this transaction will be equal to $20. Therefore, we can write this transaction as below;

$$CC + VC - MP = Profit\ (surplus\text{-}value)$$

$$10 + 10 - 40 = 20$$

As we see, the capitalist is taking $40 from the consumer, which is $20 more than the original cost. If we consider that the fair wage of the employee was $15 instead $10, this means that our capitalist did not pay enough to the employee, which in terms of dollars is equal to $5; otherwise the fair total cost of producing the shoes would be $25. Instead of selling the shoes to the consumer for $25, the capitalist sold the shoes for $40, which is $15 more than the real fair cost of the shoes (commodity). The consequence is that by taking $15 more from the consumer and by paying $5 less to the employee, our capitalist is cashing $20 more than what originally was spent for the production of the shoes.

As we saw, the $20 profit (wealth) has two parts: the first part is $5 (first potential energy – FPE), which is the employee's labour, which was not paid enough. Then the second part is $15 (second potential energy – SPE), which is the consumer's money (labour) taken. As soon as the commodity starts circulating from production to distribution,

---

251 Marx, *Capital*, Vol. I, 202.

these potential energies turn to the kinetic energy of wealth accumulation. Hence, in the capitalist mode of production, the monetary identity of any commodity, from its production up to its consumption, will be as such:

$$CC + VC - MP = \text{Profit (surplus-value)} = \text{FPE (employee)} + \text{SPE (consumer)}$$

$$10 + 10 - 40 = 20 = 5 + 15$$

At first glance, what we see is that the capitalist is robbing both the employee and consumer. But this is not the whole story.

So let us first examine this situation through the Marxism. For Marx, as the variable capital, the source of the profit, surplus-value, is the labour. He said, "The labour adds fresh value to the subject of his labour by expending upon it a given amount of additional labour."[252] If, based on Marx's idea, we take $20 profit from the capitalist and give it to the employee, up to the $5 that was not paid to the employee, our action is fair for establishing justice. But in this case, the remaining $15, which was taken from the consumer, still will be robbed from the consumer. However, this time the robber is not the capitalist; it will in fact be the employee who is putting that $15 in his pocket. Hence, the injustice of capitalism will be replaced by the injustice of the employee. Meanwhile, the participation of the capitalist in circulation, production, and distribution will indeed remain unappreciated. This will be another form of injustice established against the capitalist and consumer. Thus, we understand that Marxism is not the answer that can fix our problem. Therefore, for a solution, we have to look somewhere else.

Let us now assume that every individual will be refunded the share that was collected unfairly. As we have seen, starting with the employee, the unpaid share was $5. Therefore, by paying back the employee's $5, the real cost of the production of the shoes will become $25. In order to show our appreciation for the participation of the capitalist in the

---

252 Marx, *Capital*, Vol. I, 193.

production and distribution process, we will pay $5 to the capitalist. Hence, our production cost will rise to $30. Now our consumer can pay only $30 that is $10 less than previous price, which is indeed a fair price for the shoes.

There is no doubt that we can celebrate the justice that we have successfully established. But is this truly the solution that we were looking for? Even more importantly, would this new situation be livable or sustainable. We will examine this new situation. We will respect the order as it was above.

The employee: What a "significant" difference the $5 can make in the life of an employee. The employee could eat more fast food or order one more T-shirt from Amazon. Thus, this justice will not make any significant change in the employee's life.

The consumer: This situation will not be very different from that of the employee. With $10 remaining in the consumer's pocket, our consumer can buy one more cosmetic item or one more useless pair of sandals. The situation for the consumer is not very different either. So, this justice will not make any significant change in the consumer's life.

The capitalist: By paying $5 to the capitalist, we have shown our appreciation, but would that be enough to support, encourage, and even more importantly to provide the capitalist with the necessary financial freedom and resources to continue the natural curiosity and energy with which the capitalist takes risks to try new scientific and industrial innovation and development to improve business and production? Of course, it will be very hard to have an affirmative answer to this question. Most probably our capitalist will become frustrated and run away in order to save whatever still remains in their hand.

But let us come back to the real world. So far as we were examining the various possibilities, we didn't mind crossing the lines and even sometimes going beyond the limits. Nevertheless, our examples were exaggerated in order to bring out all the possibilities, even though some or all of them could go beyond the limits. Whereas we are aware that they are all totally naïve and imaginary ideas and that in the real world, applying these tiny, severe rules would mean that a state is interfering in every detail of its citizens' lives. This would result in nothing but destroying democracy and establishing dictatorship and tyranny. This would definitely not provide modern humans with a smart life. Here, we have reached to the point that we must get to the core of our issue and set the record straight.

CAPITALISM AND MODERN HUMAN SOCIETY

apitalism without capitalists, employees, and consumers does not exist. We have already talked quite enough about employees and consumers, and now is the time to talk about capitalists. Therefore, we will start our inquiry by asking this question: Who is a capitalist?

A capitalist is an individual member of human society. A capitalist is a thief but not a traditional one. A traditional thief robs and runs away, and sometimes never comes back again. But capitalist is a thief who robs and never goes away. In fact, a capitalist wishes to rob eternally. A capitalist is also a very well-equipped thief. The tool of a capitalist for robbing is called a commodity. A traditional thief always takes and leaves and never gives anything. But a capitalist thief always gives something first (commodity), and then robs, stays, and continues giving and robbing. We have already shown how a capitalist robs employees and consumers, and therefore, astronomically accumulates wealth and capital. Capitalists have a very well-organized system within which all capitalist activities can be administered, grown, and continued. In *The Communist Manifesto*, Karl Marx and Friedrich Engels explain very well what capitalism is and what capitalism has done and is doing to human society. Below we will read them as they tell us everything in detail.

Modern industry has established the world-market, for which the discovery of America paved the way. This market has given an immense development to commerce, to navigation, to communication by land. This development has, in its time, reacted on the extension of industry; and in proportion as industry, commerce, navigation, railways extended, in the same proportion the bourgeoisie developed, increased its capital, and pushed into the background every class handed down from the Middle Ages.[253]

Further, they said:

It has been the first to show what man's activity can bring about. It has accomplished wonders far surpassing Egyptian Pyramids, Roman aqueducts, and Gothic cathedrals; it has conducted expeditions that put in the shade all former Exoduses of nations and crusades.[254]

They then continued with a very important point: "The bourgeoisie cannot exist without constantly revolutionizing the instruments of production, and thereby the relations of production, and with them the whole relations of society."[255] They explained how all this is happening: "All that is solid melts into air, all that is holy is profaned, and man is at last compelled to face with sober senses, his real conditions of life, and his relations with his kind."[256] They also said that capitalism is not a local matter. As we read: "The need of a constantly expanding market for its products chases the bourgeoisie over the whole surface of the globe. It must nestle everywhere, settle everywhere, establish connexions everywhere."[257] And as well, we can hear them, with a very good feeling, say that capitalism is not nationalist, for as they said,

---

253 Engels and Marx, *Manifesto,* King Solomon edition, 43.

254 Engels and Marx, *Manifesto,* King Solomon edition, 44.

255 Engels and Marx, *Manifesto,* King Solomon edition, 45.

256 Ibid.

257 Ibid.

capitalism needs the whole world. They wrote: "To the great chagrin of Reactionists, it has drawn from under the feet of industry the national ground on which it stood."[258] And they continued: "National one-sidedness and narrow-mindedness become more and more impossible, and from the numerous national and local literatures, there arises a world literature."[259]

They further explained how capitalism had helped humans to flourish:

> The bourgeoisie, by the rapid improvement of all instruments of production, by the immensely facilitated means of communication, draws all, even the most barbarian, nations into civilization. The cheap price of its commodities are the heavy artillery with which it batters down all Chinese walls, with which it forces the barbarians' intensely obstinate hatred of foreigners to capitulate. . . .The bourgeoisie has subjected the country to the rule of the towns. It has created enormous cities, has greatly increased the urban population as compared with the rural.[260]

And finally, genius Karl Marx and super-smart Friedrich Engels, in just one spellbinding phrase, tell us how capitalism has enlightened humans' life and society, as we read: "The bourgeoisie, during its rule of scarce one hundred years, has created more massive and more colossal productive forces than have all preceding generations together."[261]

If we take in consideration that *The Communist Manifesto* was published in January 1848, that is equal to 175 years ago. Somewhere we read that Marx and Engels wrote that capitalism had existed for only a scant one hundred years. Thus if we add the two numbers 100 + 175, this tells us that the capitalism we are living with today is about 275 years old. In fact, we know a capitalism that is almost three times older

---

258 Ibid.

259 Engels and Marx, *Manifesto,* King Solomon edition, 46.

260 Ibid.

261 Engels and Marx, *Manifesto,* King Solomon edition, 47.

than the capitalism that Marx and Engels knew. Nevertheless, in 1848, Marx and Engels were mesmerizingly talking about capitalism and they had not yet seen electricity, a telephone, automobile, and airplane— never mind a space shuttle, computer, smart car, or smart phone. It is worth mentioning that today, every six months or so, youngsters around the world sleep overnight on the street in front of Apple stores' doors in order to be the first to purchase the newest iPad or iPhone. This is to say that still, after about 300 years; capitalism is continuing to create more massive and more colossal inventions and creations.

Here it will be useful if we examine a data. In 1950, the world economy was about US$9 trillion. And in 2022, the world economy was about US$90 trillion. In about seventy years, the capitalist world economy has grown almost ten times. With this information, we can imagine that in 1848, when Marx and Engels were writing *The Communist Manifesto,* that capitalism had not reached even 5% of its growth. If we compare 5% growth with a human life, and we imagine that a person lives 100 years, thus 5% would be equal to a five-year-old child. In fact, 175 years ago, in 1848, in thinking of a socialist or communist revolution, Marx, Engels, and some of their friends were dreaming of collapsing capitalism, which was just a five-year-old child. Isn't it lamentable? Here we can ask a very serious question: Could it be considered progressive if someone or a group of people think of imposing a miscarriage to human's history and civilization? For the life of capitalism, even in our time, has not reached to its final day.

HUMAN LABOUR AND COMPENSATION

We have already shown how the capitalists are stealing from employees and consumers. And from the other side, we have said that the life of capitalism is not finished yet. Hence, we are naturally looking for justice between oil and fire. Luckily, we have the treasurial power institution, a reliable shelter, that can provide refuge. But first we have to examine wealth tax. In some countries, they have wealth tax, which is different from income tax. In these countries, if a citizen has wealth that reaches a certain value, the citizen must pay a wealth tax, according to the law.

Wealth is value; indeed, it is use-value. Wealth is good, and wealth is important. The bigger the wealth, the better its positive effect to society. It is very important for any society to have wealthy people, especially people who know how to accumulate wealth, and particularly capital wealth that goes to science, industry, and production. Here is where we can see the value of capitalists in human society. For capitalists are individuals, who are either naturally gifted or because of their character are able to have a certain vision and certain sensitivities that provides them with specific courage, understanding, risk capacity and tolerance. These together make them able to do things that others would hesitate to do. Therefore, despite of all the negative points that are very true, capitalists are elements of growth and development in human society. They know how to build, progress, and reproduce wealth. Thus, human civilization must value and appreciate their presence.

In some countries, they levy a tax on wealth. Taxing wealth is not a good idea because the power institution that collects the tax is the executive power. Thus, the tax money becomes cash flow in the pocket of the government, the government spends the money, and then it disappears forever. Instead, wealthy people must pay interest on their wealth to society. It must be the treasurial power institute that collects the wealth interest from wealthy people. It will also be the treasurial power that will advise the executive and legislative powers on the rate and conditions that must become laws. Money collected from wealthy citizens would go to the fund and stay there to serve society in the present and future. Consequently, employees and consumers and their families would profit from the wealth that would be accumulated, protected, and also invested for the well-being of the entire nation. We have already examined this matter earlier.

CONCLUSION TO PART II:
MODERN HUMAN AND SMART LIFE

There is absolutely no room for any doubt regarding humans' scientific and industrial achievements. Technologically and scientifically, humans have crossed all borders and indeed every day are crossing new borders. In fact, humans in science and technology have become totally borderless. Humans have not only learned how to land smoothly on the planet Mars, more than 88 million kilometres from Earth, but on the surface of Mars, humans are remotely driving a human-made robotic vehicle. On December 25, 2021, the James Webb Space Telescope was launched. This is the most powerful telescope ever made and it can see a very remote distance in space. Here on our planet Earth, every day we see new things in every sphere, field, domain, and specialty. Car makers, shoemakers, cosmetic products, fast foods, travel agencies, clothing stores and boutiques, and millions of others are advertising day and night on every surface they can find about new products.

In science and technology, humans want everything new. Whatever is old goes quickly to the scrap yard. But humans' attitudes toward culture, ideologies, religions, and traditions is not the same. Humans still believe in some ideas or beliefs or traditions that are more than one, two, or even three thousand years old. Every day, humans of the twenty-first century are paying extremely heavy prices for old, obsolete, and expired ideas, which will never do any good to humans.

Of course, any activity or endeavour seeking freedom and justice is definitely noble. Nevertheless, no attempt will achieve any tangible and sustainable result unless supported by a realistic, genuine theory and laws that can be applied through suitable social mechanisms and institutions. Without this, humans will end up wasting life in a tail-chasing effort.

Hence, modern human needs a modern and smart way of thinking and living. Nothing is modern and nothing is smart in the past. Therefore, modern human should never seek emancipation and redemption in the past. Smart is now, and modern is in future. Thus, only idiots, losers, and charlatans look for glory in the past. The past does not exist anymore. The old fashions, old tools, old methods, and old installations will never provide modern human with growth and development. In order to thrive, modern humans must invent, discover, and build new things and go forward and grow up. The idiots, losers, and charlatans never grow up; they only grow old, and then they decay and disappear. Therefore, modern humans should stay away from this plague.

ACKNOWLEDGEMENTS

More than a decade ago I read Bryce Courtenay's book *The Power of One*, which is a witty and delightful story, a schoolboy's observation of human life and society, with all its goods and bads. There was also an interesting point in his acknowledgements. There Courtenay wrote, "We always think of a book as a lonely business: black coffee, white paper and time. Yet no book gets under way without a support crew, those people who are the real-life characters who help to make it happen."[262] Indeed, I believe all books are included in Courtenay's remark.

First, my professor friend, the late Nasser Pakdaman, who taught me economics privately at home; in his place or mine, while travelling in the train or in Queen's University dormitory room (Kingston, Ontario), or in his office in Jussieu Campus, Université Paris 7éme, and sometimes in parks or in coffee shops in Paris, Montreal, or Frankfurt am Main. He also edited my book in 1991, *The Poverty and Wealth of Nations*. I am greatly appreciative for everything I learned from him in economics, demography, and statistics.

---

262 Bryce Courtenay, *The Power of One* (New York: Ballantine Books, 2008).

I am immensely indebted to professor Hassan Mansoor, who generously and patiently read and over read my writings, sometimes eruditely explaining things or advising me, and sometimes very candidly criticizing me.

I am also deeply indebted to Isabel Wagner, who taught me German for that I could read *Das Kapital* in its original language (Karl Marx's mother tongue). She also generously spent time reading *Kapital* with me and helping me to understand it

I am grateful to my daughter Maude Paquet, who for years tirelessly ordered my books and kept assuring me that I would have them on time.

I am thankful to Emily Perkins for her very kind and professional attention toward my book. For about a year or may be more, she stayed in contact with me, checking the progress of my work and advising me for publication and answering my questions.

I appreciate Elizabeth Siegel's work in reading and editing my manuscript and writing me very useful notes.

BIBLIOGRAPHY

Arendt, Hannah. *The Human Condition* (Chicago: The University of Chicago Press, 2018).

Aristotle. *Politics*, book one (Chicago; London: The University of Chicago Press, 2013).

Courtenay, Bryce. *The Power of One* (New York: Ballantine Books, 2008).

Derrida, Jacques. *Specters of Marx* (New York; London: Rutledge, 2006).

Descartes, René. *Principals of Philosophy* (New York: Springer Publishing Company, 2012).

Dooley, Peter C. *The Labour Theory of Value* (New York; London: Rutledge Taylor & Francis Group, 2005)

Engels, Friedrich. *Anti-Dühring* (Moscow: Progress Publishers, 1947).

Fukuyama, Francis. *The Origins of Political Order* (New York: Farrar Straus & Giroux, 2011).

Hegel, George Wilhelm Friedrich. *Encyclopedia of the Philosophical Science* (New York: Cambridge University Press, 2010).

———. *The Philosophy of History* (New York: Dover Publications, 2004).

Hurley-Walker, Natasha. Science Daily Research News, January 27, 2022: 74.

Locke, John. *The Conduct of Understanding* (Whithhorn, UK: Anodos Books, 2017).

Marx, Karl. *A Contribution to the Critique of Political Economy.*

———. Capital, volumes I – III (New York: International Publishers, 1967).

———. *Das Kapital* (München: Anaconda Verlag, 2009).

———. *Le Capital*, Livre 1 (Paris: Garnier-Flammarion, 1969).

———. The German Ideology (New York: Prometheus Books, 1998).

———. *Theses on Feuerbach* (New York: Prometheus Books, 1998).

———. *Value, Price and Profit*. Liverpool Socialist Party.com.

Marx, Karl, and Engels, Friedrich. *The Communist Manifesto*, King Solomon (Asturias-Spain: Entreacacias S.L., 2021).

Mazhari, Nima. *Les Ambassadrices* (Montreal: Stanké, 2001).

Mill, John Stuart. *The Principles of Political Economy* (Scotts Valley: Create Space Publishing, 2016).

Montesquieu, Charles-Louis de Secondat. *De L'Esprit des Lois* (Paris: Flammarion, 1979).

———. *The Spirit of Law* (Connecticut: Prometheus Books, 2002).

Piketty, Thomas. *Capital* (London: The Belknap Press of Harvard University Press, 2017).

Ricardo, David. *Principles of Political Economy and Taxation* (New York: Dover Publications, 2004)

Schramm, Wilbur. *The Process and Effect of Mass Communication* (Chicago: University of Illinois Press, 1974).

Smith, Adam. *The Wealth of Nations* (New York: Bantam Books, 2003).

LINKS

"Baby's First Breath," SickKids Hospital (2009), https://www.about-kidshealth.ca/article?contentid=420&language=english#.

"Beginners' Guide to Financial Statement," U. S. Securities and Exchange Commission, 2007, https://www.sec.gov/reportspubs/investor-publications/investorpubsbegfinstmtguidehtm.html.

"Civil Law vs. Common Law." *Diffen*. https://www.diffen.com/difference/Civil_Law_vs_Common_Law.

"Comparing Prokaryotic and Eukaryotic Cells," Biology for Majors I, *Lumen*, https://courses.lumenlearning.com/wm-biology1/chapter/reading-comparing-prokaryotic-and-eukaryotic-cells-2/.

"Fundamental Force," Energy Education (2014), https://energyeducation.ca/encyclopedia/Fundamental_force.

Institute for Quality and Efficiency in Health Care. "What Does Blood Do?" National Center for Biotechnology Information. National Library of Medicine. August 29, 2019. https://www.ncbi.nlm.nih.gov/books/NBK279392/.

International Centre for Radio Astronomy Research. "Mysterious object unlike anything astronomers have seen before." ScienceDaily. https://www.sciencedaily.com/releases/2022/01/220126122424.htm.

Koch, Charles H. Jr. "The Advantages of the Civil Law Judicial Design as the Model for Emerging Legal Systems," *Indiana Journal of Global Legal Studies* 11, No. 1 (2004), https://www.repository.law.indiana.edu/ijgls/vol11/iss1/6.

Koffman, Brian. "What is Bone Marrow?" *CLL Society.* September 29, 2016. https://cllsociety.org/2016/09/what-is-bone-marrow/.

Lacomte, Lucie. "Party Discipline and Free Votes." Publication No. 2018-26-E. Ottawa: Legal and Social Affairs Division, Parliamentary Information and Research Service, June 28, 2018. https://lop.parl.ca/staticfiles/PublicWebsite/Home/ResearchPublications/InBriefs/PDF/2018-26-e.pdf.

Lynch, Matthew. "What You Need to Know as an Educator: Understanding the 4 Main Branches of Philosophy," *The Edvocate* (2016), https://www.theedadvocate.org/need-know-education-understanding-4-main-branches-philosophy/.

Marx, Karl. "Reflections of a Young Man on the Choice of a Profession." Libcom.org. April 10, 2015. https://libcom.org/library/reflections-young-man-choice-profession.

National Institute of Neurological Disorders and Stroke. "Brain Basics: Understanding Sleep." National Institutes of Health. Bethesda, MD: NIH. https://www.ninds.nih.gov/health-information/public-education/brain-basics/brain-basics-understanding-sleep.

O'Connor, C.M. & Adam, J. U. *Essentials of Cell Biology* (Cambridge, MA: NPG Education, 2010: 5. https://www.nature.com/scitable/ebooks/essentials-of-cell-biology-14749010/.

"Rule of Four," Mathematics Department, San Francisco Unified School District, https://www.sfusdmath.org/ruleoffour.html.

"SFUSD Math Core Curriculum," Mathematics Department, San Francisco Unified School District. https://www.sfusd.edu/departments/mathematics-department-page/sfusd-math-core-curriculum.

"The Four Basic Mathematical Operations," Universal Class, https://www.universalclass.com/articles/math/pre-algebra/the-four-basic-mathematical-operations.htm.

Wikipedia, s.v. "biomolecule," last modified January 6, 2024, https://en.wikipedia.org/wiki/Biomolecule.

Wilkinson, Alissa. "Hollywood's writers are on strike. Here's why that matters." *Vox.* July 17, 2023. https://www.vox.com/culture/23696617/writers-strike-wga-2023-explained-residuals-streaming-ai.

———. "The Hollywood writers' strike is over — and they won big." *Vox.* September 28, 2023. https://www.vox.com/culture/2023/9/24/23888673/wga-strike-end-sag-aftra-contract.

Wonderopolis. "How Are Rocks Made?" Wonder of the Day #1620. https://wonderopolis.org/wonder/How-Are-Rocks-Made.

Printed in the USA
CPSIA information can be obtained
at www.ICGtesting.com
LVHW092326300824
789746LV00016B/57/J

9 781038 300591